"WE ARE LINCOLN MEN"

*Abraham Lincoln
and His Friends*

DAVID HERBERT DONALD

SIMON & SCHUSTER

NEW YORK   LONDON   TORONTO   SYDNEY   SINGAPORE

SIMON & SCHUSTER
Rockefeller Center
1230 Avenue of the Americas
New York, NY 10020

For information regarding special discounts for bulk purchases,
please contact Simon & Schuster Special Sales at
1-800-456-6798 or business@simonandschuster.com

Designed by Karolina Harris

Manufactured in the United States of America

1   3   5   7   9   10   8   6   4   2

Library of Congress Cataloging-in-Publication Data
Donald, David Herbert, 1920–
"We are Lincoln men" : Abraham Lincoln and his friends / David Herbert Donald.
p.   cm.
Includes bibliographical references and index.
1. Lincoln, Abraham, 1809–1865—Friends and associates. 2. Lincoln, Abraham,
1809–1865. 3. Presidents—United States—Biography. 4. Male friendship—
United States—Case studies. I. Title.
E457.2.D66 2003
973.7'092'2—dc22
[B]
2003055648

ISBN 0-7432-5468-6

Frontispiece: Abraham Lincoln (daguerreotype), July 11, 1858, by Polycarpus von
Schneidau. Chicago Historical Society (ICHi-30373).

For
my grandchildren,
Aleta Groh Donald
and
Maia Groh Donald

CONTENTS

All I can do is to urge you to put friendship ahead
of all other human concerns, for there is nothing
so suited to man's nature, nothing that can mean
so much to him, whether in good times or in bad.

CICERO, "ON FRIENDSHIP"

PREFACE

IN the 1880s, when John Hay and John G. Nicolay were collaborating on their biography of Abraham Lincoln, they discussed the tone and bias of the work. Fierce Republicans both, they did not want to "write a stump speech in eight vols," but instead "to write the history of those times like two everlasting angels—who know everything, judge everything, tell the truth about everything and don't care a twang of their harps about the one side or the other." But then Hay added a demurrer: "There will be one exception. We are Lincoln men all the way through."

This is a book about Lincoln men—people who thought of themselves as special friends of Abraham Lincoln. There can be no doubt that much of the time, Lincoln himself so considered them. They are figures whose lives were inextricably intertwined with Lincoln's. They were his closest friends.

It came as a surprise to me that they were so few in number. Of course, there were dozens—indeed, hundreds—of others who claimed to be Lincoln's friends. Throughout his life, many people stepped in to assist him when he needed their help. They loaned him money, they employed him as their lawyer, and they voted for him in elections. He is often pictured as a self-made man who had to struggle to get to the top, but William H. Herndon, his law partner for sixteen years, insisted,

with only a little exaggeration, that "no man ever had an easier
time of it in his early days—in . . . his young struggles than
Lincoln had. He always had influential and financial friends to
help him; they almost fought each other for the privilege of
assisting Lincoln." After Lincoln's assassination, when
reporters asked old-timers in Illinois how he had been able to
rise so rapidly without family connections, without wealth,
without education, they received the explanation that Lincoln
"had nothing only plenty of friends."

In turn, Lincoln referred to dozens of his neighbors, his
associates, and even some of his political opponents as friends.
In his early years, adopting the Quaker manner of his ances-
tors, he frequently began letters with salutations like "Friend
Diller," "Friend Thomas," and "Friend White." Many of his letters ended with "Your friend, as ever." His correspondence is
sprinkled with phrases like "my personal friend" and "my personal friend of twenty years standing." In a few instances, he
referred to acquaintances as intimate friends—some of whom
remain as obscure as Benjamin A. Watson, a Springfield con-
fectioner, and George C. Beilor, or Bestor, who may have been
a mayor of Peoria.

But the evidence is overwhelming that only a handful of
these friends were on intimate terms with Lincoln. Those who
knew him best came to realize that behind the mask of affabil-
ity, behind the facade of his endless humorous anecdotes,
Lincoln maintained an inviolable reserve. Even Herndon, who
was associated with him for so many years, found him "incommunicative—silent, reticent—secretive," and he often had to
guess what his partner thought or wanted. He was, Herndon
summarized, "the most shut-mouthed man" who ever lived.

In pursuing my research, I found myself confronting a riddle: How could a man who had no friends also be a man who had nothing but friends? In attempting to solve it, I steeped myself in the extensive literature on the nature and significance of friendship. The best introduction is *The Norton Book of Friendship,* edited by Eudora Welty and Ronald A. Sharp—a copy of which my dear friend, Eudora Welty, sent me shortly before her death. It offers a rich and rewarding sampling of letters, poems, and essays describing notable friendships. Next, I explored the considerable psychological literature on friendship, which proved especially valuable in showing the importance of close friendships in one's early years. I have been greatly influenced by Harry Stack Sullivan's *The Interpersonal Theory of Psychiatry,* and I have also learned much from *Making a Friend in Youth,* by Robert L. Selman and Lynn Hickey Schultz, and from *Parents and Peers in Social Development,* by James Youniss.

Presently, I discovered that most ideas about friendship derive from philosophical analyses. It is easy to trace a line of intellectual descent from Emanuel Kant to Michel Montaigne to St. Thomas Aquinas to Cicero, all of whom wrote treatises on friendship. And, in turn, their ideas derive from the *Nicomachean Ethics* of Aristotle.

Over the centuries, Aristotle's typology of friendship has remained fundamental. There are, Aristotle shows, three basic kinds of friendships. There are "enjoyable" friendships, in which people associate simply for the pleasure they derive from each other's company; there are "useful" friendships, in which each party has something to gain by associating with the other; and there are "perfect" or "complete" friendships, in which there is free sharing of ideas, hopes, wishes, ambitions, fears. Such a complete friendship can exist only between good people similar in virtue, each of whom wishes for his friend good things—not because his friend is useful or even enjoyable but simply because he is good. It hardly needs saying that such friendships are rare.

I found Aristotle's categories useful in classifying the hundreds of people who claimed to be Lincoln's friends. A great many of his political supporters were clearly useful friends—people who could help him (and sometimes be helped by him) in running for office or winning a court case. Others were enjoyable friends, like the wild Clary's Grove boys with whom he raced and wrestled in New Salem, Illinois.

The list of the men who might be considered Lincoln's "complete" friends is much shorter. He would have found it easy to agree with Henry Adams's observation: "One friend in a lifetime is much; two are many; and three are hardly possible." For a number of men who thought themselves as intimates of Lincoln, there is too little evidence to explore, or to refute, their claims of close friendship. Ward Hill Lamon, Norman B. Judd, Leonard Swett, Gideon Welles, Edwin M. Stanton, Frederick Douglass, and Ulysses S. Grant all knew Lincoln well, but surviving records do not tell us how frequently they saw him, what they talked about, what confidences, predictions, and fears they shared.

I have chosen to focus on six figures who were undoubtedly close to Lincoln and who have left full, revealing reports of their association: Joshua F. Speed, William H. Herndon, Orville H. Browning, William H. Seward, John Hay, and John G. Nicolay. Each saw a different side of Lincoln, and taken together, their accounts present a rounded picture of Lincoln at various stages of his development. They also tell much about Lincoln's difficulty in making, and in holding, intimate friends.

It will be noted that I have not included any women in this list, and readers may reasonably ask why I do not offer an account of his relationship with his wife, Mary Todd Lincoln. Obviously, there was, for at least part of their marriage, an intimacy that Lincoln did not find elsewhere, but I am convinced that the closeness of husband and wife is basically different from that of friends. At any rate, Mary Lincoln is such an important, and difficult, figure in Lincoln's life that she deserves separate treatment.[1] Apart from that, my omission stems from the fact that Lincoln was never really comfortable around women, and, except for a few elderly matrons in New Salem, he did not confide in them. Toward the end of his life, he assumed an air of gallantry toward some women—an air that infuriated his jealous wife—but he never developed a special friendship for any of them.

I found that an examination of Lincoln's close friends required me to rethink some puzzling questions in the Lincoln story: Why did Abraham Lincoln, as a boy, not have a close friend, or "chum"? Did Lincoln have a love affair with Ann Rutledge? Did Lincoln have a homoerotic relationship with Joshua Fry Speed? How reliable are William H. Herndon's recollections of his friendship with Lincoln? Why did Lincoln never offer a cabinet post, or a seat on the Supreme Court, to his closest wartime friend, Orville H. Browning? Did William H. Seward largely direct American foreign policy during the Civil War, or did Lincoln use his friendship to manage Seward? Why did Lincoln come to depend so heavily on his two private secretaries, John G. Nicolay and John Hay? To such questions, there are no simple or definitive answers in the historical record, and a biographer has to rely on his understanding of Lincoln's character, on his knowledge of the period, and, in the end, on his intuition. I have tried to authenticate every factual statement in the following pages, but where the evidence is conflicting or lacking, I have offered judgments that are admittedly speculative.

From time to time, all the major figures in this book had disagreements with Lincoln, but all of them remained loyal to him throughout his life, and after his death, all venerated him as our greatest President. My title is a tribute to that loyalty.

David Herbert Donald
Lincoln, Massachusetts
December 31, 2002

"A Strange, Friendless, Uneducated, Penniless Boy"
Lincoln's Early Friendships

EVERYBODY liked the boy, but he had no special friends.[1] Years later, after Abraham Lincoln was assassinated, old residents of Kentucky and Indiana remembered what a good boy he had been. "He was a modest and Sensitive lad—never coming where he was not wanted," Elizabeth Crawford recalled; "he was gentle, tender and Kind."[2] Dozens said they had been his friends, but no one claimed to have been his intimate.

I

NOT much can be said about Lincoln's playmates in Kentucky, where he spent his first seven years. Nearly all the stories about his boyhood are apocryphal. For instance, the Reverend

James Duncan recalled how with three dogs he and young Abraham chased a groundhog into a cleft in the rocks along the side of a creek. After working in vain for nearly two hours to force the creature out, Lincoln ran off about a quarter of a mile to the blacksmith shop and returned with an iron hook attached to the end of a pole, which he used to pry the creature out. The problem with this memory is that Lincoln would have been only two years old at the time.[3]

The only fairly authentic anecdote concerning Lincoln's Kentucky playmates recounts an adventure when he was about seven. He and Austin Gollaher were playing in Knob Creek, which ran near the Lincolns' cabin, and decided to cross it to look for some young partridges Lincoln had seen the previous day. Neither boy could swim. Gollaher succeeded in "cooning" his way across on a small sycamore pole, but when Abraham followed, he fell off into deep water, and Gollaher had to rescue him. "He was almost dead," Gollaher remembered years later, "and I was badly scared. I rolled and pounded him in good earnest" until he began to breathe again.[4]

When Abraham was about six, he trudged off to school with his older sister, Sarah, more in order to keep her company on the two-mile walk than in any expectation that he would learn to read and write. But Gollaher, looking through the golden haze of memory, said Abraham was "an unusually bright boy at school, and made splendid progress in his studies." During the few months he and Sarah attended school, another Kentuckian remembered, "He alwa[y]s appear[e]d to be very quiet during play time" and gained something of a reputation for liking solitude and for keeping his clothes cleaner than the other boys his age.[5]

But when all these stories are put together, they add up to

very little. As his cousin Dennis Hanks correctly judged, "Abe Exhibited no special traits in Ky."[6]

II

SOUTHERN Indiana was not a place that encouraged young Abraham Lincoln to make close friends. When Thomas Lincoln moved his family from Kentucky to Perry County (later subdivided to form Spencer County), Indiana, in 1816, they settled in a wild region. The public land to which Thomas staked his claim in the Little Pigeon Creek area was so remote that for part of the distance from the Ohio River, he had to hack a path through unbroken forest for his family to follow. Dangerous animals prowled in the woods. Many years later, when Abraham Lincoln revisited the region, he was moved to verse:

> When first my father settled here,
> 'Twas then the frontier line:
> The panther's scream, filled night with fear
> And bears preyed on the swine.[7]

There was little opportunity in this rough frontier region for young Abraham Lincoln to make friends with other children of his own age. Though he was only eight years old, he was large for his age, and his labor was needed to help clear away the undergrowth and chop down enough trees so that his father could plant corn. As he remembered it, he "had an axe put into his hands at once; and from that till within his twenty-third year, he was almost constantly handling that

most useful instrument—less, of course, in plowing and har-
vesting seasons."[8]

After about a year, the family seemed fairly well settled,
especially when Thomas Sparrow and his wife, Elizabeth
Hanks Sparrow, Nancy Hanks Lincoln's aunt and uncle,
moved from Kentucky and built their own cabin near the
Lincolns'. Dennis Hanks, Elizabeth Sparrow's eighteen-year-
old illegitimate nephew, accompanied them, and he enlivened
both households with his irrepressible good spirits and endless
loquacity.

Then disaster struck. People in the Little Pigeon Creek
community began to be afflicted with the mysterious ailment
they called milk sickness that was later discovered to be caused
by milk from their cows that ran wild in the forest and had
been eating the luxuriant but poisonous white snake-root
plant. Dizziness, nausea, and stomach pains were followed by
prostration, coma, and, usually within seven days, death. Both
Thomas and Elizabeth Sparrow died. Then Nancy Hanks
Lincoln fell sick and died on October 5, 1818, leaving behind
her husband, her daughter, aged eleven, and Abraham.

The death of his mother was a critical event in Abraham
Lincoln's life. There is no way to measure the effect of such a
loss on a nine-year-old. Lincoln himself left no direct record of
his grief over his mother's death, but there is evidence to suggest his deep sense of loss. In the 1840s, when he revisited his
old Indiana neighborhood, he was moved to mournful verse:

> I range the fields with pensive tread,
> And pace the hollow rooms,
> And feel (companion of the dead)
> I'm living in the tombs.[9]

During the Civil War, in an attempt to console the bereaved child of a friend killed in battle, he wrote: "In this sad world of ours, sorrow comes to all; and, to the young, it comes with bitterest agony, because it takes them unawares. . . . I have had experience enough to know what I say."[10]

Death is always traumatic for small children, and in Abraham's case the blow was the more severe because his mother's death, at the age of twenty-five or twenty-six, was both premature and unexpected. There was no long period of illness during which her husband and children could reconcile themselves to the inevitable. The loss was the more devastating because of its finality. Though a religious woman, Nancy Hanks Lincoln apparently had no belief in an afterlife (nor did her son ever develop one), and on her deathbed she gave her children no assurance that she would see them in heaven but "told them to be good and kind to their father—to one another and to the world."[11] There was no possibility for a healing period of mourning. Nancy Lincoln, like her aunt and uncle, was placed in a coffin her husband hastily constructed of rough boards and, without ceremony, was buried on a knoll a quarter of a mile from the cabin. No stone or other marker was erected over her grave.

Children experience the death of a parent with confused emotions. There is, of course, the immense and overwhelming sense of loss, but there is also often concealed anger at having been abandoned. Always there is a sense of guilt—guilt over being a survivor when a mother or father has been taken—which can be accompanied by a wholly irrational feeling that, especially in the case of a mysterious disease like the milk sickness, somehow the child may have done something or neglected to do something that caused the parent's death.[12]

Psychoanalysts agree that when a parent dies, a child needs most "the comforting presence of his surviving parent or of a known and trusted substitute."[13] But the undemonstrative Thomas Lincoln, who had to struggle simply to keep food on the family table, was not a man who could extend such comfort to his orphaned children, and there were no neighbors who could serve as mother substitutes.

The sense of abandonment that the Lincoln children felt because of the death of their mother induced fear that their father too might leave them. Indeed, within a year of Nancy's death, Thomas Lincoln did go back to Kentucky, leaving his two small children unprotected except for their teenage cousin, Dennis Hanks. When Thomas Lincoln returned with a new wife, Sarah Bush Johnston Lincoln, she found Abraham and Sarah dirty, hungry, and clad in tatters. The children became devoted to this warm and outgoing woman, a widow with two daughters and a son Abraham's age, who quickly brought order to the Lincoln household, but she arrived before Abraham had time fully to accept the loss of his mother. His father had remarried before an itinerant preacher read a funeral service over Nancy Hanks Lincoln's grave.

In such circumstances, children often have difficulty in making close connections with others. It is as if once their most intimate link, to a parent, has been destroyed, they are fearful lest they invite another devastating hurt.

III

During this period of incomplete mourning, Abraham was saved from social isolation by the presence of Dennis Hanks, engaging, garrulous, and self-promoting. Dennis was later to claim he had great influence on young Abraham. "I taught Abe his first lesson in spelling—reading and writing," he boasted. "I taught Abe to write with a buzzards quillen which I killed with a rifle and having made a pen—put Abes hand in mind [mine] and moving his fingers by my hand to give him the idea of how to write."[14] (He claimed also to have sparked Lincoln's interest in the law: "I bought the Statute[s] of Indiana and from that he Lerned the principles of Law and allso My Self.") Most of these claims were fabricated or highly exaggerated, though certainly the two worked together on the farm and hunted rabbits together. But Dennis was nearly ten years older than his cousin, and he was more like a benevolent uncle than a close friend.

Abraham never developed a warm friendship for his step-brother, John D. Johnston, who was about his own age. The reasons are obscure. Though Sarah Bush Johnston Lincoln was even-handed in her treatment of both boys, her husband was not; as a relative remembered, he "always appeared to think much more of his stepson John D. Johnston than he did of his own Son Abraham."[15] Perhaps Thomas Lincoln felt more temperamentally kin to John D., who was rather dull and lazy, if good-tempered, than he did to Abraham; possibly he felt threatened by Abraham and was unwilling to share the male role of authority with his talented son. At any rate, a relative recalled, he "never showed by his actions that he thought much of his son Abraham when a Boy, he treated [him] rather unkind than otherwise." Inevitably the two boys became rivals rather than friends. Dennis Hanks said they were enemies.[16]

Outside of Abraham's family circle, there were few boys of his own age in the Little Pigeon Creek community. The Lin-

coln family had no nearby neighbors. Spencer County was almost uninhabited when the Lincolns arrived, with a total population of only about 200 in an area nearly the size of the state
of Rhode Island. In 1820, about forty families lived within a
five-mile radius of the Lincolns' cabin; this means there were
fewer than two families per square mile. Louis A. Warren, who
made a careful study of the early land records and the 1820
census, calculated that at the time Abraham was eleven years
old, there were seven, or possibly eight, families that lived
within a mile of the Lincolns, and these included only ten boys
(besides Abraham and John D. Johnston) and nine girls between the ages of seven and seventeen. It is not possible to as-
certain the ages of the individual children, but these figures
suggest that within a mile radius, there were, at most, only one
or two other boys of Abraham's age, none living so close that
they could see each other and play with each other daily.[17]

The Little Pigeon Creek neighborhood was not even a village, and there was nothing like a community center, but
Abraham did have a chance to meet other children when he,
with his sister and the three Johnston children, attended the
school that Andrew Crawford opened in a cabin about a mile
from the Lincoln house. It closed after one term of three
months. The next year, he enrolled in James Swaney's school,
about four miles from home, but the distance was so great that,
because of his farm chores, he attended only sporadically. The
following year, he went for about six months to a school Azel
W. Dorsey opened in the same cabin where Crawford had
taught. His formal schooling then ended and, all told, as he
himself summarized, "the ag[g]regate of all his schooling did
not amount to one year."[18]

The somewhat sporadic services of the Little Pigeon Creek

Baptist Church, which his father, stepmother, and sister joined in 1823, offered other opportunities for meeting children of his own age. Though not a member, Abraham listened to the sermons and after the service would often rally the other boys and girls around him. Then, climbing on a tree stump, he would repeat—or sometimes parody—the minister's words.

He became a leader of the children in the area, in part because he matured earlier than most others. Lincoln experienced the onset of puberty in his twelfth—possibly in his eleventh—year, when he began to shoot up in height. He became "a man though a boy." When the other children his age got into squabbles or engaged in pranks, Lincoln would say, "Leave off your boyish ways and be more like men."[19] More mature than the other students, he was nearly always at the head of his class. One of them thought Lincoln "got ahead of his masters—[They] Could do him no further good: he went to school no more."[20] His excellence in his school work could have caused jealousy, but it didn't because he was generous in helping other children. Kate Roby remembered that once Schoolmaster Crawford stumped the class by insisting that they spell "defied," threatening to keep the children in school day and night until they got it right. After unsuccessfully trying every variant she could think of, she chanced to spy tall Abraham Lincoln through the window, who smiled and pointed his finger to his eye. Taking the hint, she immediately changed the letter "y" into an "i," and Crawford had to let the class out.

The absence of playmates—important at any age—was of crucial importance at this stage of Lincoln's development. In late childhood and early adolescence, most boys find a close friend—a "chum," to use the term favored by psychoanalyst Harry Stack Sullivan—from whom they are inseparable and

with whom they share confidences, secrets, desires, and ambitions. By giving a boy a perspective on himself different from
that offered by his family members, a chum can help in the difficult process of self-recognition and can help him to develop an
autonomous personality.[21] When there are very few children of
the same age in a community, some boys never find such an intimate friend, and the failure can have serious consequences for
the rest of their lives. Boys who do not have chums often have
difficulty later in establishing close, warm friendships, and
there is some evidence that such boys are more likely to suffer
from depression in later years.[22] Lincoln never had a chum.

IV

IN 1831, when Lincoln, at the age of twenty-two, left his family and settled in New Salem, Illinois, he was—as he later
described himself—"a strange, friendless, uneducated, penniless boy."[23] What he meant by "strange" is so obscure that the
editors of his *Collected Works* thought that he meant to say
"stranger." But to have Lincoln call himself a "stranger"
requires that his self-description be changed to "a stranger, [a]
friendless, uneducated, penniless boy." Lincoln chose his
words carefully and such emendations are unwarranted.
Probably Lincoln meant precisely what he said: to residents of
New Salem who saw him for the first time, he did indeed seem
strange. He had already attained his full height of six feet and
nearly four inches, which made him a head taller than almost
anybody else in the New Salem community. Rail-thin, with
elongated arms and huge feet, he flapped around like some
enormous immature bird when he walked. His clothing added

to the oddity of his appearance: a cheap chip hat, perched precariously on his mass of black hair that had the texture of a horse's tail; a flimsy jacket or coat, so short that it left his midriff unprotected; and jeans that lacked six or more inches of reaching his heavy work shoes. He was, one observer said, "as ruff a specimen of humanity as could be found."[24] New Salem had never seen his like before.

He arrived in New Salem by accident, and he knew nobody in the community. Working for Denton Offutt, he, John D. Johnston, and his cousin John Hanks, who lived off and on with the Lincolns, were guiding a flatboat loaded with barrels of wheat, corn, and bacon down the Sangamon River, and it became lodged on the milldam at New Salem. When the boat began taking on water, Lincoln worked frantically with the others to lighten the load in the stern. As the boat started to right itself, he went ashore, borrowed an augur, and bored a hole in the bow. After the water poured out of the hole, he plugged it. Then the whole boat was lifted and eased over the dam. Impressed by Lincoln's ingenuity, Offutt swore that, once the trip down the Mississippi was concluded, he would set up a store in New Salem, with Lincoln as its manager. In July, Lincoln returned, but Offutt had not yet come back, and there was no store.

In September, when Offutt did arrive with his stock of goods, Lincoln set to work as his clerk, assisted by William G. ("Slicky Bill") Greene. They both slept on a cot in the little store; it was so narrow, Greene remembered, that "when one turned over the other had to do likewise."[25] Henry McHenry later recorded that Lincoln made "a good—obliging clerk and an honest one: he increased Offut[t']s business much by his simplicity—open—Candid—obliging and honest."[26]

Soon Lincoln came to know all the hundred or so inhabitants of the village, and, because business at the store was seldom pressing, he joined in their amusements. He liked to run in foot races, and he promptly demonstrated that with his long legs, he could outjump any other man in the village. Offutt's store became the place where the men of the town met daily to exchange news and gossip and to regale each other with jokes and anecdotes. Lincoln seemed to have an inexhaustible supply of both, and men gathered around him when he began one of his tall tales, recounted with great gusto.

He found easy acceptance in this small, closely knit trading community, but initially it was not certain that he would be as well received by the farmers and laborers from the surrounding countryside, who came to New Salem to trade, have their corn ground at the grist mill, and have a few drinks at one of the "groceries" (as saloons were then called).

Wild and undisciplined, these young country men virtually terrorized the more sedate residents of New Salem. Worst of them all were the "Clary's Grove boys," who lived in a hamlet several miles southwest of New Salem. They were not innately vicious—that is, they did not rob, steal, or murder. If the spirit moved them, they would help an invalid or a widow when a pond needed to be dug or a ditch to be trenched. But they were, as James Short, one of the New Salem residents, called them, "roughs and bullies," who made it a practice to entice any stranger into a game of cards, when—fairly or unfairly— they would win all his money and often beat him up afterward.[27]

Indeed, fighting was a favorite pastime, as it was all along the frontier. Sometimes these brawls served simply as a vent for excess energy, like a gymnastic exercise; but frequently, they were dead serious and included choking, hair pulling, and eye gouging. Often there was little or no pretext to set off a fight, which could involve the whole gang. A fight became a kind of initiation rite for a newcomer, to establish his place in the pecking order.

Inevitably the Clary's Grove boys turned their attention to Offutt's new clerk. Offutt himself provoked them by boasting that Lincoln was not merely the smartest but the strongest man in the town. Caring nothing for Lincoln's mental accomplishments, the Clary's Grove boys vowed to test his ability to fight.

Jack Armstrong, their leader, challenged Lincoln. Stout and burly, Armstrong was a tricky veteran of scores of contests, and he was a formidable fighter. Lincoln demurred. He disliked the tactics of the Clary's Grove boys, who favored rough-and-ready wrestling, with no rules and no holds barred. "I never tussled and scuffled and will not," he said, "dont like this wooling and pulling." He enjoyed "scientific" wrestling, a style in which opponents, following agreed-on rules, begin by taking holds and attempting to throw each other. Urged on by Offutt and others who placed bets on the outcome, the two men agreed to wrestle, not to fight.[28]

The outcome of the contest became a matter of legend in New Salem. According to some accounts, Lincoln was victorious; according to others, Armstrong "legged" Lincoln—a tactic forbidden by wrestling rules—and illegally brought him down. Some remembered that Armstrong's followers, angered by the defeat of their champion, tried to gang up on Lincoln, who vowed that he would lick them all, but only by fighting them one at a time. Others recalled a controversy over whether Offutt lost his bet, since Armstrong did bring Lincoln down, though by an outlawed maneuver. Douglas Wilson's scrupulous account of this episode in *Honor's Voice* concludes that the evidence is so confused and contradictory that it will never be possible to determine precisely what happened.

But of the importance of the fight in shaping Lincoln's years in New Salem, there can be little doubt. With some exaggeration, John Todd Stuart, Lincoln's future law partner, said, *"This was the turning point in Lincoln's life."*[29] This test of Lincoln's strength and courage earned him the admiration of the Clary's Grove boys, and Jack Armstrong became, and remained, his lifelong follower.

V

LINCOLN'S place in the New Salem social hierarchy was ensured. Oddly enough, the rough country boys were not put off by his idiosyncratic refusal to smoke and drink or by his peculiar fondness for books and reading. Perhaps his deficiencies in these areas were made up for by his ability to spin yarns, often scabrous or scatological. More were doubtless impressed by his strength. He could hurl a maul or a cannon ball farther than any competitor. Rowan Herndon claimed Lincoln could lift a box of rocks weighing between 1,000 and 1,300 pounds.[30] According to one frequently reported anecdote, he squatted beside a barrel of whiskey, raised it by the chimes, and drank out of the bung hole.

The rough boys about town began to accept him not merely as an equal but in some sense as a leader who appealed to their better instincts. For instance, he put a stop to Jack Armstrong's plan to cure one of the town's chronic drunkards by nailing him in a barrel and rolling it down the steep cliff into the Sangamon River. Another time, when the boys, well lubricated after an election celebration, bet a feeble-minded resident that he could not ride his pony through a bonfire they had built, Lincoln made them call the bet off and send the man home, slightly scorched but, in general, none the worse off.

The next year (1832), the young men of the New Salem area gave a clear demonstration of the place Lincoln held in their regard. That spring, the Sauk and Fox Indians violated the treaty they had signed with the U.S. government to remove across the Mississippi River and returned to Illinois to reclaim their tribal lands. Illinois Governor John Reynolds called out the militia to help the federal troops resist the invasion. Like other able-bodied white males, Lincoln was obliged to enlist, and he did so willingly because Offutt's store had, in Lincoln's words, "winked out" and he had no job. On April 21, he and the other recruits from the New Salem neighborhood were sworn into service, and, as was customary, they proceeded to elect their own officers. William Kirkpatrick, a wealthy sawmill owner, had announced his candidacy for captain and expected to be elected, but someone also nominated Lincoln. When the voting took place, each candidate stepped out in front on the village green, and his supporters fell in behind him. To Kirkpatrick's surprise, two-thirds of the recruits lined up behind Lincoln, and most of the others soon followed.

It was a success that delighted Lincoln, because he relished being esteemed by his peers. As Charles Strozier has said, it marked him as being first among equals, not just a friend of the soldiers but their leader. Years later, in 1859, after he had been elected four times to the state legislature and once to the U.S. House of Representatives and after he had twice been his party's candidate for the U.S. Senate, Lincoln said that his election as militia captain was "a success which gave me more pleasure than any I have had since."[31]

The story of Lincoln's brief service in the Black Hawk War—he served for one month as captain of his company, until it was disbanded, and then reenlisted for another few weeks as a private in another company—is not memorable, but what is significant is the high esteem, approaching veneration, in which his men held him. It was not due to any special military skill or knowledge. Lincoln knew nothing of military science. When he was drilling the company by making them march across a field, he discovered that they were about to run into a fence with a narrow gate. Unable to remember the proper command, he ordered the company to halt, disband for two minutes, and re-form on the other side of the fence. Nevertheless, the men continued to admire his physical strength and his skill as a wrestler. In a series of contests, he was never thrown, or "dusted," as the phrase went, and his men thought he could beat anyone. The supporters of Lorenzo Dow Thompson, of a St. Clair County regiment, also believed their champion was invincible. So a contest was arranged, and, as Lincoln remembered many years later, "the whole army was out to see it." To the surprise of Lincoln's backers, many of whom had bet on the outcome of the contest, Thompson threw him not once but twice. When some protested that Thompson's holds were illegal, Lincoln silenced them and told them that his opponent had played fair. "Why," he said later, "that man could throw a grizzly bear."[32]

Rather against their will, Lincoln's men were also impressed by his moral as well as his physical courage. When an old Indian, bearing a certificate of good conduct from American authorities, stumbled into their camp, some of the Illinois volunteers wanted to kill him, saying that he was a spy. Lincoln stepped between his men and the shivering Indian and said that anyone who wanted to hurt the visitor would have to lick him first. Grumbling, the men let the Indian slip away.

Nonetheless, Lincoln remained very popular among the men in his company, who were considered "the hardest set of men" in the army.[33] They knew, as Rowan Herndon observed, that "he Could out jump the Best of them he Could out Box the Best of them he Could Beat all of them on anicdote." "Lincoln was their idol," another soldier recalled, "and there was not a Man but what was obedi[e]nt to every word he spoke and would fight [to] his death for Lincoln."[34] In their recollections of this period in Lincoln's life, the theme is unvaried. "Lincoln was a man I always loved," observed John M. Rutledge. "I was with him in the Black Hawk war he was my Captain a better man I think never lived on the earth."[35] According to one soldier, he "was idolized by his men and generally by all the Regiment . . . to which he belonged."[36] "All the men in the Company—as well as the Regiment to which he and they belonged loved him well," claimed another, "almost worshipped him."[37]

Long after the Black Hawk War, the loyalty of these men to Lincoln remained unshaken. Although most of them were Democrats and he was a Whig, they regularly supported him for public office. When he traveled Sangamon County campaigning for the state legislature, some of them accompanied him, at times lending muscular as well as moral support when audiences were unruly. But it is notable that even after Lincoln's death, when the temptation to claim closeness to the martyred President was almost irresistible, very few of these men claimed that Lincoln was their friend, and none professed any degree of intimacy with him.

VI

In his description of his arrival in New Salem, Lincoln also referred to himself as a boy. He was, in fact, twenty-two years old, an age when most young men had settled on a career and a good many were married and had begun families.[38] But Lincoln gave a first impression of coltish youthfulness. "Uncle" Johnny Potter was working on a high rail fence when he first saw Lincoln, who asked whether he could have something to eat. Mrs. Potter gave him boiled eggs for breakfast. When he was finished, Lincoln came out and "straddled over that five-rail fence as if it wasn't in the way at all." Out in the road, he turned back and said, "There's only one egg left; I believe I'd better make a clean thing of it." He straddled the fence again, got the egg, and "went off—laughing like a boy, shuffling the hot egg from one hand to the other and then peeling and eating it."[39] Lincoln evidently thought of himself as still immature, with all the exciting possibilities and all the dangers of manhood still ahead of him.

Later, when he was only in his forties, he would be called "Old Abe," but during his New Salem years, people thought of him as a boy. His appearance of immaturity—his susceptibility to the wild moods of a belated adolescence, his inability to deal with practical matters like buying clothes and doing his laundry, his willingness to drift from one occupation to another, whether it was storekeeper, riverboat man, soldier, postmaster, or surveyor—brought out the maternal instincts of

New Salem matrons, and he looked to them as mother substitutes.

Shy with young women, he found it easy to talk with them, because most were older than he and, being married, could not be considered objects of sexual interest. Mentor Graham's daughter recalled that he frequently asked her mother "for advice on different questions—such as Love—prudence of movements etc—girls—etc etc."[40]

After the great wrestling match, Hannah Armstrong, Jack Armstrong's wife, took a strong interest in Lincoln, who became a frequent visitor. "Abe would Come out to our house," she remembered, "drink milk and mush—Corn bre[a]d—butter." He would bring her children candy and rock the cradle of her baby while she laundered his clothes. To keep briars from ruining his trousers, she "foxed" them with two buckskins—that is, she sewed the skins on the front of the garments, to keep them from being shredded.[41] Their friendship was so close that her roughneck husband kept up a running joke that Lincoln was the father of her youngest son. It was a story, one contemporary remembered, that "plagued Lincoln terribly."[42]

Elizabeth Abell, the wife of Dr. Bennett Abell, was another New Salem matron who found this disheveled and disorganized young man immensely appealing. Mrs. Abell, whom William Butler described as "a cultivated woman—very superior to the common run of women" on the frontier,[43] also did Lincoln's laundry and "foxed" another pair of his pants. She thought him "the best natured man I ever got acquainted with" and described him as "sensitive"—but also as "backward."[44]

Those were not traits that especially endeared him to the young women in the New Salem community, and, indeed, he showed very little interest in them. Even in Indiana, he had the reputation of not liking girls much because they were "too frivalous."[45] In New Salem, according to James Short, "he didn't go to see the girls much. He didn't appear bashful, but it seemed as if he cared but little for them." Once when a Virginia family with "Three stilish Daughters" stayed at the Rutledge tavern, where Lincoln was also boarding, he absented himself from the table for two or three weeks, doubtless embarrassed by his homely appearance and perhaps by his deficient table manners.[46]

But there are two apparent exceptions to Lincoln's failure to find friends among the young women of New Salem. According to William H. Herndon, his law partner, Lincoln fell deeply in love with Ann Rutledge, daughter of one of the founders of New Salem. Though she was promised to another man, she reciprocated his affection and—as the story goes— they arrived at some kind of understanding, if not an actual engagement. Then, in the terrible summer of 1835, Ann died, and Lincoln was devastated.

It is hard to know what to make of this story, which was first hinted at in an 1862 article in the *Menard Axis,* an obscure, anti-Lincoln newspaper, but was not widely known until Herndon began interviewing New Salem old-timers after Lincoln's death. Herndon's extravagant rhetoric, including assertions that Lincoln was so distraught after Ann Rutledge's death that "his mind wandered from its throne" and that he never loved another woman, including his wife of twenty-three years, made some historians skeptical, yet others strongly supported Herndon's story. It was not until 1945, after Herndon's papers had been opened to the public, that the great Lincoln scholar, J. G. Randall, was able to make a close analysis of the evidence. His brilliant appendix to his *Lincoln the President,* called "Sifting the Ann Rutledge Evidence," concluded that Herndon's story was largely myth. Unsupported by credible evidence, it did "not belong in a recital of those Lincoln episodes which one presents as unquestioned reality."[47] As Professor Randall's research assistant, I fully endorsed that view in my first book, *Lincoln's Herndon,* and tried to explain why Herndon promulgated this myth.

In recent years, there has been a tendency to reverse this judgment against Herndon's story, and John Y. Simon and Douglas L. Wilson have published well-reasoned studies that argue for the essential credibility of the Ann Rutledge story (minus Herndon's speculations about Lincoln's mental instability and his alleged lack of affection for his wife). Their close reading of Herndon's numerous interviews relating to Ann Rutledge persuaded me that Professor Randall's analysis had perhaps been too rigorous in demanding firsthand testimony of two independent witnesses. Using that criterion, a historian would have to discard almost everything reported about Lincoln's first thirty-one years. Consequently in my *Lincoln* (1995), I gave a mild endorsement to the basic Ann Rutledge story (without accepting Herndon's rhetorical embellishments).

In the years since, I have reconsidered my position. This rethinking was not, for the most part, the result of the discovery of new evidence. Both Professor Randall and his critics used the same documents—mostly interviews that Herndon conducted. But the 1998 publication of *Herndon's Informants,* ably edited and exhaustively annotated by Douglas L. Wilson and Rodney O. Davis, has made it possible more easily and systematically to examine all the testimony that Herndon collected on this subject. Looked at anew, it is impressive for its contradictions. Members of the Rutledge family were certain that there had been a firm engagement between Lincoln and their sister; Mrs. Abell, who may have been Lincoln's closest confidant in New Salem, professed to know nothing about a love affair, though she testified to Lincoln's genuine grief at Ann's death.

With one exception, all this confusing and contradictory evidence that Herndon collected was secondhand, recollected months and even years after Lincoln's assassination and, of course, thirty or more years after Ann Rutledge's death. No letter from Ann Rutledge is known to exist, and her name is never mentioned in the thousands of pages of Lincoln's published correspondence. Only Isaac Cogdal, a Menard County farmer and stonemason, claimed to have spoken personally with Lincoln about his alleged love affair. In an interview Herndon recorded in 1865 or 1866, Cogdal said he visited Lincoln in his office during the months after he was elected President in 1860, and the two friends began reminiscing about "old times and old acquaintances" in New Salem. Presently Cogdal felt emboldened to ask: "Abe is it true that you fell in love with and courted Ann Rutledge?" "It is true," replied Lincoln, "true indeed I did. I have loved the name of Rutledge to this day. . . . I loved the woman dearly and sacredly: she was a handsome girl—would have made a good loving wife . . . I did honestly—and truly love the girl and think often—often of her now."[48]

This statement has remained a linchpin in accounts endorsing the Ann Rutledge story, even though Professor Randall cautioned that it had "unLincolnian quality."[49] Recently it has come under more sustained attack from C. A. Tripp, who questions the timing and the accuracy of Cogdal's reported interview with Lincoln. In a careful computer-aided analysis of all of Lincoln's known writings and sayings, Dr. Tripp shows that Lincoln never used several key words Cogdal attributed to him, or adopted the pattern of phrasing Cogdal reported, and concludes that Cogdal's "entire testimony reeks of fraud."[50]

The whole subject is—as Lincoln said in a very different context—so "environed with difficulties"[51] that it is hard to reach a reasoned judgment. My present negative opinion rests in part on a reexamination of Herndon's evidence and of Dr. Tripp's analysis, but in larger part, it derives from the context of what we know about Lincoln's friends and associates. At no other point in Lincoln's early life did he express his deep affection—much less his love—for any woman. He was not prepared for intimacy.

Doubts about his romance with Ann Rutledge are reinforced by examination of the one other instance in which he was interested enough in a woman to propose marriage. Several New Salem matrons, concerned about his lonely and forlorn condition, vainly attempted to match him with a Miss Short and a Miss Berry, but Mrs. Abell was more successful in promoting his interest in her sister, Mary Owens. Handsome and well educated, this daughter of a wealthy Kentucky family made a great impression when she visited her sister in 1833 or 1834, and Lincoln is supposed to have told Mrs. Abell that "if ever that girl comes back to New Salem I am going to marry her." When she did return, a half-hearted courtship began, only to end in farce. Granting Lincoln's "goodness of heart," Mary Owens found him "deficient in those little links which make up the chain of woman's happiness." He found her greatly changed since her earlier visit and complained of her age, "her want of teeth, weatherbeaten appearance in general." To the relief of both parties, their romance—if it could be called that—ended, and Lincoln concluded "never again to think of marrying; and for this reason; I can never be satisfied with any one who would be blockhead enough to have me."[52]

It is clear that in his New Salem days Lincoln's attachments were to older, married, and hence unavailable, women. He needed a mother more than he needed a wife.

VII

LIKE older women, older men—or at least those who were more settled in occupation and family, more established in their businesses—also often volunteered to help this lonely, friendless young man. Denton Offutt became his first patron in Illinois. Though Offutt was, as one New Salem resident said, "a wild—rec[k]less-careless man,—a kind of wandering horse tamer," he was perceptive enough to see great possibilities in Lincoln and put him, without any experience at all, in charge of his general store and then of his grist mill. "By God," he predicted, "Lincoln will yet be President of these U.S."[53] Other men also trusted him. When Lincoln returned from the Black Hawk War without a job, Rowan Herndon sold him half-ownership of his general store, with no cash payment. "I believed he was thoroughly honest," Rowan Herndon explained, "and . . . I accepted his note in payment of the whole. He had no money, but I would have advanced him still more had he asked for it."[54]

When the store, which Lincoln owned jointly with William Berry, failed and he was left without a job, friends again intervened to help him. One secured for Lincoln the appointment as postmaster of New Salem, and another persuaded John Calhoun, the chief surveyor for northern Sangamon County, to name Lincoln his deputy, even though he knew nothing of surveying. While learning his new trade, Lincoln was invited to live for six months with Mentor Graham, the local schoolmaster.[55]

Successful in his new occupations, Lincoln again ran into trouble when his notes—mostly incurred through the purchase of the store and the contents of an adjacent one that the Clary's Grove boys drove out of business—fell due. His financial distress was the greater because Berry, his partner, had died, and he felt obligated to pay all the indebtedness of their firm. In the judgment against him, the court ordered the sale of all his assets, including his horse and his surveying compass, flagstaff, chain, and other surveying equipment, without which he could not make a living. Quietly, James Short, a New Salem neighbor, bought them up and returned them to Lincoln.

Not all the help Lincoln was offered was material or financial. In addition to giving him room and board, Mentor Graham shared with him his meager knowledge of arithmetic and geometry, which he needed to become a surveyor. Jack Kelso, a man of some education, with whom Lincoln boarded for a time, stimulated him to read Shakespeare and Burns. It seemed to one New Salem resident that they were "always together—always talking and arguing."[56] Kelso was less successful in interesting Lincoln in fishing, his other passion, but the two men would often sit for hours on the bank of the Sangamon River and "quote Shakespear."

Bowling Green, the local justice of the peace, was also fond of Lincoln, who boarded with him too for a time. Always interested in legal proceedings and thinking of the law as a possible profession, Lincoln faithfully attended the hearings at Green's court. Looking for amusement, the corpulent Green delighted in Lincoln's sense of humor and in some cases allowed him to make comments, which, as one resident recalled, produced "a spasmotic [sic] shaking of the fat sides of the old law functionary."[57] He came soon to recognize the young man's shrewd intelligence and clear, logical mind. "There Was good Material in Abe," he told friends, "and he only Wanted Education."[58] Abner Y. Ellis, who knew Lincoln well, reported that Bowling Green was "his allmost second Farther [sic]," and recalled that Lincoln "Used to say that he owed more to Mr Green for his advancement than any other Man."[59]

Even more important was the interest that John Todd Stuart took in the young man. The two served in the Black Hawk War, and after the expiration of their one month of obligatory service, both reenlisted as privates. Stuart, a college-educated Virginian, already established as a lawyer in Springfield, saw great promise in this young frontiersman who was so fond of books and reading. Learning that Lincoln had considered studying law but was discouraged because he lacked formal education, Stuart urged him on and offered to lend him books from his own law library. He also promoted Lincoln's political career. As a staunch Whig, he recognized that his party had a very poor chance in strongly Democratic Menard County unless the Whigs ran someone like Lincoln, who had no telltale political record, though he strongly favored Whiggish policies like governmental support for internal improvements and—even more important—had a loyal personal following. Though Lincoln was defeated in his first race for the state legislature in 1832, he was victorious in the 1834 election, when, with Stuart's consent, he maneuvered to secure votes of both Whigs and Democrats.

Once elected, Lincoln realized that he had to pay some of

his debts and buy clothes appropriate for a legislator. He approached Coleman Smoot, a well-to-do farmer and stock raiser of the Indian Creek neighborhood, saying, "You must loan me money to buy Suitable Clothing for I want to make a decent appearance in the Legislature."[60] Unhesitatingly, Smoot loaned him two hundred dollars, quite a large sum at that time, being more than half a month's salary of the governor of the state. He asked for no security, because he knew that Lincoln had nothing of value to secure the loan.

VIII

BY the time Lincoln left New Salem for Springfield, he had literally hundreds of supporters and admirers who thought of him as their friend. Over and over again, in their letters and in their later recollections, they expressed their admiration and affection for Lincoln. "His friendship," wrote William Engle, "was undying, it was eternal . . . ; it was truly friendship in marble and marble in Clay."[61] "I was Lincolns frend," wrote Henry Clark; "he was my frind."[62] "Lincoln was a man I always loved," echoed John M. Rutledge.[63]

Certainly many from Lincoln's Indiana and New Salem years regarded him as their close friend, but it is less clear how attached he felt toward them. In a number of cases in his later life, mostly when he was making recommendations for appointments, he spoke of a correspondent as "my intimate and personal friend." But there is only one such reference to any of his New Salem acquaintances: he said the son of Dr. Bennett Abell and Elizabeth Abell was "the child of very intimate friends of mine."[64]

By temperament and early training Lincoln grew up as a
man of great reserve, unable to reach out in the broad, good
fellowship that so many politicians cultivate as they strive to be
everyone's closest friend. In his early life, he had never had
anyone in whom he could confide, and that was not a barrier
he could break down as an adult. Herndon, who worked daily
in the same law office with Lincoln for sixteen years, concluded, "He was the most reticent and mostly secretive man
that ever existed: he never opened his whole soul to any man:
he never touched the history or quality of his own nature in the
presence of his friends."[65]

Indeed, Lincoln was so self-contained that he rarely seemed
to reciprocate the affection of those who admired and assisted
him. Some thought him incapable of friendship. "L[incoln] did
forget his friends," John Todd Stuart told Herndon. "There was
no part of his nature which drew him to acts of gratitude to his
friends."[66] Others tried to explain his lack of strong personal
attachments. "He was the warm friend of few men," concluded
Illinois Governor Richard Oglesby, "but he was the true friend
of Mankind."[67] "He was by some considered cold hearted or at
least indifferent towards his friends," agreed Joseph Gillespie,
long a political associate. "This was the result of his extreme
fairness. He would rather disoblige a friend than do an act of
injustice to a political opponent."[68] Leonard Swett, who did
much to promote Lincoln's nomination for President in 1860,
agreed that "beneath a smooth surface of candor and an apparent declaration of all his thoughts and feelings," Lincoln was a
very private man, without intimate friendships: "He handled
and moved man *remotely* as we do pieces upon a chessboard."[69]

II

"HE DISCLOSED HIS WHOLE HEART TO ME"
Lincoln and Joshua F. Speed

THE first time Lincoln met Joshua Speed was on April 15, 1837.[1] Admitted to the bar just six weeks earlier, he rented a horse, thrust all his belongings into the saddlebags, and rode into Springfield from New Salem, ready to begin a new phase of his life. Speed later told of their meeting so many times that he could repeat it by rote: Lincoln came into the general store of Bell & Co., on the courthouse square, to price the furnishings for a single bed—mattress, sheets, blankets, and pillow. Speed, who was part owner of the store, took out his slate and calculated the cost at $17.00.

Lincoln said, "It is probably cheap enough; but . . . I have not the money to pay. But if you will credit me until Christmas, and my experiment here as a lawyer is a success, I will pay you then." He added, in a tone of deep sadness, "If I fail in that I will probably never be able to pay you at all."

Moved by his visitor's melancholy, Speed suggested a solution: "I have a very large room, and a very large double-bed in it; which you are perfectly welcome to share with me if you choose."

"Where is your room?" Lincoln asked.

"Up stairs," replied Speed, pointing to the stairway that led from the store.

Without saying a word, Lincoln picked up his saddlebags, went upstairs, set them on the floor, and came down, his face beaming, and announced: "Well Speed I'm moved."[2]

I

THIS charming story, which Speed recounted over and over again in the years after Lincoln's assassination, has been repeated by nearly every Lincoln biographer, and it is essentially correct. But a little background information is needed to explain why a Springfield merchant should offer to share his bed with a total stranger who happened to wander into his store.

First, as Speed told his friend Cassius M. Clay, his initial conversation with Lincoln was a good deal more extensive.[3] As Speed gave the price of the mattress, the blankets, and the other furnishings, Lincoln walked around the store with him, inspecting each item, and making a memorandum of the cost. In the course of their conversation, Lincoln explained that he had recently been admitted to the bar and had come to Springfield to become John Todd Stuart's partner. He hoped to fit up a small law office and adjacent sleeping room. Indeed, he had already contracted with a local carpenter to build him a single bedstead.

What is more important for understanding the story, it was probably true that Lincoln had not met Speed up to this point, but the storekeeper knew perfectly well who Lincoln was and, indeed, had a good deal of information about him. Speed had heard Lincoln speak in a celebrated 1836 debate in Springfield. He was so effective that George Forquer, a wealthy Springfield resident who had recently left the Whig party to join the Democrats and had been appointed register of the Land Office as a reward, felt it necessary to take Lincoln down, ridiculing him in every way he could. Lincoln, in reply, referred to the lightning rod Forquer had just erected over his splendid Springfield house and told the audience: "I would rather die now, than, like the gentleman change my politics, and simultaneous with the change, receive an office worth three thousand dollars per year, and then have to erect a lightning-rod over my house, to protect a guilty conscience from an offended God."[4] Speed must also have known that Lincoln had served two terms in the Illinois state legislature and was one of the most prominent Whig politicians in the state.

Even so, the two young men were not personally acquainted when they first met.

II

INITIALLY, Speed and Lincoln seemed to be unlikely friends. Lincoln was twenty-eight. Speed, who was born in 1814, was five years younger. Slim and trim, he had, in the days before he began wearing disfiguring whiskers, a handsome face with regular features. The son of a wealthy Kentucky planter, he had been brought up at Farmington, one of the great historic houses of Kentucky, just outside Louisville. A member of a large and caring family, he revered his father, adored his mother, and was fondly affectionate to his numerous brothers and sisters. Carefully educated at the best private schools in the West, he had attended St. Joseph's College in Bardstown for a while before he decided to make his own way in the world. After clerking in a large Louisville store for two or three years, he set out in 1835 for Springfield, where he bought a part interest in the general store of Bell & Co.[5] Though far from Kentucky, he kept up an affectionate correspondence with his father and mother, writing them regularly and informing them, in his somewhat heavy-handed style, that "nothing gives me more pleasure than a consciousness that I have done nothing to forfeit the love or esteem of my parents."[6]

Lincoln, in contrast, was thin and gaunt, and he was still very rough in dress and appearance. He brought to his friend-ship with Speed no record of distinguished ancestry, no history of education and polish. He had nothing to offer except innate good manners, an eager desire to please, and a sensitivity to the needs of others. Both men were drivingly ambitious—Speed for wealth and comfort, Lincoln for fame.

For the next four years, Speed and Lincoln slept in the same bed, above the general store on the town square in Springfield. From time to time, they shared the big room above the store with Billy Herndon, who clerked for Speed, and with Charles Hurst, who also worked in the store. But much of the time, they were alone. The arrangement put Lincoln in closer con-tact with another person than any he had ever experienced.

As Lincoln settled in, he charmed Speed and his clerks with his endless fund of anecdotes, and, as the word spread, other unattached men in Springfield—mostly young lawyers and clerks—began to gather in Speed's store after hours, clustering around the big stove to listen to Lincoln's tales and jokes. They met so regularly that Speed called the group "a social club without organization."[7] Soon the members began presenting their own stories and poems for criticism, and they engaged in informal debates.

When the stove grew cold and the other men went home, Speed and Lincoln were left together, to talk endlessly about everything. They discussed books and literature. Lincoln loved Shakespeare and Burns, some of whose poems he could recite from memory, while Speed favored the poetry of Lord Byron. They both had a taste for melancholy—one might say mor-bid—verse and liked to quote William Knox's "Oh, Why Should the Spirit of Mortal Be Proud?" At the same time they both had a lively sense of humor. Lincoln in these early years was given to burlesque, and his endless anecdotes always had a point; Speed's humor tended to be understated. They shared an intense interest in everything going on in Springfield and central Illinois. In 1841, when Speed was out of town, Lincoln sent him a long letter detailing the alleged murder of one Archibald Fisher, who lived in Warren County. The case fasci-nated Lincoln—the fuller account that he prepared five years later revealed that Fisher was not murdered after all—and he was so sure that Speed shared all his interests that he minutely described the investigation for his friend.[8]

Much of the time, Lincoln and Speed talked politics; they were ardent anti-Jacksonians and supporters of Henry Clay. Complaining of the "trained bands" of Democrats, so well organized that they carried election after election, they signed and helped distribute an 1840 campaign circular announcing that the Whig Committee, to which they both belonged, planned "to organize the whole State, so that every Whig can be brought to the polls in the coming presidential contest."[9] They discussed at length the value of internal improvements— the building of canals and railroads with government funds— which Whigs generally supported and Democrats opposed. Referring to the governor of New York who was responsible for the completion of the Erie Canal, Lincoln, usually so reticent about his political goals, confided to his friend that "his highest ambition was to become the De Witt Clinton of Ills."[10]

But mostly they talked about themselves. Analyzing his roommate, Lincoln concluded that he was *naturally of a nervous temperament,*" which, he judged from Speed's confidences, he probably inherited from his mother.[11] For his part, Speed noted both the kindness of Lincoln's heart and his "nervous sensibility."[12] Once he remarked that Lincoln's mind was "a wonder," because impressions were easily made upon it and were never erased. "No," replied Lincoln, "you are mistaken—I am slow to learn and slow to forget. . . . My mind is like a piece of steel, very hard to scratch any thing on it and almost impossible after you get it there to rub it out."[13] Summarizing their friendship after Lincoln's death, Speed was sure of their total intimacy: "He disclosed his whole heart to me."[14]

III

INEVITABLY questions arise about the nature of this friendship and the influence that it had on Lincoln. Lincoln's letters to Speed in 1842 and 1843 (Speed's letters for these years have unfortunately been lost) make it clear that the two young men shared their most personal feelings, especially about courtship and marriage. It may well be true that, as Lincoln's official biographers, John G. Nicolay and John Hay, asserted, Speed was "the only—as he was certainly the last—intimate friend that Lincoln ever had."[15] But Speed himself was careful to make no great claims that he influenced Lincoln's ideas or policies. After Lincoln's death, he explicitly denied reports that he had helped draft some of Lincoln's speeches, and when Herndon questioned him, he made it clear that he saw the President infrequently during the Civil War years and did not think of himself as a White House intimate. Herndon's verdict on this point is sound. Jealous when other biographers claimed that Lincoln "poured out his soul to Speed," he correctly pointed out that Speed had little, if any, influence on Lincoln's political views. Scornfully, he added that "except in his love scrapes"—in which Speed had been a willing co-conspirator—"Lincoln never poured out his soul to any mortal creature."[16]

Recently, another question has been raised: Was the close relationship between Lincoln and Speed a homosexual one? Or, since the word *homosexual* did not come into use until the 1870s, could it be called a "homoerotic" one? To be blunt, did they have sex together? It was not until the gay liberation movement that these subjects began to be discussed, and with increasing frankness.[17] On a publicity tour that I undertook in 1995–1996 to promote my biography of Lincoln, I was astonished to discover the question most frequently asked was whether Lincoln was gay.[18] The subject deserves careful and cautious discussion.

First, it ought to be noted that no contemporary ever raised the question of sexual relations between Lincoln and Speed. Herndon, who sometimes slept in the same upstairs room over

Speed's store, never mentioned the possibility, though he discussed at length his ideas about Lincoln's sexual interests in
women. Charles Hurst, another of Speed's clerks, who also
slept in the room, never referred to any sexual or even physical
intimacy between the two men. Though nearly every other possible charge against Lincoln was raised during his long public
career—from his alleged illegitimacy to his possible romance
with Ann Rutledge, to the breakup of his engagement to Mary
Todd, to some turbulent aspects of their marriage—no one
ever suggested that he and Speed were sexual partners.

In these still primitive, almost frontier, days in Illinois, it was
anything but uncommon for two or more men to share a bed.
Space was at a premium, and privacy was not much valued or
expected. Unmarried men who worked on farms, or in livery
stables, or in country stores regularly slept in the same beds.
Primitive hotels often offered transients only the option of
sharing a bed with other guests. Even when respectable
lawyers rode the circuit, traveling from county seat to county
seat, they tumbled unceremoniously into bed together. There
was no sexual implication in these sleeping arrangements.

Of course, both Lincoln and Speed knew that men did
sometimes have sex with each other. They had only to read the
Bible to be aware of that. In his Indiana years, Lincoln wrote a
scurrilous poem, "The Chronicles of Reuben," in which he
ridiculed a neighbor he did not like and claimed that, unable
to find a wife, he wed another man. But such relationships
were not merely infrequent; they were against the law. There
were surprisingly few legal cases involving what was called
"sodomy," "the crime against nature," or—where an animal was
a party—"buggery." Jonathan Ned Katz has made a careful
search of all the appeals cases heard during the nineteenth

century by the high courts of twenty-five states and by the federal courts, and has identified only 105 that may have concerned what we call homosexual activity. Only two of these were in Illinois.[19]

During the first half of the nineteenth century, close relations between a man and a woman prior to, or outside of, marriage were frowned on, but intimacies between two people of the same sex—especially if they were young—were readily tolerated. There are a surprising number of well-documented cases of love among young men.[20] Young Ralph Waldo Emerson nearly swooned with passion over Martin Gay, whom he thought the most handsome student at Harvard College, but he was too inhibited to make his love known.[21] Daniel Webster was deeply in love with James Hervey Bingham, a classmate at Dartmouth, with whom he continued on intimate terms long after graduation. He addressed Bingham as "Dearly Beloved," and ended his letters with affectionate phrases like: "Accept all the tenderness I have. D. Webster."[22] The letters between such male lovers are full of references to sleeping together, kisses, caresses, and open longing for each other. There can be no doubt that these were erotic relationships, but with rare exceptions, they do not appear to have been sexual relationships.

The Lincoln-Speed connection did not fall even into that category. Nearly all of the documented erotic relationships between males were between young men—in effect, boys who had reached the peak of their physical powers but were far from ready to assume the role of husband and breadwinner.[23] In contrast, when Lincoln and Speed came together in 1837, neither was a youth: Lincoln was twenty-eight years old and Speed was twenty-three. Nor, when appraising their relationship, can one find anything to suggest a passionate or erotic connection between the two. There is an extensive correspondence between Lincoln and Speed during the 1840s (consisting almost entirely of Lincoln's letters to Speed; Speed's replies have to be conjectured from Lincoln's responses), but, unlike the letters between other enamored males that have been preserved, they are totally lacking in expressions of warm affection. To be sure, Lincoln closed one of his letters, "Yours forever"—but this was the same phrase he used in writing to his law partner and to an Illinois congressman.

The evidence is fragmentary and complex, but my judgment is strongly influenced by the opinion of Charles B. Strozier, the psychoanalyst and historian, who concludes that if the friendship had been sexual Lincoln would have become a different man. He would, Dr. Strozier writes me, have been "a bisexual at best, torn between worlds, full of shame, confused, and hardly likely to end up in politics." What finally convinced me that the relationship between Speed and Lincoln was not a sexual one is an anecdote from late 1864, when Lincoln found it necessary to replace his attorney general and chose Joshua's brother, James Speed. James Speed, he told Titian J. Coffey, the U.S. assistant attorney general, was "a man I know well, though not so well as I know his brother Joshua. That, however, is not strange, for I slept with Joshua for four years, and I suppose I ought to know him."[24] I simply cannot believe that, if the early relationship between Joshua Speed and Lincoln had been sexual, the President of the United States would so freely and publicly speak of it. In my judgment, these two young men were simply close, warm friends, who came close to achieving Montaigne's definition of complete comradeship, a relationship in which "all things being by effect common between them: wills, thoughts, judgments, goods, . . . honour, and life."[25] I do not know whether Speed had earlier, or subsequent, friendships of this nature, but it is clear that this was the first—and perhaps the only—time Lincoln had ever arrived at such a degree of intimacy with any other person.

IV

AT the same time that Lincoln and Speed were living together, both men were eagerly trying to get married. They were in love with the idea of being in love. They were interested in any eligible woman and were so excited by the courtship game that they often felt, as Joshua wrote his sister, "like a tea kettle that is lifting its top and losing its contents by the constant boiling and evaporation."[26] Both flirted with Sarah Rickard, the sixteen-year-old sister-in-law of William Butler, with whom they boarded. Lincoln's attentions to Sarah were probably not serious; after all, he was just extricating himself from what he considered an unsuitable connection with Mary Owens and was hardly likely to make the same mistake so quickly. But years later, Sarah remembered that he talked of marriage, offering "the accounts of the patriarch Abraham's marriage to Sarah" to support his cause. She brushed off his advances, saying she was too young to marry and that she thought of Lincoln "almost like an older Brother."[27] Speed was more deeply involved with the young woman and, after he left for Kentucky, asked Lincoln to report on Sarah's well-being.

But neither was very serious about Sarah because both were looking for brides in the best social circles in Springfield. It may seem preposterous to talk of social classes in a little town that had only about 1,500 residents, but there were exclusive groups, like that of the wealthy and influential Ninian W. Edwards, who owned a large mansion in the southern part of Springfield and who, with his wife, Elizabeth, gave elaborate and fashionable parties. Speed, because of his wealth, his distinguished lineage, and his personal charm, was welcomed in these elite circles. He was, as Herndon said, "a lady's man in a good and true sense."[28]

Acceptance of Lincoln was more problematical because he seemed so rough and socially maladroit. He wanted to meet women, but after his first month in Springfield, he complained that only one had even spoken to him. But presently he too began to get invitations. Everybody in Springfield was aware that he was a coming man. One of the "Long Nine" representatives—so called because they were all very tall—who had lobbied successfully to transfer the state capital from Vandalia to Springfield, he was already a figure of political importance. And it was no secret that he had moved from New Salem to Springfield to become the law partner of John Todd Stuart, one of the most prominent attorneys in the city, who was closely connected to the Edwards circle.

The two bachelors met young women primarily at the Saturday soirées at the Edwards mansion. Elizabeth Edwards was a matchmaker. She had already helped two of her sisters find eligible husbands, and she welcomed a third, Mary Todd, when she came for a long visit. Ninian Edwards also had relatives visiting from time to time, such as the beautiful and pious Matilda Edwards. Mary and Matilda formed "the grand centre of attraction" in Springfield society, as James C. Conkling wrote. "Swarms of strangers who had little else to engage their attention hovered around them, to catch a *passing smile*."[29]

Young women in the Edwards circle thought Speed handsome, romantic, and highly eligible. He flirted with many but centered his attention on Matilda. By December 1840, Mary Todd shrewdly observed that Speed's "ever changing heart . . . is about offering its young affections at [Matilda's] shrine." He seems to have been genuinely in love, but, even though Ninian Edwards favored the match, she refused him.[30] Possibly she suspected that he was a roué. Many years later, he himself spread the highly improbable rumor that he was at this very time keeping a pretty young girl in Springfield.[31] Whatever the reason, he tried to rationalize his failure. "I endeavor to persuade myself that there is more pleasure in pursuit of any object, than there is in its possession," he wrote his sister. "This general rule I wish *now* most particularly to apply to women. I have been most anxiously in pursuit of one—and . . . if my philosophy be true I am to be most enviably felicitous, for I may have as much of the anticipation and pursuit as I please, but the possession I can hardly ever hope to realize."[32]

Meanwhile, Lincoln concentrated his attention on Mary Todd. They were, as Mrs. Edwards recalled, an odd couple. When they were together, "Mary led the conversation—Lincoln would listen and gaze on her as if drawn by some superior power, irresistably [*sic*] so." He "could not hold a lengthy conversation with a lady—was not sufficiently educated and intelligent in the female line to do so," she remembered, but he "was charmed with Mary's wit and fascinated with her quick sagacity—her will—her nature—and culture."[33]

As Lincoln and Speed played the mating game, they naturally exchanged confidences. Henry David Thoreau once remarked that friends "cherish each other's hopes. They are kind to each other's dreams." Both of these young men thought they wanted to marry, but they had forebodings, probably related to doubts about their sexual adequacy. Charles Strozier, the psychohistorian, believes it is possible that both were virgins.[34] Lincoln's anxiety may also have referred to a fear of losing autonomy; he had never been intimate with any woman or, indeed, except for Speed, with any other person. Also, he and Speed shared what Lincoln called "the peculiar misfortune" of dreaming "dreams of Elysium far exceeding all that any thing earthly can realize," and they recognized that marriage might mean disappointment.[35]

While Speed's pursuit of Matilda Edwards failed, Lincoln's courtship of Mary Todd advanced almost too rapidly. He first wrote to her in the fall of 1840, when he was in southern Illinois campaigning for the Whig presidential ticket headed by General William Henry Harrison, and when he returned to Springfield, the ties between them grew stronger. He became one of her regular attendants at parties, on horseback rides, on jaunts to neighboring towns. By the winter of 1840, they were engaged.

Once Lincoln made the commitment, however, he began to have doubts. With no regular income except a beginning law practice, he was not sure he could afford a wife and family. Maybe he was not ready for marriage. Maybe Mary was not the right one for him. He shared his doubts with Speed, who considered them "foolish."[36] Unpersuaded, Lincoln wrote Mary Todd a letter breaking off the engagement. When Speed saw it, he told Lincoln to burn it. Saying, "Once put your words in writing and they Stand as a living and eternal Monument against you," he advised Lincoln: "If you think you have *will* and Manhood Enough to go and see her and Speak to her what you say in that letter, you may do that."[37]

Lincoln did go to see Mary and told her that he did not love her.* She broke into tears. To comfort her, he drew her down onto his knees and kissed her. When he got back to his room, he told his friend what had happened, and Speed said it was "a bad lick, but it cannot now be helped." They assumed the engagement still held, and in the next week or so in the new year, Lincoln continued to go about his business in the state legislature.

But at about the same time he learned that Speed was going to return permanently to Kentucky. Perhaps Matilda Edwards's rejection precipitated Speed's decision to leave Springfield, but it could hardly have been unexpected. The death of his father in the spring of 1840 left his family desolate, and Speed wrote to his mother: "If it would be any consolation to you in your affliction to have me with you, you have only to let me know and I will be with you and shed with you 'tear for tear.'"[38] She did want him at home, and Speed made arrangements to sell his share of the general store on what Lincoln later called "that fatal first of Jany. '41." While attempting to cope with this news, Lincoln received a letter from Mary, who had been brooding over his reason for asking to be released from their engagement. Believing that he was in love with another woman—probably Matilda Edwards—she accepted his decision, letting him know "that she would hold the question an open one—that is that She had not Changed her mind, but felt as always."[39]

---

*It is not possible to establish an exact chronology for these events. Biographers, including myself, have generally assumed that Lincoln's later phrase, "that fatal first of Jany. '41," referred to his break with Mary Todd. But Douglas L. Wilson, in a brilliant piece of historical detective work, has established that the break could not have occurred at that time. Indeed, Mary Todd may not even have been in Springfield on that date. He suggests that the phrase may refer to some unknown crisis in Speed's affairs. Wilson, "'That Fatal First of January,'" in his *Lincoln Before Washington*, pp. 99–133.

The news devastated Lincoln. Though he had earlier longed to end his commitment to Mary Todd, he now began to suspect—just as he had after Mary Owens turned him down—that he loved her more than he had thought. Even more important, he was haunted by "the never-absent idea" that he had made Mary unhappy. "That still kills my soul," he told Speed. "I cannot but reproach myself, for even wishing to be happy while she is otherwise."[40] All this vacillation cost him confidence in his ability to keep his resolves once they were made, which was, he wrote Speed, "the only, or at least the chief, gem of my character."[41]

Losing both his only intimate friend and his fiancée within a matter of days was more than Lincoln could bear, and he collapsed. Taking to his bed for about a week, he was unwilling to see anyone except his doctor and Speed, who had not yet left for Kentucky. Years later, Speed said he thought Lincoln might commit suicide and felt obliged "to remove razors from his room—take away all knives and other such dangerous things."[42] Speed's fears were unwarranted, but they indicate how deeply he was implicated in Lincoln's affairs and anxieties.

Deeply troubled, Speed warned Lincoln that he would die unless he got a grip on himself. Lincoln responded that he was not afraid of dying—indeed, that he would be more than willing to die, but for his regret "that he had done nothing to make any human being remember that he had lived" and that he had not done anything to make the world better for having lived in it.[43]

Just what specific advice Speed offered his friend is unknown, but my guess is that he told Lincoln that he should either end his relationship with Mary Todd or marry her. Lincoln acknowledged the correctness of the advice but could not act on it. Unable to make a choice, he was, as he wrote his law partner, John T. Stuart, "the most miserable man living. If what I feel were equally distributed to the whole human family, there would not be one cheerful face on earth."[44] More than a year later, he still could not decide. "Before I resolve to do the one thing or the other," he confessed to Speed, "I must regain my confidence in my own ability to keep my resolves when they are made."[45]

V

BY the end of January, Lincoln resumed his duties in the Illinois House of Representatives and attended to his legal cases, though in a somewhat lackadaisical fashion. Confident that Lincoln was recovering, Speed felt able to leave Springfield in May, after extracting a promise from his friend to visit the Speed family that summer. Partly because Lincoln was entering into a new law partnership with Stephen T. Logan, he was not able to get away until August.

For nearly a month, he stayed at Farmington, the Speed mansion, a few miles outside Louisville. It was the first vacation he had ever had and his introduction to the luxury and leisure of Southern society at its best. Farmington was a handsome fourteen-room brick house, built, according to tradition, after a plan that had been drawn up by Thomas Jefferson, who was an old friend of Mrs. Speed's family back in Virginia, and it was surrounded by beautiful grounds.[46] He had a little difficulty in getting used to the elegance and formality of the Speeds' way of life. At one dinner, featuring a saddle of mutton, when the relish was passed, he made the mistake of keeping it at his plate until he observed that others, on the opposite side of the table, were sharing it. Embarrassed, he asked Joshua why he had not told him better, and his friend replied: "I expected you to look at me Linco[l]n and do as I do."[47]

Despite his faux pas, Lincoln remembered his stay at Farmington as an idyllic time. Mrs. Speed gave him one of the spacious bedrooms, and a house slave was assigned to take care of his every need. Day after day, he took long walks with Joshua, and at least once they took a carriage ride to call on Fanny Henning, a young woman in whom Joshua had become deeply interested. From time to time Lincoln would go into Louisville, where James Speed, Joshua's brother, had a thriving law practice. "He sat in my office, read my books, and talked with me about his life, his reading, his studies, his aspirations," James recalled. "He was earnest, frank, manly, and sincere in every thought and expression."[48]

But mostly he stayed close to Farmington, where Mrs. Speed, aware that her guest seemed exhausted and melancholy when he arrived, did her best to comfort and cheer him. Before he left, she presented him with an Oxford Bible, assuring him it was the best cure for depression that could be found. "I intend to read it regularly when I return home," he promised, adding, as he saved both his manners and his religious skepticism, "I doubt not that it is really . . . the best cure for the 'Blues' could one but take it according to the truth."[49]

Others in the Speed household also did their best to cheer him up. He long remembered "the delicious dishes of peaches and cream" that the Speeds served guests. He liked all of Joshua's brothers and sisters, who exerted their Southern charm to make him feel part of the family. One of them, for example, involved him in an attempt to give a name to her homestead. He developed a special liking for Mary Speed, and they became "something of cronies." In one game they played, he remembered, he "was under the necessity of shutting you up in a room to prevent your committing an assault and battery upon me."[50]

He also tried to help Joshua. When the two young men called on Fanny Henning, an orphan who lived nearby with her uncle, John Williamson, Joshua found he could make no headway with his courtship because Williamson, an ardent Whig, insisted on engaging his visitors in a political discussion. By prearrangement, Lincoln, a die-hard Whig, pretended to be a Jacksonian Democrat and ensnared Williamson in such a lengthy political argument that Joshua was able to escape for a few minutes of private conversation with Fanny. He proposed and was accepted.[51]

All in all, this was one of the happiest times in Lincoln's life, hardly marred by a miserable toothache and the botched job a Louisville dentist made in trying to extract the tooth. Another ache he managed to conceal for many years. In September, accompanied by Joshua, who needed to return to Springfield to finish his business dealings, he took the steamboat *Lebanon* down the Ohio River. Aboard were twelve slaves who were being sold down the river, separated from wives, children, and family; to prevent any from trying to escape they were, Lincoln observed, chained together, "strung together precisely like so many fish upon a trot-line." Yet, he wrote in a letter to Mary Speed, they seemed remarkably happy, playing the fiddle almost constantly, dancing, singing, and cracking jokes. They were "the most cheerful and apparantly happy creatures on board."[52] Perhaps Lincoln's assessment reflected his own happiness, now that he had recovered from his prolonged depression. More likely, I think, it showed what he thought it was proper to include in a letter to a lady. In his heart, as he wrote Joshua in 1855, the sight of the slaves shackled together with irons was "a continual torment." He was sure that it was equally outrageous to "the great body of the Northern people," who kept silent and crucified "their feelings, in order to maintain their loyalty to the constitution and the Union."[53]

VI

BACK in Springfield with Speed, Lincoln learned to his surprise that his friend was beginning to have doubts about his engagement to Fanny Henning. It was a feeling Lincoln found unreasonable, because he thought Fanny "one of the sweetest girls in the world," even though she did have a tendency toward melancholy.[54] During the winter of 1841–1842, he spent hours trying to persuade Speed that his fears of marriage were unjustified. It was, as Gary L. Williams has remarked, as if Lincoln and Speed were playing a game of doctor and patient. Just one year earlier, it was Lincoln who was the patient and Speed the doctor; now, in a complete reversal of roles, Speed was the patient and Lincoln the doctor.[55]

In January 1842, as Speed prepared to return to Kentucky, Lincoln wrote him a long letter of analysis and advice, preferring the written to the spoken word because he feared Speed would forget his diagnosis "at the verry time when it might do you some good." During the months ahead, he predicted, Speed was going to worry, over and over again, whether he loved Fanny as much as he should. This fear originated in Speed's "nervous debility," which was likely to be exacerbated by exposure to bad weather on his journey home and by the absence of business and conversation with friends ("like Lincoln" was implied).[56]

In this and in a series of weekly letters throughout February, Lincoln attempted to convince his friend that his fears were unwarranted. The thought of Fanny's "heavenly *black eyes*" should be enough to dispel Speed's worries.[57] Then, too, Speed's extreme anxiety when Fanny fell ill ought surely forever to "banish those horid doubts . . . as to the truth of your affection for her." "Why Speed," Lincoln continued, "if you did not love her, although you might not wish her death, you would most calmly be resigned to it." Apologizing for this "rude intrusion upon your feelings," Lincoln reminded Speed of his own experience: "You know the Hell I have suffered on that point, and how tender I am upon it."[58]

As the time for Speed's wedding approached, Lincoln continued to worry that his friend's nerves might fail him at the last minute—just as his own had failed when he was engaged to Mary Todd. Again, he urged Speed to get involved in some business right away, to divert his attention from his anxieties over marriage. If Speed could manage to get through the wedding "ceremony *calmly,* or even with sufficient composure not to excite alarm in any present," he was sure to be all right, and Lincoln predicted that within two or three months he would be "the happiest of men."

Unconvinced, Speed, only three days before the wedding, wrote that he continued to have "forebodings" and that he was still haunted by something "indescribably horrible and alarming," which made him sure that the Elysium of which he had dreamed so much was "never to be realized." Rather inappropriately Lincoln advised his friend to remember a saying of his father, Thomas Lincoln: "If you make a bad bargain *hug* it the tighter."[59] And Speed must have taken cold comfort from Lincoln's warning that after he was married, "it is even yet possible for your spirits to flag down and leave you miserable."[60]

But on the day after the wedding, Speed wrote another letter, which Lincoln opened "with intense anxiety and trepidation." He was so excited, he wrote, that "I have hardly yet, at the distance of ten hours, become calm."[61] Having feared the worst, Lincoln was delighted that the letter—and presumably the wedding—"turned out better than I expected." A month later, when Speed wrote that his marriage made him far happier than he had ever anticipated, Lincoln replied that the news gave him "inexpressible" joy and brought him "more pleasure, than the total sum of all I have enjoyed since that fatal first of Jany. '41."[62]

These letters—the most intimately personal letters that Lincoln ever wrote—stemmed from his desire to comfort and encourage his closest friend, but they also had another purpose. Quietly and privately, mutual acquaintances had begun bringing Lincoln and Mary Todd together, with the injunction: "Be friends." They rediscovered the interests they had in common, both in poetry and in politics, and by fall they were ready to renew their engagement. But before taking the final step, Lincoln felt he had to know how Speed's marriage was working out. In October, eight months after the Speeds' wedding, he dared ask his friend an intimate question: "Are you now, in *feeling* as well as *judgment,* glad you are married as you are?" Lincoln recognized that from anyone else, this would be "an impudent question not to be tolerated; but I know you will pardon it in me."[63]

Evidently Speed responded positively, because Abraham

Lincoln and Mary Todd were married on November 4, 1842.

For the rest of his life, Speed remained convinced that he had played a central role in bringing about their union. "If I had not been married and happy—far more happy than I ever expected to be," he told Herndon, "He would not have married."[64]

VII

ALONG with Lincoln's happiness that Speed's marriage was successful, there was an element of sadness. He worried that in the future, Joshua and Fanny would be "so exclusively concerned for one another, that I shall be forgotten entirely." He had hoped that the Speeds would make their home in Springfield, but he learned that Fanny was unwilling to leave her relatives and friends. "I shall be verry lonesome without you," he told Speed. "How miserably things seem to be aranged in this world," he exclaimed. "If we have no friends, we have no pleasure; and if we have them, we are sure to lose them, and be doubly pained by the loss."[65]

Lincoln's fears were justified. After Speed married Fanny the two close friends began to drift apart. There was not then, or ever, a rift between them, but Speed increasingly turned to his wife, rather than to his friend, for emotional support. Rather to his surprise, he discovered that Fanny's presence was "necessary both to my health and happiness." When they were briefly separated during the single term he served in the Kentucky legislature, he felt desolate, and when she joined him, he was ecstatic. "Were it not that my senses tell me that it is winter," he told his mother, "I would almost think that spring has come."[66] "My earthly treasure is in you," he wrote Fanny, in his somewhat florid style, a number of years later; "not like the treasures only valuable in possession; not like other valuables acquiring increased value from increased quantity; but, satisfied with each other, we will go down the hill of life together, as we have risen."[67]

Speed busied himself by becoming a farmer on a thousand-acre tract in what was called the Pond Settlement, some thirteen miles outside Louisville. Lincoln said frankly that he had "no sympathy" for Speed's new career. "*I* have no farm, nor ever expect to have; and, consequently have not studied the subject enough to be much interested with it. I can only say that I am glad *you* are satisfied and pleased with it."[68] For his part, Speed continued to retain Lincoln (who was now a member of the Logan and Lincoln partnership) to collect a number of small notes and other debts due him for his storekeeping days in Springfield, but he was evidently bored by the minutely detailed financial reports that Lincoln kept sending him of collections, interest payments, and overdue mortgages. Recognizing that Lincoln was acting as his agent, not as his friend, he nevertheless slightly begrudged the commission he charged. Asking for a report on one collection, he ended his letter: "Your *toll* you will keep of course. Make it as light as you can."[69]

Both men repeatedly affirmed their desire to see each other again, and they exchanged frequent invitations to visit. But there were always problems. "I reckon it will scarcely be in our power to visit Kentucky this year," Lincoln lamented in 1843, adding, "I most heartily wish you and your Fanny would not fail to come" to Springfield, where the Lincolns and the Speeds could "all be merry together for awhile."[70] The two men passed along greetings from their respective spouses. "Mary . . . continues her old sentiments of friendship for you," Lincoln assured Speed.[71] "Mary joins in sending love to your Fanny and you," he ended another letter.[72]

Just how cordial these wishes actually were is hard to tell. Fanny Speed did not write to the Lincolns after she was married, and no letters exist from Mary Lincoln to either Joshua or Fanny Speed. In general, Mary did not look kindly on most of Lincoln's female acquaintances, and she knew—for all her husband's protestations of hospitality—that she had no way of properly entertaining the Speeds so long as she lived in the one room at the Globe tavern that the Lincolns rented during the early months of their marriage.

When Mary became pregnant with her first child, there was just a hint of something less than amiability in her view of the Speeds. Hearing the news, Joshua apparently remembered an earlier conversation, or perhaps a promise, and asked about the prospect of having a namesake in the Lincoln household. Lincoln replied evasively, and Mary named the first son, born on November 2, 1843, Robert Todd Lincoln, after her father.

Over the years, correspondence between Lincoln and Speed diminished to a trickle. Speed's letters to Lincoln during this period have been lost, but Lincoln's are full of expressions like, "It has been a long time since I wrote you last, but you have not been forgotten nevertheless."[73] By 1846 their letters had become so infrequent that Lincoln grieved over "allowing a friendship, such as ours, to die by degrees," and urged that they both pledge to write each other regularly.[74]

In time, the two old friends began to drift apart politically. Both Whigs, they initially agreed on all the issues of the day, including slavery, which had not yet become a major national concern. Always opposed to slavery, Lincoln in 1837 had cosponsored a resolution in the Illinois legislature condemning the South's "peculiar institution," and at that time Speed admitted the abstract wrong of slavery.

But by the 1850s, as sectional tensions grew stronger, their agreement in theory broke down in practice. In 1854, when Stephen A. Douglas introduced the Kansas-Nebraska bill, which would permit the introduction of slavery into national territory from which it had been barred by the 1820 Missouri Compromise, Lincoln was outraged, and within two years he moved into leadership of the new Republican party, dedicated to containing slavery. At the same time, Speed was drifting in the opposite direction. He came from a family of slaveholders. At his death, his father had owned fifty-seven slaves,[75] a large holding for Kentucky, and Joshua inherited four of them. Unlike his brother James, who called slavery "the greatest national sin"[76] and freed his bondsmen, Joshua had no moral repugnance to owning slaves. Indeed, over the years, he felt the need to buy others to work his large farm, so that by 1850 he had eighteen slaves. Even after he gave up farming and moved to Louisville, where he engaged in extremely profitable ventures in real estate and railroads, he continued to own between eight and fourteen slaves, and at one point his partnership with his brother-in-law, Speed & Henning, advertised "Valuable Slaves for Sale."[77] Slave ownership became for him a right, not an evil to be tolerated. He wrote Lincoln that "as a christian," he would "rather rejoice" if the inhabitants of Kansas decided to exclude slavery, but he insisted on their legal right to admit it. Sooner than yield that, he would see the Union dissolved.[78]

Because Speed had no political ambitions, his differences with Lincoln did not lead to a rupture of their friendship. After serving his one term in the Kentucky legislature and finding that it did "nothing of general importance," Speed willingly withdrew to private life.[79] So when Lincoln received the Republican nomination for President in 1860, Speed could warmly congratulate him as "a warm personal friend, though as you are perhaps aware a political opponent." He expressed a belief that, if elected, Lincoln would "honestly administer the government—and make a lasting reputation for yourself." He added that Fanny was warmly supportive of Lincoln and ended with an invitation for the Lincolns to visit Kentucky.[80] Lincoln replied that he was not surprised that Mrs. Speed—for so Fanny had become in their infrequent correspondence—was his political supporter: "with her nature and views, she could not well be otherwise." Declining Speed's invitation because of the press of business, he asked plaintively: "Could not she and you visit us here?"[81]

That fall, when Lincoln was elected, Speed again sent his "sincere congratulations upon your elevation to the highest position in the world—by the suf[f]rage of a free people. As a friend, I am rejoiced at your success—as a political opponent I am not disappointed. The result is what I expected."[82]

VIII

IN congratulating the President Elect, Speed took occasion to warn Lincoln of the grave dangers ahead. In Kentucky, the Republican ticket had received only 1,365 votes—1 percent of the total—and in most states of the Deep South none. Disloyalty and disunionism were rampant. He alerted Lincoln to the basic problem: "How to deal with the combustible material lying around without setting fire to the edifice of which we are all so proud and of which you will be the chief custodian is a dificult [sic] task." He offered, entirely as "a private citizen seeking no office for himself nor for any friend he has," to visit Lincoln and give him "some information as to men and public sentiment here which may be valuable." "I will deem it no disrispect [sic], and not take it unkindly if you decline the interview," he concluded hesitantly. "Be as frank as the free commerce of friendship dictates."[83]

Eagerly, Lincoln accepted the offer and suggested that Speed meet him in Chicago on November 22, 1860, where he already had some other interviews arranged. Mary Lincoln planned to go to Chicago with her husband, he wrote his old friend, "and therefore I suggest that Mrs. S. accompany you."[84] When the Speeds reached the Tremont House, they found the entrance so crowded with journalists and political hangers-on that they could get in only by showing Lincoln's letter. The President Elect warmly greeted them and, seeking to get away from the crowd, went to Speed's room. Throwing himself across the bed, he looked worn-out and exhausted. For an hour or more, while the two ladies shopped, the two men reminisced about their days in Springfield. Then, turning to the business at hand, Lincoln asked: "Speed what are your pecuniary conditions—are you rich, or poor?" Clearly he intended to offer him an office in the new administration that he was forming. Unfortunately, he was less clear in saying that he badly needed a close, trusted friend like Speed as his confidant and adviser in Washington. Responding to only the first of Lincoln's purposes, Speed replied: "Mr Presdt. I think I know what you wish. I'll Speak Candidly to you—My pecuniary Conditions are good—I do not think you have any office within

your gift that I can afford to take."[85] If he sensed Lincoln's second purpose, he took no notice of it.

With that tacit rejection, Lincoln changed the subject and
told Speed how much he needed a Southern man in the cabinet he was constructing. One frequently mentioned possibility
was James Guthrie, the immensely wealthy Kentucky railroad-
man who had once served as secretary of war. Not wanting to
make any formal offer, lest it lead to a public rebuff, he asked
Speed, a friend of Guthrie, gingerly to raise the possibility with
him. As it turned out, Guthrie said he was not available
because of age and health.[86]

Speed's refusal to join Lincoln's administration was a blow to
the President personally, but in the years ahead, it proved an
immense advantage to the country. As the states of the Deep
South seceded, Lincoln's most immediate task was to retain
the loyalty of the border states. The situation in Kentucky was
urgent. Though a majority of Kentuckians were undoubtedly
loyal to the Union, many had close ties to the South. Governor
Beriah Magoffin was sympathetic to the Confederate cause,
and the state guard, the only armed force in the state, was led
by an unabashed secessionist, Simon Bolivar Buckner. It was
necessary for Lincoln to strengthen the Union cause in
Kentucky, but any overt move might drive the state into the
arms of the Confederacy. Providentially, Lieutenant William
Nelson of the navy turned up at the White House with a plan.
A Kentuckian by birth, an enormous man as tall as Lincoln
himself but weighing three hundred pounds, "Bull" Nelson
proposed secretly to distribute five thousand guns from the
federal arsenals to loyalists in his home state. Greatly relieved,
Lincoln directed Nelson to consult with Joshua Speed, who
would help him identify prominent influential Kentucky loyal-

ists, and he authorized the shipment of the guns, in care of Speed, to Jeffersonville, Indiana, across the Ohio River from Louisville. Acting with great secrecy, Joshua, together with his brother James, arranged for Nelson to meet with other prominent Unionists in Frankfort, where they worked out a plan for distributing the federal guns after they were smuggled across the Ohio. Speed was chosen to countersign each requisition. News of the arrival of these "Lincoln guns," as they were soon called, brought about a major shift in public opinion in Kentucky. "Our friends speak out with boldness and confidence," Speed wrote Lincoln, "while the secessionists hang their heads—and are in a state of trepidation and fear."[87]

So indispensable had Speed become that in May 1861, when Lincoln named General Robert Anderson, who had been forced to surrender at Fort Sumter, to command the Department of the Ohio, he specifically instructed him to consult Joshua Speed. "I have the utmost confidence in his loyalty and integrity," he told Anderson, "and also in his judgment on any subject which he professes to understand." Speed, he added, would prove "a most agreeable companion, and at the same time a most valuable assistant in our common cause."[88]

In the months—indeed, in the years—ahead, Speed became the President's most trusted intermediary in Kentucky. "A quiet, observant, courageous man," as the adjutant general of Kentucky characterized him, Speed rallied the Unionists with his soft-spoken, modestly presented arguments, but he did not hesitate to use a stronger tone when necessary. After two of the largest banks in Louisville balked at lending money to support the raising of troops for the Union, Speed, one of the wealthiest men in the city, was called in to persuade them. "His interview with the hesitating officials was brief," his biographer wrote, "but it was pointed and earnest. It was successful."[89]

Speed wrote Lincoln frequently during the early months of the war. "Genl. Anderson needs at least one thousand Regulars with as many Western regular Officers to command Volunteers as you can spare," he telegraphed Lincoln in September 1861; "any movement must be vigorous to be useful."[90] He promised: "We can get men enough, if we had arms."[91] Recognizing that getting action from the slow-moving federal bureaucracy required personal intervention, Speed came to Washington himself and persuaded Lincoln to escort him to the office of the Adjutant General, Lorenzo Thomas, to make sure that arms, equipment, and officers were supplied promptly to General Anderson's department.[92]

The President almost always accepted Speed's recommendations of loyal Kentuckians for civilian or military appointments, forwarding his letters to the appropriate departments with endorsements like: "Let the request of my friend, J. F. Speed be granted, if it is consistently possible."[93] If there was special urgency about a request, Speed knew exactly how to attract Lincoln's interest. When General Jeremiah T. Boyle began infringing on the civil liberties of Kentuckians, Speed gave Lincoln the grounds on which he sought Boyle's removal: "First I desire the Govt saved. Second Ky saved to the Union. third and not much less than either I desire *you* to be the instrument by which all these results are attained."[94] Again, when he urged Lincoln to appoint a court-martial for General Thomas L. Crittenden, a fellow Kentuckian who was censured for his conduct at the battle of Chickamauga (September 19–20, 1863), he ended his petition: "I earnestly ask this as *your* friend and a friend of the cause."[95]

IX

UNFLAGGING in his support of Lincoln's military actions, Speed was often critical of his domestic policies, especially as they related to slavery. He was especially upset because he feared Lincoln was behind the proclamation that John C. Frémont, the Union general in command at St. Louis, issued in August 1861 placing Missouri under martial law and declaring the slaves of all rebels free. For a time, Speed was so horrified that he could not eat or sleep, and he sent a barrage of letters and telegrams to the President attacking "that foolish proclamation,"[96] which he privately called the act of "a mi[li]tary popinjay."[97] If Frémont's proclamation was allowed to stand, he assured Lincoln, "cruelty and crime would run riot in the land [and] the poor negroes would be almost exterminated." It would also "crush out any vestage [*sic*] of a union party in the state," he predicted, though he assured Lincoln it would not affect his own loyalty, "for I do not intend that the act of any military chieftain or any administration shall drive me from my fidelity to my government."[98]

Greatly relieved when Lincoln overruled Frémont, Speed continued to worry about the increasing Northern pressure on the President to act against slavery. While he was in Washington, he became aware of what he called "a large and powerful party of the Ultra men . . . being formed to make war upon the President," but he had little success in persuading Lincoln that he should form a counter-coalition with the few Southern men still in the Congress, the Northern Democrats, and some conservative Republicans to fight the radicals in the next congressional election. Lincoln refused to consider his Republican political associates potential enemies. "He is so honest himself," Speed lamented, "that he is slow to believe that others are not equal[l]y so."[99]

Speed became so discouraged that in December 1861, he wrote a curious letter to his old friend Joseph Holt, a fellow Kentuckian who had served as President James Buchanan's last secretary of war, urging him to reenter public life, especially if Lincoln offered him a cabinet post. "Your chances for the highest position within the gift of the people at the next election are better than those of any other man," he assured Holt. "No man now has so firm a hold upon the popular heart."[100] The letter is hard to explain in view of Speed's sustained friendship for Lincoln, whom he was thus privately proposing, after less than one year in office, to replace with Holt. It is his only expression of disloyalty to Lincoln that I have discovered. Perhaps it stemmed from Speed's exhaustion and despair after spending several weeks in Washington combating the inertia of an administration that seemed unable to act. Perhaps Speed remembered that no President since Andrew Jackson had been elected to a second term, and he was therefore thinking of a likely successor to Lincoln. Or perhaps Speed was simply playing on what he knew to be Holt's insatiable vanity.

Whatever the reason, this note of implied disloyalty does not appear in Speed's other correspondence, even when he was thoroughly dissatisfied with the President. In the summer of 1862, as pressure grew for the President to act against slavery, Lincoln and Speed discussed the emancipation proclamation that he was preparing. Speed was initially opposed and told Lincoln so. The President explained that he was acting from military necessity and predicted that Speed would come to recognize the wisdom of the act when he saw "the harvest of good which he would erelong glean from it." But what quieted Speed's dissent was Lincoln's reminder of the conversation they had so many years ago, when he lamented that he had done nothing to improve the world or impress his name on history. Earnestly he told Speed: "I believe that in this measure (meaning his proclamation) my fondest hopes will be realized."[101]

X

DIFFERENCES over policy did not disrupt the friendship between Lincoln and Speed. Worried that he so often found the President looking haggard and care worn, he tried to cheer him up with presents of Kentucky delicacies, sending on one occasion six hams to the White House. Another attempt to brighten Lincoln's spirits had unfortunate consequences. Speed introduced to the White House two "agreeable ladies," Mrs. Cosby and Miss Nettie Colburn, "both mediums and believers in the spirits."[102] Mary Lincoln, grieving over the death of their second son, Willie, fell into the trap of attending Nettie Colburn's spiritualist séances.

Lincoln, for his part, always welcomed Speed's visits to Washington, though they became less frequent as affairs in Kentucky stabilized. He made a point of inviting Joshua and Fanny Speed to the Lincolns' first Thanksgiving dinner in the White House in 1861.[103] At a time when Speed was still upset over the Frémont proclamation, Lincoln took pains to send his photograph to Speed's mother, inscribed: "For Mrs. Lucy G. Speed, from whose pious hand I accepted the present of an Oxford Bible twenty years ago."[104]

That Bible played a part in one of the most frequently

quoted of Speed's anecdotes about Lincoln during wartime. In the summer of 1864, according to Speed's *Recollections*, published twenty years after Lincoln's death, the Lincolns invited Speed to the Soldiers' Home, an airy retreat several miles from the White House, where they tried to escape the summer heat of Washington. Arriving near nightfall, Speed discovered his old friend sitting at a window intently reading his Bible. Recalling Lincoln's early questioning of Christianity, Speed remarked, "I am glad to see you so profitably engaged."

"Yes," said Lincoln, "I am profitably engaged."

"Well," Speed continued, "if you have recovered from your skepticism, I am sorry to say that I have not."

Looking at his old friend earnestly and placing his hand on Speed's shoulder, Lincoln replied: "You are wrong Speed, take all of this book upon reason that you can, and the balance on faith, and you will live and die a happier and better man."[105]

Perhaps the story is true. It is certainly correct to say that Lincoln turned to the Bible for reflection and consolation as the seemingly endless war wore on. But I have nagging doubts about it. The story has a precision and detail that are generally lacking from Speed's recollections of wartime. It is not clear how much Speed knew about Lincoln's early beliefs, since he told Herndon that in Springfield he never discussed religion with Lincoln. And, finally, the anecdote makes Speed, not Lincoln, the skeptic, though Lincoln never joined any church, while Speed became a devout member of the Kentucky Methodist Church, to which he and his wife eventually made bequests of more than $375,000.

But about another of Speed's stories there is no ground for doubt. Early in 1865, Lincoln, hearing that Speed was about to return to Kentucky, summoned him to the White House.[106]

Waiting in the President's office until his hour for visitors was over, Speed thought the President looked jaded and weary. He listened as Lincoln took care of his last two petitioners, women from western Pennsylvania who asked him to release a prisoner—the son of the older woman, the husband of the younger—arrested for resisting the draft. When he granted their petition, the younger woman rushed across the room and began to kneel. Impatiently, Lincoln told her, "Get up, get up; none of this." The older woman, with tears in her eyes, gave him her hand and said, "Good-bye, Mr. Lincoln, we will never meet again till we meet in Heaven."

"I am afraid that I will never get there," the President said as he escorted them to the door, "but your wish that you will meet me there has fully paid for all I have done for you."

After the women left, the President drew his chair close to the hearth and, pulling off his boots, put his feet so close to the fire that they steamed. "Speed," he said, "I am a little alarmed about myself; just feel my hand." Speed found it cold and clammy. "I am," he said, "very unwell—my feet and hands are always cold—I suppose I ought to be in bed." Speed scolded that he was exhausted and should not spend his time on petitioners like these two women. "How much you are mistaken," replied the President; "I have made two people happy to-day." "Speed," he went on, "die when I may I want it said of me by those who know me best . . . that I always plucked a thistle and planted a flower where I thought a flower would grow."

It was the last time that Speed saw his friend.[107]

III

"I Could Read
His Secrets"

Lincoln and William H. Herndon

SPEED'S departure left Lincoln without an intimate friend.[1]
Of course, he knew dozens of people in Springfield and had a
free and easy relationship with young men like William Jayne,
James H. Matheny, and James C. Conkling, whom he saw
almost daily. These were men whom we could call "enjoyable"
friends—men from whom nothing was required or expected
except the pleasure of their company. They talked together
when they met on the streets of Springfield, they occasionally
took walks in the woods together, and from time to time some
of them played "fives," an early version of handball, using a
vacant lot and bouncing the ball against the walls of one of the
brick stores on the square. Some years later, Lincoln developed
a similar friendship with Ward Hill Lamon, a big, burly lawyer
who lived in Danville and was often Lincoln's associate in

Vermilion County law cases. Lincoln liked Lamon for his dirty stories and for his endless repertoire of popular songs. Not the greatest lawyer, not a man of letters, and, indeed, not the brightest man in the world, Lamon had a dog-like devotion to Lincoln. He accompanied Lincoln as President Elect on his journey to Washington in 1861 and, named marshal of the District of Columbia, served as a self-appointed bodyguard to the President, at times sleeping on blankets outside the door of his bedroom in the White House to protect him from would-be assassins. Lincoln referred to him as "my particular friend."[2]

Lincoln had numerous other acquaintances who might be characterized as "useful" friends—men with whom he worked closely on political and legal affairs. With many of his political allies, his relations were courteous but largely formal. For instance, after it became clear that he could not win election to the U.S. Senate in 1855, he strongly supported Lyman Trumbull, but he never professed friendship for the antislavery former Democrat. His relations with Gustave Koerner, the leader of the large German-American population in southern Illinois, were cordial but not affectionate; Koerner concluded that Lincoln was not "really capable of what might be called warm-hearted friendship."[3] He worked closely with Ebenezer Peck, of Chicago, in the Illinois state legislature and in Whig politics, but after he became President, he refused to support Peck's application for office, frankly telling him—as Peck remembered it—"that a man had occasion sometimes, to put his foot in the face of his best friend in order to lift himself a round higher on the ladder of ambition."[4] Even David Davis, the judge on whose circuit Lincoln traveled year after year, who was the mastermind behind the movement to nominate Lincoln for President in 1860, fell into this category of the useful associate. "Lincoln was a peculiar man," Davis recalled after Lincoln's death; "he never asked my advice on any question. . . . Lincoln . . . had . . . no Strong Emotional feelings for any person—Mankind or thing. He never thanked me for any thing I did."[5]

I

NOT until Lincoln chose William H. Herndon as his new law partner in the fall of 1844 did he have another friend in whom he could confide freely and confidentially.[6] Lincoln's partnership with Herndon was different from his two previous partnerships, first with John Todd Stuart and then with Stephen T. Logan. In the earlier associations, he was the junior partner to older and more experienced men. With both Stuart and Logan, his relationship was friendly and agreeable but not intimate. During his association with Stuart, the senior partner was away in Washington, as a congressman, for much of the time. In Lincoln's years with Logan, his political ambitions conflicted with those of his partner, and, as an acquaintance said later, Lincoln learned that a partnership wouldn't work when both members wanted to run for Congress.

In choosing a new partner, Lincoln did not try to join any of the established lawyers in Springfield, who probably would have welcomed him. Mary Lincoln hoped he would renew his association with her kinsman, Stuart, but Lincoln was tired of being a junior partner. He never explained his choice of Herndon, and Herndon himself was surprised when Lincoln invited him to be his partner.

Lincoln knew Herndon well. Archer Herndon, Billy's father,

ran the Indian Queen, one of the earliest hotels in Springfield, and as a boy Billy had worked for him. After attending the local schools and after an unsuccessful year at Illinois College in Jacksonville, Billy Herndon returned home and began clerking in Joshua Speed's store. He was paid seven hundred dollars a year—a good sum for those days—and slept in the room upstairs with Speed, Lincoln, and, often, another clerk. Along with Lincoln, he participated in the discussions around the big pot-bellied stove, after the store closed, and he took part in the informal debates the group held on political and other topics. Both men also belonged to "a Kind of Poetical Society," before which they presented their own verse,[7] and both were charter members of the Young Men's Lyceum, where they delivered carefully prepared addresses.

Herndon was a hard-working and ambitious young man, but his energy was as yet unfocused. After he married Mary Maxcy in 1840, he recognized that he had to choose an occupation and, at Lincoln's suggestion, decided to study law in the office of Logan & Lincoln. For the next three years, he continued to work as a store clerk during the day while he read law at night. He was, he recalled later, "studious—too much so for my own health—studied 12 to 14 hours a day."[8] Finally, in November 1844, he passed the perfunctory Illinois bar examination.

Even before Herndon was formally admitted to the bar the next month, Lincoln selected him to be his partner. To some extent, political considerations probably influenced his choice. A split had developed in the Illinois Whig party between the old, established leadership, which included men of consider-able wealth and experience, such as Stuart and Lincoln's brother-in-law, Ninian W. Edwards, and the "Young Turks," who wanted a more democratic party that could rival the

Jacksonians in appealing to the masses. Improbably enough, they associated Lincoln with the old guard, primarily because of his marriage into the Todd-Edwards clan. Lincoln was both amused and irritated when voters called him "a member of the aristocracy." "Well that sounds strange to me," he said, remembering his hardscrabble beginnings. As for his family, he added, "I do not remember of but *one that ever came to See Me and While he Was in town he Was accused of Stealing a Jews Harp.*"[9] Nevertheless, most of the young Whigs looked to Edward D. Baker, Lincoln's personal friend but political rival, as their leader. Herndon stood out for his sustained loyalty to Lincoln, who, he said, "was my man always above all other men on the globe."[10]

But there were other reasons for selecting Herndon. Watching the young man study, Lincoln, who was all too aware of his own deficiencies as an office manager, concluded that Herndon might not make much of a lawyer but would certainly be efficient in keeping books, filing papers, and keeping track of a firm's business. Some years later, he ruefully observed that he was doubly in error, because Herndon proved as indifferent to such matters as he was but turned out to be a fine lawyer.[11]

Lincoln also recognized that Billy was "a laborious, studious young man . . . far better informed on almost all subjects than I have ever been."[12] He knew Herndon was a man who loved books and learning. Eventually Herndon collected one of the best private libraries in Springfield. Through the firm of C. S. Francis & Co. of New York, he bought the works of English historians like Lecky, Buckle, and Froude; the translated writings of Feuerbach, Fichte, and Kant; works on political economy by John Stuart Mill, Henry C. Carey, and Francis

Wayland; and everything that Ralph Waldo Emerson, Henry Ward Beecher, and Theodore Parker published. He read enthusiastically and undiscriminatingly. Ready to share what he learned with anyone, he bubbled over with talk about new ideas, new authors. He was an exciting man to have around.

II

THE Lincoln and Herndon partnership was a business arrangement, to which initially the two men made very different contributions. Nearly a decade younger than Lincoln and still inexperienced, Herndon at the outset had the duties of keeping a rudimentary set of books for the firm, of searching out authorities for Lincoln in the nearby state library, and of toting books to the courtroom where his partner might need them. But soon he began to take charge of the law office he and Lincoln rented in the Tinsley Building, across the street from the state capitol. For the partnership, he bought a desk for $20.00 and basic legal reference books in the amount of $54.65. Presently, the firm owned a set of Illinois Reports, copies of the Illinois statutes, such standard volumes as Blackstone's *Commentaries,* the four volumes of James Kent's *Commentaries on the Constitution,* Simon Greenleaf's textbook on evidence, and Joseph Story's *Commentaries on Equity Jurisprudence.*[13] Herndon was also responsible for supervising the occasional student who read law in the Lincoln & Herndon office. When a student was accepted to work with the partners, Lincoln would greet him with a hearty, "Glad to see you, young man," but it was Herndon who directed his studies and prodded him into mastering Blackstone.

In time, Herndon attracted his own clients, and the firm became one of the most successful in Springfield. Their practice was a general one. Though a majority of their cases had to do with debt collection—and they represented both creditors and debtors—they did not specialize in any one area and represented clients in cases that ranged from hearings before a local justice of the peace to trials before the Illinois Supreme Court and the federal courts in Illinois. Within two years after Lincoln & Herndon was formed, the firm was handling more than two hundred cases a year. Over the life of the partnership Lincoln and Herndon appeared in nearly 1,500 cases together.[14]

In most of these cases, the papers were signed "Lincoln & Herndon," and the partners often cooperated in preparing them. Many years later, Herndon claimed that Lincoln rarely drafted documents and that he was responsible for drawing up the papers and writing the briefs in most of their cases. But the thousands of documents recently collected by the Lincoln Legal Papers prove beyond question that Lincoln did at least half of this clerical work and was deeply and directly involved in the firm's cases on all levels. Nevertheless, it probably is true that Herndon did most of the legal research for the partnership. Lincoln was not well versed in legal technicalities, while Herndon became skilled in searching out citations and authorities. He kept careful memoranda of briefs and authorities for cases the firm handled and prepared a notebook containing a kind of legal index of the principal precedents on such topics as Corrupt Motives, Trusts, and Physical or Moral Nuisances.

In the Sangamon County Circuit Court, where they argued a heavy majority of all their cases, Lincoln and Herndon worked together, though they rarely appeared in the same courtroom in the same case. In a handful of cases, Lincoln and Herndon represented opposite sides in court. Lincoln argued much more frequently than his partner before the Illinois Supreme Court, in part because Herndon for several years served as deputy clerk of that court, a position that prevented him from appearing before it as an attorney. Herndon rarely appeared in federal district or circuit court.

Because Springfield did not offer enough business, both men traveled to other counties when the judge of the circuit court made his semiannual peregrination around his district. On the circuit, after the court adjourned, the judge and the lawyers usually gathered in the local tavern, and, Herndon recalled, "story telling—joking—jesting would be kept up till 1 or 2 o'c[lock] in the night." Often the lawyers "slept with 20 men in the same room—some on old ropes—some on quilts— some on sheets—a straw or two under them."[15] Sometimes Lincoln and Herndon had to sleep in the same bed. Lincoln's long legs usually stuck out over the floorboard, and he would keep Herndon awake while he read by tallow candlelight.[16] Lincoln enjoyed traveling the circuit and was often away from home for weeks at a time; Herndon did not like this "rough— semi barbarous" life and usually confined his practice outside Sangamon County to adjacent Menard County.

Just as the firm was getting established, Lincoln ran for Congress, and during his term in the House of Representatives (1847–1849), Herndon struggled to keep the business afloat. While Lincoln was away in Washington, the number of cases handled by the firm dropped by almost 50 percent and—what was even more ominous—there was an even greater decline in the number of new clients it attracted. When Lincoln returned, he realized that most of the firm's work was now due to Herndon's exertions, and he suggested that he had no right to share in the profits. Reminding Lincoln how he had helped when his partner was young and inexperienced, Herndon replied that he "could afford now to be grateful if not generous" and asked that the partnership be continued.[17]

Moving to somewhat more spacious quarters on the west side of the capitol square, both partners began to work hard to bring in new business. Their success depended in no small part on the advent of the railroads, which inevitably became entangled in litigation with the counties and towns through which they passed and with the owners of the land they needed for right of way. During the 1850s, the firm of Lincoln & Herndon appeared in at least 133 cases concerning railroads—sometimes representing the roads, sometimes opposing them. The most famous of these cases involved the Illinois Central Railroad; Lincoln & Herndon, as attorneys for the railroad, received what was then the enormous fee of $5,000 for their services. It, like all their other fees, was divided equally between the partners.

The two partners were almost exact opposites in temperament. Despite a deep poetic streak, Lincoln's mind was coolly logical, and he longed for the day when "reason, cold, calculating, unimpassioned reason," would rule the world.[18] Herndon was intuitive; he fancied that he could "see to the gizzard of things" and could predict the future because he felt it in his bones. Half jocularly, Lincoln would sometimes ask when he came to the office in the morning: "Billy—how is your bones philosophy this morning?"[19] Lincoln was a fatalist who virtually dripped melancholy as he walked; Herndon was an inveterate optimist, styling himself as a "progressive—somewhat of a radical," who believed "in the universal progress of all things,

especially of man's up going." Lincoln was quiet, a man of few
words, although from time to time he interrupted his fits of
introspection with stories and gales of laughter; Herndon
spoke rapidly and freely, but he had no sense of humor.
Herndon found Lincoln "incommunicative—silent, reticent—
secretive—having profound policies—and well laid—deeply
studied plans." He himself had no reticence and endlessly
expounded his responses to what he was reading, whether it
was history, philosophy, or political economy.

Inevitably there were strains in the relationship between two
such dissimilar partners from time to time. Herndon believed
that children should be well mannered and carefully disci-
plined. On the infrequent occasions when his children visited
the law office, they were expected to sit quietly and play
silently. But when Lincoln brought Willie and Tad, his two
youngest boys, to the office, Herndon thought they behaved
like "little devils." With the exaggeration of a memory fifty years
after the event, he claimed they "would take down the books—
empty ash buckets—coal ashes—inkstands—papers—gold
pens—letters, etc., etc., in a pile and then dance on the pile."
To all this their father was oblivious. "Had they s—t in
Lincoln's hat and rubbed it on his boots, he would have
laughed and thought it smart."[20]

At times, the partners also had differences over public questions. Herndon recalled that they "frequently disagreed on
measures and men, never on principle," and their disputes over
subjects like the need for protective tariffs were sometimes hot
but always friendly.[21] Lincoln, who sought fully to master a
problem, would dwell on an idea and "doubly explain" things to
his partner, who complained privately "that he used to bore me
terribly by his methods, processes, manners, etc., etc." On the

other hand, Herndon's highfalutin language and discourses upon esoteric subjects bored Lincoln. "If you wished to be Cut off at the knee," Herndon remembered, "just go at Lincoln with abstractions—glittering generalities—indefiniteness— mistiness of idea or expression." He would "become vexed and sometimes foolishly so." He used to say: "Billy dont shoot too high—shoot low down, and the common people will under- stand you."[22]

Herndon idealized his partner. He not merely felt grateful to Lincoln; he considered him his mentor, an older man who was a friendly, safe counselor. A man of extremes—indeed, a man who sometimes fell off the edge—Herndon found a steadying influence in his relationship with Lincoln. "He was," Herndon explained, "the great big man of our firm and I was the little one. The little one looked *naturally* up to the big one."

Lincoln too gained from their association. Herndon became much more than a useful friend; he fulfilled one of Lincoln's basic psychological needs. Lincoln liked being the senior fig- ure, the master, and he nurtured Herndon's intense idealiza- tion just as he had encouraged it among his soldiers in the Black Hawk War. His reward was a devotion that was almost worshipful.

Many years later, after Lincoln's death, Herndon came to see that his partner had had weaknesses. Indeed, he believed that Lincoln was "very deficient" in some ways as a lawyer because, he said, he "never thoroughly read any elementary law book" and "knew nothing of the laws of evidence—of pleading or of practice. . . . [He] was purely and entirely a case lawyer— nothing more."[23] He objected when other biographers called Lincoln a great lawyer. Unless Lincoln had ample time to pre- pare his case, to learn the facts and the law by heart, and then to feel that he was in the right he was only "a 2nd rate lawyer."[24] Sometimes he fretted that Lincoln, as the senior partner who appeared in the most publicized cases, received a dispropor- tionate share of public attention, and he grumbled—with some justice—that his own considerable accomplishments as a lawyer were overlooked. Friends told him that Lincoln "got the credit of all wise acts and good things, and you [i.e., Herndon], for your part, got the disgrace for all the foolish ones done by the firm or either of you."[25] In his bleaker moods, it seemed to Herndon he had allowed himself to be exploited by his partner. Lincoln, he judged, "was a remorseless trimmer with men; they were his tools and when they were used up he threw them aside as old iron and took up new tools."[26]

But these were passing moods, and for the most part the two men worked together amicably. Each knew the other's strengths and weaknesses. "We never had any personal contro- versy or disagreement," Herndon recalled. "I believe we under- stood each other perfectly."[27] They got along well in part because Herndon had a deep respect for his partner. And Lincoln, in turn, took great care not to adopt a tone of censure or superiority when addressing Herndon. Theirs was never quite a relationship of equals. As the senior partner, Lincoln usually called his junior "Billy"; Herndon always referred to him as "Lincoln" or "Mr. Lincoln."

III

MORE than a legal partnership, Lincoln & Herndon was also a political alliance. Both men were earnest, stalwart Whigs, and in election after election they stood side by side in battling the Jacksonian Democrats, who normally controlled the state. Herndon was far more active than Lincoln in local politics and served as mayor of Springfield in 1855, but he did not aspire to higher office. Lincoln took no interest in local offices but enjoyed playing a role in state politics. After repeated maneuvering, he won election in 1846 as the only Illinois Whig in the U.S. House of Representatives, where he served for a single term, and twice he actively sought election to the U.S. Senate.

While Lincoln was in Washington, Herndon kept him informed as to public opinion in central Illinois. Initially Lincoln's conduct in the House of Representatives elicited a good deal of praise, which Herndon promptly reported to his partner. There was some sentiment, though, that the new congressman had not attracted enough attention to himself in the debates. When Herndon reported this feeling, Lincoln responded dryly: "As you are all so anxious for me to distinguish myself, I have concluded to do so, before long,"[28] and he promised to make a speech.

He never made that speech, but in January 1848, he got the floor to make another, which brought him more notoriety than praise. Speaking at the very end of the Mexican War, which Whigs generally condemned and Democrats defended, Lincoln challenged President James K. Polk's claim that the Mexicans had begun the war by shedding American blood on American soil. With lawyer-like pertinacity, he attempted to grill the President as to whether the spot where that bloodshed had occurred was on Mexican, rather than American, soil. He hoped to demonstrate that Polk was the aggressor. His "Spot" resolutions, followed closely by a biting attack on the President's credibility, were part of an orchestrated Whig attempt to oust the Democrats in the next election, but back in Illinois, Lincoln seemed to be disloyal. After all, his country was still at war with Mexico. Herndon reported this rising opposition to his partner.

Herndon's letters have not been preserved, but they were apparently quite sharp in tone. He not merely informed Lincoln that many of his former supporters were offended by his course but challenged his partner's argument that Polk had exercised unconstitutional, even dictatorial, power. Herndon insisted that the spot on which the first fighting had occurred was irrelevant since the President, as commander in chief, had the responsibility to act if he learned that the country was about to be invaded.

Lincoln was clearly hurt by his partner's criticism, and in the only extensive group of letters he wrote to Herndon that has survived, he tried to justify his position. His letters—addressed to "Dear William," not to "Dear Billy"—were not angry but reasoned. Expressing sadness that he was obliged to disagree with his partner, Lincoln made it clear he did not think Herndon understood either the constitutional or the political questions posed by the war with Mexico. He especially objected to a passage in one of Herndon's letters claiming that the younger Whigs of Springfield and Sangamon County were tired of having "old fogies" as their leaders. Gently, Lincoln chided his partner. He was, he supposed, one of the old fogies himself—he was forty years old—but he had always encouraged younger men to participate in politics and to speak out for themselves.

Then, with a new presidential election pending, he urged Herndon to use his influence among these young Whigs to organize and stage meetings where everyone could play the part he played best—"some speak, some sing, and all hollow"—for the 1848 Whig presidential candidate, General

JOSHUA FRY SPEED at about the time he
first met Lincoln in 1837
Robert Todd Lincoln said Speed was "the most intimate friend
his father had ever had."
The Filson Historical Society

JOSHUA FRY SPEED AND FANNY HENNING SPEED,
a painting by George P. A. Healy
Lincoln wrote that the Speeds' marriage in 1842 gave him "more
pleasure than the total sum of all I have enjoyed since that fatal
first of Jany. '41."
The Filson Historical Society

WILLIAM H. ("BILLY") HERNDON
Deeply discouraged by his defeat in his second race for the
United States Senate in 1859, Lincoln said: "I expect everyone
to desert me except Billy."
Illinois State Historical Library

ORVILLE HICKMAN BROWNING
Awarding Lincoln the LL.D. degree on behalf of Knox College,
Browning enjoined the President Elect: "You will, therefore, . . .
consider yourself a 'scholar,' as well as a 'gentleman,' and
deport yourself accordingly."
Illinois State Historical Library

WILLIAM HENRY SEWARD
When Secretary of State Seward threatened to upset Lincoln's cabinet
by resigning, the President outmaneuvered him, saying: "I can't afford
to let Seward take the first trick."
Illinois State Historical Library

JOHN GEORGE NICOLAY
As Lincoln's private secretary, Nicolay, it was said, "never said anything
worth quoting" and had the rare "gift of hearing the other fellow talk."
Illinois State Historical Library

JOHN HAY
Frances Seward described Lincoln's assistant personal secretary as
"small, with light hair, faint moustache, round face, brilliant
complexion, and fine, dark eyes. Is twenty-four & looks nineteen.
Has a clear voice and converses fluently."
Illinois State Historical Library

Lincoln and his private secretaries
Picture History

Zachary Taylor.[29] Herndon did help organize the Taylor movement in central Illinois, but his heart was not in the campaign.

IV

WHEN Lincoln's single term in Congress ended in 1849, Lincoln and Herndon settled down to their law practice and for the next four years paid only marginal attention to politics. But in 1854, Stephen A. Douglas introduced his Kansas-Nebraska bill, which repealed the Missouri Compromise of 1820 and allowed settlers in the western territories to decide whether to permit or prohibit slavery. Both partners were alarmed and vigorously reentered the political arena. Aroused by reports that armed bands of Southerners, principally from Missouri, were invading Kansas, intimidating free-state residents and attempting to set up a territorial government that would protect slavery, Herndon joined a little group in Springfield that promised to supply arms and ammunition to the antislavery settlers. Lincoln, always more cautious, warned against insurrection and bloodshed but pledged fifty dollars to the antislavery cause, to be used only when Logan, his former law partner, whom he knew to be a very conservative man opposed to violence, authorized it. He never did.

That episode illustrated the difference between Lincoln and Herndon on questions concerning slavery and, in particular, the extension of slavery into the national territories. Lincoln worked quietly within the Whig party, seeking to join forces with anti-Douglas Democrats and the small but articulate Free-Soil element in northern Illinois. He hoped the coalition would elect him to the U.S. Senate. Herndon, who subscribed to the major abolitionist newspapers in the country, expressed his opposition to the Kansas-Nebraska Act by beginning a correspondence with Eastern antislavery leaders like William Lloyd Garrison, editor of *The Liberator,* and Charles Sumner, the famous antislavery senator from Massachusetts. His longest and most fruitful correspondence was with Theodore Parker, the noted Boston minister, to whom he poured out his ideas on questions political and philosophical. Parker wrote him encouraging notes and sent him copies of his addresses. In one of them, he defined democracy as "Direct Self-government, over all the people, for all the people, by all the people."[30] Herndon showed it to Lincoln, who stored away the words for later use.

Herndon's antislavery connections enabled him to serve as a conduit between his partner and abolitionist leaders, who did not really know Lincoln. For instance, Zebina Eastman, editor of the *Morning Star* in Chicago, came to Springfield to learn whether, as an abolitionist, he could trust Lincoln, who also opposed slavery but obdurately refused to abandon the Whig party. He talked at length with Herndon and went away reassured by Herndon's pledge: "Mr. Lincoln is all right."

After Lincoln failed to secure election to the Senate in 1855, he and Herndon drifted into an alliance with the new Republican party, dedicated to opposing the extension of slavery. Herndon later exaggerated his role in bringing Lincoln into the new party; they moved together at about the same speed, and at the major organizing convention of the party in Illinois in 1856, Lincoln made the main address while Herndon served as corresponding secretary.

Over the next few years, Herndon loyally supported Lincoln's political aspirations. As the election of 1858 approached, Lincoln saw a chance to replace Stephen A. Douglas in the U.S. Senate. The unpopular Kansas-Nebraska Act had led to the creation of rival proslavery and antislavery governments in Kansas, and Illinois Republicans were outraged when President James Buchanan urged that the state be admitted to the Union with a constitution that protected slavery. Then, to almost universal surprise, Douglas broke with the President and opposed the admission of Kansas. Some Republicans in the Northeast, who had previously lambasted Douglas as a tool of the proslavery forces, now began praising him, and Horace Greeley's influential *New York Tribune,* which had a large circulation in the West, suggested that Douglas's heroic stand for freedom entitled him to another term in the Senate.

Both Lincoln and Herndon were concerned that their careful work of organizing an antislavery Republican party in Illinois might be undermined. Lincoln deplored the "constant eulogising, and admiring, and magnifying" of Douglas in the columns of the *New York Tribune* and feared it portended "sacrificing us here in Illinois." Both partners were alarmed when Senator Lyman Trumbull told them that certain Republican leaders in Washington had "a DISPOSITION to sell out Illinois" and support Douglas's bid for reelection.[31] Though Lincoln said little, Herndon *"inferred"* that his partner wanted him to go East to tell the misguided Republicans there that Douglas, despite his recent actions, was still an unprincipled man, not a friend of freedom. Herndon, who for years had longed to visit the historic sights and meet the great intellectual leaders with whom he corresponded, jumped at the chance and set out on a mission to Washington, New York, and Boston. He talked at length with Trumbull, Greeley, and

Douglas himself and believed that after his one-man crusade, "things began more and more to work for Lincoln's success."[32]

When Illinois Republicans nominated Lincoln to run against Douglas for the U.S. Senate, he conferred with Herndon in drawing up his acceptance speech. Over the years in their office discussions, Herndon had repeatedly argued "that this Continent was not broad enough nor long enough to contain the principles of Liberty and the despotism of Slavery" and that "one or the other must go to the wall and die there."[33] Lincoln decided to make this idea the theme of his address. Coming to the office early one morning, he said: "Billy, I want now to read my speech, and after I am done, I want your opinion of it in all directions." He read what became known as his "House Divided" speech, predicting that the United States could not permanently endure as a nation half slave and half free. This was radical doctrine— almost as radical as the prediction William H. Seward made four months later of "an irrepressible conflict" between slavery and freedom—but Herndon warmly endorsed it, telling Theodore Parker that it was "compact—nervous—eloquent: . . . the best Executive Expression of the ideas of . . . Republicanism . . . that I have seen."[34]

A few days later, when Lincoln read the speech aloud to a group of his Republican advisers, most thought it too radical, too far in advance of the times, and some said it was "a d——d fool utterance." Herndon, the last man called on for an opinion, leapt up impatiently. "By——God," he swore, "deliver it just as it reads. . . . The speech is true—wise and politic; and will succeed—now as in the future."

In the campaign that followed, Herndon turned their law office into a Republican war room, where speakers were scheduled, speeches were drafted, and platforms revised. Lincoln was out on the stump much of the time, and in his absence Herndon managed his campaign. He had no formal assignment or title, but he gathered what Lincoln wanted him to do "from his facts, acts, hints, face, *as well as what he did not do nor say.*" "He moved me by a shrug of the shoulder—by a nod of the head—by a flash of the eye," he recalled. "I acted for him through signs and symbols—not through his requests made in language."[35]

None too scrupulous when it came to politics, Herndon was, he confessed, better versed in "the details of how we get along" than his partner. Recognizing that the pro-Buchanan Democrats might draw enough votes from Douglas to give the Republicans the edge, he encouraged his father and his brother, the lame and irascible Elliott, to take a major role in the anti-Douglas Democratic group, and, he reported with some satisfaction, "they make 'no bones' in telling me what they are going to do."[36]

But Lincoln was defeated once more. Though Republicans won in the popular vote, they did not gain control of the state legislature, which, before the Seventeenth Amendment (1913), elected U.S. senators. The Democratic majority chose Douglas. Depressed, Lincoln told friends who asked about his future plans: "I expect everyone to desert me except Billy."[37]

Loyal as ever, Herndon did what he could to boost his partner's spirits. In 1859, when Eastern Republicans invited Lincoln to give a lecture in New York City, he asked Herndon what subject he should choose. Herndon had heard his partner's lecture titled "Discoveries and Inventions," a hasty review of human discoveries from Adam's invention of the fig leaf to Watt's invention of the steam engine, and he thought it "a lifeless thing—a dull dead thing."[38] Lincoln had "no imagination, no fancy, no taste, no emotion, and no readings" that would enable him to give a popular lecture on general literary or philosophical subjects; he ought to stick to politics. Lincoln took his advice, and the result was his Cooper Union Address, which did much to promote his chances for the Republican presidential nomination in 1860.

But as Lincoln moved to win that nomination, Herndon was not one of his inner circle of councilors. Herndon's membership in the Republican state executive committee was quietly allowed to lapse, and, though he had confidently expected the position, he was not selected as a Republican presidential elector in 1860. Lincoln now needed advisers who could help him win, not alienate, voters. Herndon's reputation as an extreme antislavery spokesman and his known connections to Eastern abolitionists frightened conservative former Whigs, whose votes were necessary for a Republican victory. At the same time, his intemperate and denunciatory attacks on Douglas and his followers in previous campaigns alienated Democrats who were thinking of switching parties. Herndon also injured his partner by meddling in Illinois state politics, where Norman B. Judd, Leonard Swett, and Richard Yates were all contending for the Republican gubernatorial nomination. Lincoln, who needed the support of all three, was carefully neutral, but Herndon upset the equilibrium by claiming that Judd was guilty of misappropriating party funds. "Cannot you set him right," Judd complained to Lincoln. When Herndon denied that he had made the charge, Lincoln characteristically did not press his partner about his past utterances but secured "his solemn pledge to say nothing of the sort in the future," impressing on Herndon "that *I* would be held responsible for what he said."[39]

Herndon was not a delegate to the 1860 Chicago Republican convention that nominated Lincoln, and—contrary to his later recollections—he probably did not attend. During the campaign, he made numerous speeches in behalf of the Republican ticket. Often indiscreet and impolitic, he made radical statements that Democratic newspapers described as being "as strongly in favor of abolitionism as . . . John Brown." As Herndon repeated his speech in nearly every hamlet in the Sangamon valley, hostile newspapers denounced "The Falsities and Fanaticism of Bill Herndon" and claimed that his "heresies and false dogmas" were "traceable to the law-office of Mr. Lincoln himself." They also charged that "Mr. Herndon, Mr. Lincoln's law partner and confidential friend," while progressing from one saloon to another, admitted that his party was importing voters from other states disguised as "corn huskers" to ensure that Republicans would win in central Illinois. Whether true or not, the story doubtless did something to make sure that the Democrats—as usual—carried Sangamon County.

On election day, November 6, Herndon dropped by Lincoln's office in the statehouse and learned that his partner did not intend to vote. At this time, each political party printed its own election ballots, which included the names of the party's presidential electors as well as the nominated candidates for state and local offices. Herndon discovered that Lincoln had scruples about voting for his own presidential electors. "Lincoln you ought to go and vote," he insisted until Lincoln cut the list of presidential electors from the top of the Republican ballot and, with Herndon proudly accompanying him, went to the polls.[40]

In the weeks after the election, Herndon saw Lincoln infrequently. In his statehouse office, the President Elect was surrounded by visitors, and Herndon was disgusted by the adulation they heaped on his partner. With distaste, he observed that "men and women rushed around [Lincoln] . . . —kissed his feet—rolled in the dust—begging notice . . . begged for a hair from the tail of his old horse; the very dogs and kittens pups and chicks running around Lincoln's house assumed forms of beauty and power."[41] A proud man, Herndon wanted no place in this entourage, and in the months after the election, he went to the Lincoln house only once—"and that on business."[42]

There was not then, or ever, an estrangement between the partners. Herndon continued to assist Lincoln when he could. After Lincoln found his office too noisy and crowded and retired to a secluded second-story warehouse in order to write his inaugural address, he asked his partner to bring him the reference books he needed: a copy of the Constitution, President Andrew Jackson's proclamation against nullification, and Henry Clay's major speech on the Compromise of 1850. Herndon sent him necessary reference books and kept visitors away. But he was not one of the handful of people to whom Lincoln showed copies of the draft of his inaugural address.

During the winter of 1860–1861, as the secession crisis deepened, Herndon was increasingly out of touch with Lincoln's thinking. Paradoxically, at a time when he saw less and less of his partner, he began privately to claim more and more knowledge of Lincoln's plans. While President Elect Lincoln refrained from any public statement denouncing the secession of the Southern states, Herndon told one correspondent that his partner would "make a grave yard of the South, if rebellion or treason raises its head."[43] He was certain that Lincoln would stand against compromise "as solid as firm, as fixed as the granite hills of New England."[44] Rather than support any move to conciliate the South, he insisted, Lincoln would prefer that "his soul might go back to God from the wings of the Capitol." "I know Lincoln better than he knows himself," he assured another correspondent.[45] His partner would preserve the Union and the Constitution and insist that "the Laws be enforced at every and at all hazards."

V

THE cautious, conciliatory speeches the President Elect made on his circuitous journey from Springfield to Washington, emphasizing the absence of real issues between the North and the South and stressing the whipped-up nature of the secession crisis, infuriated Herndon. Lincoln was glossing over the seriousness of the crisis—"which was a crime under the Circumstances"—or he "never fully comprehended the situation." When the Confederates fired on Fort Sumter in April 1861, he hoped his partner finally would see the need for drastic measures. He ought to go out on the steps of the Capitol and call the people to war, announcing that slavery would be abolished and that Jefferson Davis and his fellow secessionists would be strung from the gallows.

When Lincoln instead continued his moderate course, Herndon, like many other radical Republicans, grew exasperated. He was furious when the President in the fall of 1861 overruled General John C. Frémont's order freeing the slaves in Missouri. Unlike Joshua Speed, who feared that Frémont's proclamation would cost the Lincoln administration the support of the border states, Herndon thought that its revocation would alienate the stalwart antislavery men of the North. "Good God!" he exploded. "What is Lincoln doing?" "Old Abe"—as he now patronizingly referred to his partner—was showing a shameful want of courage. "Does he suppose he can crush—squelch out this huge rebellion by pop guns filled with rose water," he fumed. "He ought to hang somebody and get up a name for will or decision—for character. Let him hang some Child or woman, if he has not Courage to hang a *man*."[46]

So vexed was Herndon with the Lincoln administration's slow and ineffectual prosecution of the war that some in Illinois suspected he was about to break with his "good old friend—Lincoln." In fact, Herndon campaigned vigorously for the Republican ticket in the 1862 election, and during the 1864 campaign only a lingering attack of bronchitis kept him from the stump. Still, the rumor was strong enough that Herndon felt it necessary to assure the President that there was no truth to reports that he was "cold towards him—his re-election." To make sure that Lincoln understood his continuing loyalty, he asked the President's private secretaries to see that he read the speech Herndon was able to make dedicating the new "Wigwam," where Springfield Republicans held their rallies, to "Lincoln—[to] Liberty and to Justice."[47]

Before Lincoln left for Washington, he asked if Herndon wanted any office under his administration. Herndon said he did not. At this time, he had one of the leading law practices in Springfield and was making a good living. In addition, his wife was seriously ill, and he did not want to leave home. He did, however, ask the President Elect to put in a good word for him with the new governor of Illinois, Richard Yates, for his reappointment as one of the Illinois bank commissioners, an undemanding job that paid about $1,000 a year.

But in January 1862, he did go to Washington to seek a job—not for himself but for a friend. His wife, Mary Maxcy Herndon, had died the previous summer, and Herndon, who could not bear to be alone, was soon wooing the beautiful Anna Miles of Petersburg, Illinois, eighteen years younger than himself. She was not much interested, but Herndon found a way to her heart through her sister, whose husband, Charles W. Chatterton, wanted a federal appointment that would offer money and adventure. Herndon volunteered to lay the whole story before Lincoln and went to Washington. Finding this roundabout courtship "wonderfully funny," the President named Chatterton agent for the Cherokee Indians.

Herndon enjoyed his stay in Washington. He visited old friends in the capital and had dinner once in the White House. Mary Lincoln snubbed him, and he bitterly resented this "very curious—excentric [sic]—*wicked woman*," who, he confided to a correspondent, had for years made Lincoln "domestically a desolate man."[48] Much of his time he spent, at Lincoln's invitation, in the waiting room of the White House and in the President's office, where he watched the endless stream of office seekers who badgered the President daily. One evening, after long hours of interviewing applicants, Lincoln wearily prophesied: "If ever American society and the United States government are demoralized . . . it will come from the voracious desire of office—this struggle to live without toil—work and labor . . ." Then, pausing for a minute, he added wryly: " . . . from which I am not free myself." Herndon failed to see the humor.[49]

Finding that living in the nation's capital was more expensive than he had expected, Herndon, embarrassingly, had to borrow twenty-five dollars from the President. When he was ready to leave, Lincoln saw him to the door of the White House, grasped him warmly by the hand, and said a fervent good-bye. It was the last time Herndon saw his partner.[50]

VI

INEVITABLY during a partnership that lasted over sixteen years, Lincoln and Herndon came to know, or infer, a great deal about the other's personal life. Sometimes Lincoln would come to the office in a somber mood, deeply depressed and unwilling to talk. On these days, Herndon would discreetly draw a curtain across the glass door to the office, lock it, and leave Lincoln alone for an hour or two to collect himself. Years later, after Lincoln's assassination, Herndon blamed Mary Lincoln for these episodes and called her "the hell-cat of the age." After open warfare broke out between Lincoln's former partner and his widow, Herndon developed a narrative of Mary Lincoln's dislike for him. Initially, he recalled, he had been much impressed by her. If this aristocratic belle from Lexington, Kentucky, was "a little proud, sometimes haughty," she was nevertheless "a shrewd girl and a sharp one, a fine judge of human nature."[51] At a party soon after they met, he had asked her to dance and, thinking to compliment her, said she seemed to glide through the waltz with the grace of a serpent. Mary snapped back that comparison to a snake was invidious and left him on the dance floor. After that, Herndon said, the two never got along.

No doubt Herndon was right in thinking that Mary Lincoln did not like him and that she would have preferred her husband to have a more gentlemanly partner. But during the years of the Lincoln and Herndon partnership, there is no record that the two exchanged harsh words.[52] From time to time, Mary Lincoln came to the law office during her husband's absence and on at least one occasion borrowed a small sum from Herndon until Lincoln returned from the circuit. It would be easy to make too much of the fact that Mary Lincoln never invited the Herndons to a meal at her house on Jackson Street. In a small town like Springfield, where people met every day in the stores or in the offices, dinner parties for neighbors were rare, and, in any event, the Lincolns' house was so small that Mary infrequently had sit-down dinners. Nevertheless, Herndon must have learned from local gossip that the Lincolns had a stressful marriage and that Mary Lincoln had a fiery temper.

Lincoln, for his part, knew a good deal about Herndon's private affairs. Growing up in a hotel with a lively bar, Herndon early developed a taste for rot-gut liquor.[53] He never became a chronic alcoholic, and he did not drink all the time. Indeed, he tried very hard to abstain; he joined the Pillars of Temperance Association and, as mayor of Springfield in 1855, attempted to ban the sale of liquor in the city limits. Still, he associated with a young, rowdy set, who passed the bottle frequently, and he admitted that he would often take a drink when he wanted to say something smart. From time to time, he fell off the wagon with a thud. Once in the 1850s, Lincoln was aroused at night to post bail for Herndon and some of his buddies, who had been on a destructive spree before they were arrested. Just as Herndon never inquired into his partner's domestic arrangements, so Lincoln never scolded Herndon for his failing. But before Lincoln left Springfield for Washington, he came by the law office for a quiet chat.

"Billy," he inquired, "how long have we been together?"

"Over sixteen years," Herndon replied.

"We've never had a cross word during all that time, have we?" Lincoln asked.

"No, indeed we have not," responded his partner.

Then Lincoln told him of efforts that other lawyers had made to supplant him in the partnership, remarking that such men were weak creatures who "hoped to secure a law practice by hanging to his coat-tail." Gathering up a bundle of books and papers, he started to leave but stopped to ask, quietly and with some embarrassment: "Billy, there's one thing I have, for some time, wanted you to tell me, but I reckon I ought to apologize for my nerve and curiosity. . . . I want you to tell me . . . how many times you have been drunk."[54] He did not expect an answer, but Herndon tried to take his message to heart.

VII

THE assassination of Lincoln was the most important event in Herndon's life. In the carnival of death that followed, there rose an insatiable demand for more information about the martyred President, and newspapermen, magazine writers, biographers, and public men began to seek out those who had known him best. Inevitably many turned to Herndon, who found himself besieged, as he said, by "enquiries and interrogations by thousands of visitors as to Lincoln." Presently, he began to plan writing a short biography of the partner whom he had idealized, because the world did not "understand the full orb of Lincoln as it swang amid the heavens of men." He would portray Lincoln "in his passions—appetites—and affections—perceptions—memories—judgement—understanding—will . . . *just as he lived, breathed*—ate and laughed."[55]

To supplement his own recollections, he interviewed dozens of people who had known Lincoln and sent letters of inquiry to others who were too distant for him to see in person. Assiduously he collected hundreds of letters and statements in what amounted to the first large-scale oral history project in the United States. At the same time, he began presenting his own memories of his slain partner in a series of public lectures. These became increasingly controversial as he revealed that his researches had led him to conclude that Lincoln's only true love was for Ann Rutledge in his New Salem days. Eventually, he came to see that he could never complete his proposed biography, and he sold a copy of his documents to Ward Hill Lamon, whose iconoclastic biography, published in 1872, gave the public a glimpse of what Herndon had uncovered in his researches.

Poor, unsuccessful in his law practice, and roundly abused for his part in the Lamon biography, Herndon retreated to a small farm north of Springfield. Not until the next decade, when he met Jesse W. Weik, a young, enthusiastic Lincoln admirer, did his interest in a Lincoln biography revive, and the two men planned to collaborate on a book. He entrusted his Lincoln Record to Weik as their basic source, but to supplement it he wrote his new literary partner not merely dozens of letters about Lincoln but numerous short monographs dealing with such subjects as Lincoln's religion, his marriage, and his law practice. The product of their collaboration, *Herndon's Lincoln: The True Story of a Great Life,* was published in 1889.

That biography, the voluminous recollections that Herndon assembled, Herndon's monographs, and his numerous letters

are basic sources for any biography of Lincoln. What is important here is that they reveal—sometimes unconsciously—a
great deal about the friendship between the two partners. They
suggest a relationship that was less intimate than what
Herndon wanted his readers to believe—and perhaps less intimate than what he himself believed.

The best and most fully realized sections of Herndon's writing—whether in his letters to Weik, in his drafts of chapters for
their biography, or in the published book—offer remarkably
vivid descriptions of Lincoln, as he looked, walked, spoke, and
worked. These sketches, which reflected Herndon's daily association with Lincoln over many years, show he was an astute
reporter. But these are essentially external characterizations.
Rarely do they attempt to reveal anything that Lincoln said in
confidence to his partner.

Though *Herndon's Lincoln* (and his other writings) contains
hundreds of anecdotes Herndon gathered, only a few of them
originated directly with Lincoln, and often these are recounted
with too much circumstantial detail to be entirely credible. For
example, there is no reason to doubt that Herndon recommended a new life of Edmund Burke to Lincoln and that, as
Herndon recalled in 1887, Lincoln refused to read it. And he
probably said something like what Herndon remembered:
"They are all alike. They all tell of the heroic deeds of their subjects. You might as well print up these biographies with blank
titles and fill in the name of any subject that you please."
Whimsically, he went on to suggest that booksellers should
have "blank biographies on their shelves always ready for
sale—so that, when a man dies, and his heirs—children and
friends wish to perpetuate the memory of the dead, they can
purchase one already written, *but with blanks,* which they can

fill up eloquently and grandly at pleasure, thus commemorating . . . the name of the dead."[56] It is a good story, and probably basically true—but not even Herndon's tenacious memory could have recalled Lincoln's exact words after so many years.

Another famous anecdote that Herndon told offers the same problem. He remembered that he had once urged his partner to speak faster and more forcibly and that Lincoln replied: "Give me your woman's little knife with its short twin blades, and give me that old jack knife, lieing [sic] over there." Opening the blade of the penknife, he showed how it traveled rapidly to reach its full but short extension; then he showed how the long blade of the jack knife moved more slowly, through a much greater space. "Just so," he remarked, "with these long convolutions of my brain—they have to act slowly— pass as it were through a greater space than the shorter convolutions that snap off quickly, but when those convolutions shoot off an idea it comes with force, and cuts its way."[57] Though the language is un-Lincolnian, the substance of the story is probably authentic, but Herndon's account was written more than a quarter of a century after he claimed to have heard Lincoln's remarks. As Don and Virginia Fehrenbacher, the experts on recollections about Lincoln, have observed, "By then, what he really remembered despite the erosive effects of time was intermingled with all that he had read and been told about Lincoln, as well as with certain inferences and speculations that he had elevated to the status of fact."[58]

Such anecdotes, which Lincoln allegedly told Herndon directly, are not only infrequent in Herndon's narrative; they are not always firsthand. For instance, *Herndon's Lincoln* offers a vivid account of the migration of the Lincoln family from Indiana to Illinois, which Herndon says "Mr. Lincoln once described . . . to me." It includes the story about how Lincoln saved a dog's life after the family pet fell behind when the ox-drawn cart forded an ice-covered stream. Rather than abandon the dog, Lincoln stripped off his shoes and socks and waded through the icy water to carry it across. The pet's frantic leaps of joy, he said, amply repaid him for all his effort. The story is a familiar and touching one—but as Herndon's letters reveal, it was not one that he gained from Lincoln. It was related to him by Jesse K. Dubois, one of Lincoln's neighbors in Springfield.[59]

In only a few instances did Herndon assert that his partner told him of deepest feelings or intimate thoughts. "Mr. Lincoln never had a confidant, and therefore never unbosomed himself to others," he wrote decades after his partner's death. He did not claim that Lincoln ever talked with him about his political ambitions or his religious views. He did assert personal knowledge that Lincoln as early as 1840 believed with almost "a religious fervor" that he was destined to become a great man.[60] He recorded Lincoln's sadness, at the end of his unsuccessful term in the House of Representatives, that he lacked the strength and power to stir up the world, saying despairingly: "How hard—Oh how hard it is to die and leave one's Country no better than if one had never lived for it!"[61] He also remembered that his partner more than once predicted to him: "I feel as if I should meet with some terrible End."[62]

Some of the few intimate conversations Herndon reported that he had with his partner are highly suspect. One concerned Lincoln's mother. Herndon remembered that while traveling with Lincoln to attend a case in the Menard County Circuit Court in Petersburg, which "required a discussion on heredi-tary qualities of mind, nature, etc.," his partner confided that his mother, Nancy Hanks, was the illegitimate child of "a

Virginia planter, large farmer of the highest and best blood of Virginia," who took advantage of his "poor and credulous" grandmother.[63] To this Virginia ancestor Lincoln attributed Nancy Hanks's "better nature and finer qualities," which distinguished her from the other members of her family. Then, in Herndon's account, he went on to speculate that children born out of wedlock were "generally smarter, shrewder, and more intellectual than others," and he attributed his own achievements to his illegitimate mother: "All that I am or hope ever to be I got from my mother, God bless her."[64]

But there are problems with this memory, which Herndon claimed Lincoln told him to keep secret until long after his partner's death. It was highly uncharacteristic for Lincoln to discuss his intimate family history; this is the only instance on record. As Herndon said, "Lincoln opened himself to no living man or woman." In addition, biographers have had difficulty identifying the case in which Lincoln and Herndon were engaged, which Herndon variously dated as between 1846 and 1852. It would have to be before 1850, because Lincoln had no cases in Menard County after that date; the sittings of that court conflicted with those in the Eighth Circuit, which Lincoln regularly attended, while Herndon represented the firm in Menard County. Careful examination of the docket of the Menard County Circuit Court for this period shows no cases involving bastardy in which either Herndon or Lincoln was engaged.

Paul H. Verduin, an indefatigable researcher, has recently attempted to reinforce Herndon's reputation for veracity. He suggests that a close reading of Herndon's words makes it likely that he was referring to an inheritance case rather than a bastardy case. He discovered in the record books of the Menard

County Circuit Court for 1847 through 1851 such a case—
Hannah Miller v. *Mary E. Miller et al.*—in which Lincoln and
Herndon were involved as attorneys.[65] The recent publication
of *The Law Practice of Abraham Lincoln,* which contains the
records of every case in which Lincoln participated, includes
details of the litigation, which dragged on for several years, and
suggests the possible date of April 1849 for Lincoln's alleged
confession to Herndon. There is, however, nothing in the surviving records of this case to suggest why it might have trig-
gered Lincoln's remarks about illegitimacy, and, indeed, there
is no positive evidence that Lincoln joined Herndon in attending the hearing in Petersburg.[66]

Equally controversial, and equally unprovable, is another
intimate confession Lincoln allegedly made to Herndon. Late
in life, Herndon told his literary collaborator, Weik, that
"Lincoln had, *when a mere boy,* the syphilis": "About the year
1835–36 Mr. Lincoln went to Beardstown and during a devilish passion had connection with a girl and caught the disease.
Lincoln told me this." After Lincoln moved to Springfield "the
disease hung to him," and, not wishing to trust local physicians, he wrote a letter to the celebrated Dr. Daniel Drake, of
Cincinnati, detailing his symptoms.[67] Dr. Drake replied that he
could not undertake to prescribe for a patient without a personal interview.[68]

For this story, which Herndon wrote more than fifty years
after Lincoln's alleged escapade and more than twenty years
after his death, there is no confirmatory evidence. Lincoln
never told it to anyone else—not even to Joshua Speed, with
whom he was sharing a bed at this time. Herndon did not
claim to have read the letter to Dr. Drake, and Speed was not
allowed to see the paragraphs that allegedly detailed Lincoln's

symptoms. The letter itself has never been found. There is no convincing medical evidence that Lincoln ever had syphilis. Certainly he never developed any of the obvious stigmata of tertiary syphilis, such as the curious spraddling walk that characterizes its victims. An examination of his aorta at the time of his death could have definitively solved the question, but doctors performed only a partial autopsy after the assassination. Modern physicians who have sifted the evidence agree that Lincoln never contracted the disease. They suggest that Lincoln may have suffered from "syphilophobia"—a fear of infection with a disease that in the nineteenth century was as incurable and deadly as AIDS.[69] The careful historian Charles B. Strozier suggests that Lincoln's confession to Herndon—if true—revealed more about his "sexual confusion and ignorance" than about the state of his health.[70]

Confidences like these—if Herndon accurately reported them—are rare in Herndon's voluminous records, and Herndon, to his credit, did not manufacture others that might have suggested an intimate friendship with his partner. "A twenty-five years acquaintance," he confessed, "convinced me that I never knew the all of Mr. Lincoln." But even if Lincoln was "a profound mystery," Herndon believed that his close, almost daily, observation of his partner over many years, his knowledge of "the science of the mind," and, especially, his intuition enabled him to understand Lincoln "inside and outside." Toward the end of his life he wrote a correspondent: "I knew the man so well that I think I could read his secrets and his ambitions."[71]

Lincoln characteristically left little record of his personal feelings toward his partner. He signed the few letters he wrote to Herndon while he was in the House of Representatives with

"Your friend as ever," but in his correspondence Lincoln referred to scores of men as friends. He found Herndon a useful and, much of the time, an enjoyable acquaintance, if not an intimate friend. Certainly he valued Herndon's loyalty. After one of Herndon's alcoholic episodes, someone asked Lincoln why he did not take another partner—someone safe and solid, like Orville H. Browning. Lincoln turned sharply on his interviewer to reply: "I know my own business, I reckon. I know Billy Herndon better than anybody, and . . . I intend to stick by him." On a last visit to the Lincoln & Herndon office before he departed for Washington, he directed Herndon not to take down the shingle that hung over the door. "Let it hang there undisturbed," he told his partner. "Give our clients to understand that the election of a President makes no change in the firm of Lincoln and Herndon."

IV

"A CLOSE, WARM, AND SINCERE FRIENDSHIP"
Lincoln and Orville H. Browning

LINCOLN came to Washington in 1861 without a single intimate friend in his entourage.[1] It is hard today to imagine that a President Elect could arrive in the national capital without a chief of staff, without a campaign manager, without a press spokesman. That Lincoln had none of these speaks volumes about the political process of the Civil War era. It tells even more about Lincoln.

As we have seen, Lincoln tried to persuade Speed to accompany him to Washington, but his old friend gently begged off. After Speed, Lincoln might have considered Herndon, who was unquestionably loyal. But in the past few years, his law partner had proved indiscreet in political affairs, and his fondness for alcohol may have caused a problem. Anyway, Mary Lincoln detested him.

Lincoln could have made David Davis his chief adviser. He had known the rotund judge of the Eighth Illinois Circuit for many years. That he was avaricious was not perhaps an obstacle, but it was troublesome that—like so many other judges— Davis tended to think himself infallible. Lincoln knew how much he was indebted to Davis for organizing the Lincoln for President movement in 1860, but he felt that Davis had been rather too active at the Chicago Republican convention. Pennsylvanians believed that Davis had promised Simon Cameron a post in the cabinet if they voted for Lincoln. In fact, Davis had made no explicit promises, and certainly Lincoln had authorized him to make none, but the misunderstanding forced him reluctantly to appoint Cameron to the War Department. After that, Lincoln was wary of Davis's advice.

Lincoln thought of naming another Illinois associate, Norman B. Judd, to his cabinet, where he could serve as both a political adviser and a personal friend. Judd, a prominent Chicago lawyer, had been associated with Lincoln in a number of cases, and the two men got along well. Lincoln lent him money to speculate in land in Iowa. Judd had been one of the principal organizers of the Lincoln-Douglas debates in 1858. But Lincoln found there were insuperable obstacles to bringing Judd into his inner circle at Washington. Former Whigs in Illinois, like David Davis and his henchman, Leonard Swett, strongly resented Judd, a former Democrat. Mrs. Lincoln took a violent dislike to him. And Lincoln himself came to realize that Judd, while a staunch political ally and an excellent casual acquaintance, was not, after all, a close personal friend. Judd had to be consoled with appointment as minister to Prussia.

I

THUS, when Lincoln reached the capital, there was no one in whom he could confide and with whom he could freely and frankly discuss his opinions and his plans. Surrounded by people all the time, he was the loneliest man in the capital.[2] No doubt, that sense of isolation contributed to his depression in the critical weeks after his inauguration, when, he said, "all the troubles and anxieties of his life had not equalled those which intervened between this time and the fall of Sumter."[3] The pressures of office, which he could share with no one, brought on headaches, and once, as Mary Lincoln said, he simply "keeled over."[4]

In early July 1861, Orville Hickman Browning arrived in Washington, appointed by the governor of Illinois to serve out the term of Senator Stephen A. Douglas, who had died in June. Browning and Lincoln had been acquainted for many years. They had both served briefly in the Black Hawk War, though they probably did not meet at that time. But in 1838, Browning, a rising young attorney from Quincy, was elected to the Illinois state legislature, where he joined the Whig contingent, of which Abraham Lincoln, now in his second term, was one of the leaders. After the capital was moved from Vandalia to Springfield, both men boarded with William Butler, the clerk of the Sangamon County Circuit Court. Browning was witness to Lincoln's bout of deep depression when he broke off his engagement to Mary Todd.[5]

It would have been hard to find two men who seemed more dissimilar. Self-educated, Lincoln came from hardscrabble beginnings, while Browning, son of a well-to-do Kentucky merchant and planter, had enjoyed a privileged childhood and attended college. Lincoln was tall, awkward, and carelessly dressed. He knew he looked odd and often made fun of his homely appearance. Browning was a strikingly handsome man, who fancied himself something of a dandy. Beneath his beautifully cut coat (in a style that would later be called Prince Albert), with a white or yellow handkerchief billowing from the pocket, he wore ruffled shirts with conspicuous cuffs. As a speaker, Lincoln was informal and used folksy language. Browning strove for—and sometimes achieved—eloquence.

But the two men soon found that they had much in common. Both were natives of Kentucky, and both had married Kentucky-born women; both were rising attorneys; both were strong Whigs, earnestly opposed to the Jacksonian Democrats; both were opposed to the institution of slavery; and both were quietly ambitious. Though they differed on some issues before the state legislature, including the vast internal improvements scheme that Lincoln favored and Browning opposed, they generally agreed in their votes.

What was more important, they came to like each other, and Lincoln greatly admired Mrs. Browning, the former Eliza Caldwell. Lively and entertaining, this stately, somewhat portly lady brought grace and decorum to the frontier Illinois capital at Vandalia. Shy and embarrassed in the presence of most women, Lincoln warmed to Mrs. Browning's "frank cordiality" and often passed his lonely evenings in the Brownings' room.[6] When Mrs. Browning failed to accompany her husband to subsequent sessions of the legislature, Lincoln joined other state representatives in sending her a mock legal petition, representing "to your Honoress, that we are in great need of your society in this town . . . , and therefore humbly pray that your honoress will repair, forthwith to the Seat of Government,"

where they pledged to pay her "due attention and faithful obe-
dience."[7] It was to Mrs. Browning that Lincoln addressed an
account of his brief romance with Mary Owens, whom he now
lampooned as "a fair match for Falstaff," whose size persuaded
him "that nothing could have commenced at the size of in-
fancy, and reached her present bulk in less than thirtyfive or
forty years."[8] Mrs. Browning took this burlesque as another of
the jokes Lincoln told to amuse her, and it was not until the
1860s that she learned that—however half-heartedly—he had
indeed asked Mary Owens's hand in marriage.

In the 1840s, when both Lincoln and Browning dropped out
of the state legislature, they remained in touch. In legal cases
they were sometimes colleagues and just as often opponents,
and they recognized each other's ability. In politics, though
they lived in different congressional districts, both promoted
Whig candidates and causes. After the railroad connected
Quincy and Springfield in the 1850s, Browning came more
often to Springfield to appear before the Illinois Supreme
Court and from time to time visited the Lincolns.

Mary Lincoln admired this handsome, well-bred Kentucky
gentleman with such excellent manners. He was one of the
few guests she ever invited to dinner in her cramped little
house on Jackson Street. She also liked Eliza Browning, who
was not so beautiful or flirtatious as to pose a threat. Perhaps
the two women found a bond in having both lost a child: in
April 1843, the Brownings' only child was stillborn, and the
Lincolns' sickly second son, Edward Baker, died in 1850, when
he was not quite four years old. The two families got along so
well that the Brownings invited the Lincolns to visit them in
Quincy. With a husband away on the circuit much of the time
and with three small children to care for, Mary could not

accept, but this was one of the few family invitations the Lincolns received.

Still, the Lincolns and the Brownings were more acquaintances than friends. Browning's extensive diary offers some hints of the nature of their relationship. Meticulously recording the weather, the state of his health, his legal cases, and his travels, Browning's diary makes no mention of the Lincolns until 1852, and thereafter their names appear infrequently, with passing references like "spent the evening at Lincolns" and "attended large & pleasant party at Lincoln's." Once or twice when both Browning and Lincoln were in Chicago on legal business, they attended the theater together, seeing such memorable plays as "Toodles" and "Dombey and Son."[9]

On political affairs, Browning's diary was somewhat fuller but more tantalizing. As Illinois Whigs slowly and reluctantly made their way into the new Republican party, Browning gained recognition as the man who could best draft resolutions that would express the moderate antislavery policy of the new party without offending either the more conservative old-line Whigs or the nativists, whose support the Republicans needed. Lincoln recognized his skill in such matters. In 1856, noting the need for "a sort of party State address" for the Republicans, he wrote his friend: "It has been suggested that you could draw up such a thing as well if not better than any of us."[10] Browning knew that he had a special talent for such work. With some self-congratulation, he reported that at the 1856 Illinois state Republican convention he served on the committee on resolutions, presented a set he had prepared beforehand, and saw them "unanimously adopted without change."[11]

Intent on recording his own very significant role in these party matters, Browning paid surprisingly little attention to the work of others. After detailing the success of his resolutions in the 1856 convention, which was chiefly notable because Lincoln delivered one of his greatest antislavery speeches, Browning merely recorded that the delegates at Bloomington were "also addressed by Lovejoy, Lincoln, Cook & others."[12] More puzzling was his diary account of the 1858 Republican convention at Springfield, where again he was asked to draft a platform, which, he noted somewhat smugly, "was adopted without dissent."[13] It was before this same convention that Lincoln delivered his "House Divided" speech. Browning must have heard it but did not mention it in his diary.

Possibly Browning was jealous of Lincoln, but, more probably, intent on his own role in the Republican party, he could not take seriously the political aspirations of his old friend. Lincoln, in his mind, was still the same awkward, unpromising man he had first met at Vandalia. In the 1858 Senate campaign to elect the successor to Stephen A. Douglas, Browning campaigned vigorously for local Republican candidates, but he took no part in planning or organizing the seven major debates between Lincoln and Douglas. When one of those debates was held in Quincy, Lincoln was a guest in Browning's home, but his host, attending to a legal case in Carthage, was not present.

As the 1860 election approached and it was evident that the Republicans stood a good chance of electing the next President, Browning warmly endorsed Edward Bates, the conservative Whig from Missouri, as a man of force and intellect, who was in "complete harmony in all our political opinions, inclusive of the tariff, and slavery in the abstract and in the Territories."[14] Browning took no part in the growing movement to promote Lincoln's nomination. So insensitive was he that in February 1860, he engaged Lincoln in a long conversation about presidential prospects, urging Bates's merits. Lincoln by this time clearly had his own chances in mind, but he did not want to offend any of his potential rivals and cagily told Browning that he might "be right in supposing Mr Bates to be the strongest and best man we can run." By the time of the Chicago convention, he added, he might "be of opinion that the very best thing that can be done will be to nominate Mr Bates."[15]

At the Illinois state Republican convention of 1860, Browning's role was once more that of resolutions maker, and he drafted a careful platform opposing extension of slavery into the national territories, opposing discrimination against foreigners, favoring a homestead act, and endorsing governmental economy. He took no part in stage-managing the convention's endorsement of Lincoln for President. When the time came to appoint delegates to the national convention who were pledged to support Lincoln, there was some objection to Browning. His support for Bates was so well known that one delegate said that naming him would be like "putting the child into the nurses arms to be strangled."

But Lincoln intervened, saying, "I guess you had better let Browning go [to Chicago]." Doubtless, he felt that Browning cared less for candidates than for party. "I am willing to forego all personal preferences," Browning confided to his diary, "and make any reasonable sacrifice to secure a triumph."[16] Lincoln knew too that Browning had many friends among conservative former Whigs, not merely in Illinois but in the border states of Kentucky and Missouri. Perhaps he hoped his long friendship with Browning would have some influence.

Whatever his reasons, his judgment was correct. Once in Chicago, Browning accepted the directions of David Davis, who acted as manager of the Lincoln campaign, and made an earnest appeal to a caucus of Indiana and Pennsylvania Republicans, stressing Lincoln's long Whig antecedents and emphasizing that his opposition to nativism would attract foreign-born voters. He ended, according to an eyewitness, with "a most beautiful and eloquent eulogy on Lincoln, which electrified the meeting."[17] Two days later, when Lincoln received a majority of the votes on the third ballot, Browning gained the floor of the convention to move that the nomination of "our noble Lincoln" be made unanimous.[18]

A few days after the convention, Browning, at the urging of Davis and other Lincoln managers, successfully urged Bates to endorse the Republican candidates, but he did so with a heavy heart. He continued to believe that Bates "would have carried the entire Republican party and the old whig party besides" and, five days after Lincoln's nomination, concluded: "We have made a mistake in the selection of candidates."[19]

II

IN the following weeks, Browning's opinion of Lincoln's chances for election improved. When one Democratic faction nominated Douglas for President and another named John C. Breckinridge, Browning wrote Lincoln that the division "must inevitably give you this state," and he eagerly joined dozens of others who campaigned for the Republican ticket.[20] He addressed 7,000 listeners at Macomb, 14,000 at Mendon, between 20,000 and 30,000 at Keokuk, and over 25,000 at Springfield.[21] His warm reception greatly cheered him. After his two-hour address in Springfield, he confided to his diary:

"My friends were in exstacies [sic] and said I made a great speech."[22]

Browning's campaign travels brought him more frequently than usual to Springfield, where he saw much of Lincoln. He was present when Thomas Hicks painted his portrait of the Republican presidential nominee, and he was delighted with the result. "I . . . cannot adequately express my admiration of the fidelity of the picture," he wrote Hicks, and he praised "the perfect and satisfactory idea which it gives of the original, and his physical, mental, and moral characteristics."[23]

In those days, propriety did not allow a candidate to campaign for himself; he was supposed to be a modern Cincinnatus, following his plow, until an eager public claimed his services. Consequently, Lincoln was often lonely and bored during the months between his nomination and the election, and he welcomed opportunities to have "a free and easy talk of an hour or two" with his old friend. Browning was pleased to discover that the presidential nominee bore his honors meekly, and found that Lincoln quickly "fell into his old habit of telling amusing stories."[24] Attempting also to be amusing in his own heavy-handed way, Browning tried to cheer Lincoln up by reporting that the board of trustees of Knox College, of which Browning was a member, had voted to confer on Lincoln the LL.D. degree. "You will, therefore, . . . consider yourself a 'scholar,' as well as a 'gentleman,'" he enjoined his friend, "and deport yourself accordingly."[25]

After the election, the two men had more serious matters to discuss. Writing Lincoln of his "great gratification at the glorious victory we have won" and invoking "the blessings of Heaven on your administration,"[26] Browning began to offer advice about appointments, strongly urging Bates for a cabinet position and warning the President Elect that "many of your most sensible, discreet and reliable friends" were opposed to the appointment of Judd to the Interior Department.[27]

During the winter, as the states of the Deep South began to secede, Browning also offered Lincoln advice about policy. "We ought not admit that the election of [a] President . . . in perfect conformity with the constitution and laws, affords any justification whatever for the attitude of hostility which some of the Southern states have assumed," he told the President Elect. Consequently, there should be no compromise on the part of the free states, which "should never consent, under any circumstances, to any concession which would tend to the recognition of slavery as a national institution, or to the reopening of the African slave trade." As for the states that were attempting to secede, they "should be treated as territories, and governments organized [for them] accordingly."[28]

During the months before his inauguration Lincoln was reticent and refused to give even a hint, whether in public statements or in private letters, of the policies he would follow, but he so trusted Browning that he discussed the secession crisis with him fully and freely. Browning was delighted to discover, after a long conversation shortly before Lincoln left Springfield for Washington, that there was "no point upon which we differed." He and Lincoln agreed that "no concession by the free States short of a surrender of every thing worth preserving . . . would satisfy the South." "Far less evil and bloodshed would result from an effort to maintain the Union and the Constitution," the two men believed, "than from disruption and the formation of two confederacies."[29]

Respecting Browning's judgment and his felicity of style, Lincoln chose him as one of the very few people to whom he

showed an advance text of his inaugural address. He accepted
Browning's suggestion that he should revise one passage that
threatened to "reclaim" federal forts that had fallen into
Confederate hands and substitute a pledge to "hold, occupy
and possess" those that remained under Union control.
William H. Seward, Lincoln's choice to become Secretary of
State, made a similar suggestion, with a view to calming
Southern apprehensions and allaying hostility. But Browning's
purpose was different. He predicted that any attempt to resup-
ply or reinforce the Union troops in Fort Sumter, one of the last
federal installations in the Confederacy, would induce South
Carolina to attack, and he wanted to make sure that in the conflict that would inevitably ensue, "the traitors shall be the
aggressors." By keeping them "constantly and palpably in the
wrong" Lincoln and his government would "stand justified
before the entire country, in repelling that aggression, and
retaking the forts."[30]

Valuing Browning's advice, Lincoln hoped that he would
accompany him on the long trip from Springfield to
Washington, but Browning begged off, pleading the pressure of
his legal business. In the end, he consented to go with the
inaugural party as far as Indianapolis, but at that point, bored
by the celebrations and festivities, he turned back.

At home in Quincy, Browning kept in close contact with
Lincoln by correspondence. As the secession crisis deepened,
he grew more and more extreme in his view that "the attempt
to break up this Union is the most atrocious piece of political
wickedness the world ever saw." He was satisfied, he wrote
Lincoln, "that it would be better . . . to maintain the union, the
constitution and the laws, even at the point of the bayonet,
than to stand acquiescently by and let all go to pieces."[31] The

cotton states had "invited their doom," he went on. "God is entering into judgment with them."[32]

When the Confederates fired on Fort Sumter on April 12, 1861, and Lincoln responded by calling out 75,000 men to crush the rebellion, Browning thought he should have called up 300,000, but he reported the enthusiastic rallying of Northerners of all parties to defend the Union and demand the "unconditional submission of the rebels." The "principal traitors" were criminals, to be dealt with according to the law. As for the hundreds of thousands of African Americans who would undoubtedly flock to an invading Union army, Browning now saw only one solution: "Give up the cotton states to them. Let them have the soil upon which they were born." Let them form themselves "into a Republic under the protection of this Government." "The time is not yet," he alerted the President, "but it will come when it will be necessary for you to . . . proclaim freedom to the slaves."[33]

In these letters addressed to the President, there appeared a new note. Previously, Browning had written to Lincoln in a fairly flat, formal style, but now his writing had a hortatory, almost evangelical tone. "Don't hesitate," he urged the President. "You are fighting for national life—for your own individual life. God has raised you up for a great work. Go boldly forward in the course his providence points you."[34]

Lincoln was not much influenced by Browning's message. When asked about Browning's proposal for turning the South into a black protectorate, he responded mildly: "Some of our northerners seem bewildered and dazzled by the excitement of the moment."[35] But doubtless he was touched by the sympathy that Browning's letters showed. "Surely no man ever assumed the reins of government beset by such complicated and oppressive difficulties as have surrounded you," Browning consoled the President and assured him, "You are adequate to the emergency."[36] His only fear was that Lincoln would permit himself to be overtaxed by the insatiable demands of office seekers. "Prompted by a very sincere friendship, and the kindest feelings," he urged the President to limit his office hours. Unless he did, "even your constitution may sink under it, and the country cannot afford to lose you now."[37]

III

WHEN Browning arrived in Washington to take his place in the Senate and attend the special session of Congress the President had summoned to deal with the war, the Lincolns eagerly welcomed him. On July 3, Browning made his first official call at the White House. Learning that the President was busy revising the message he was about to send to Congress the next day, he did not even send his name in but went to pay his respects to Mrs. Lincoln. In just a few minutes, he was told that the President had now finished his message, in which he reviewed the steps that led up to the firing on Fort Sumter, and wanted to read it to Browning. Finding it "a conclusive and unanswerable argument against the abominable heresy of secession," Browning praised it as "a most admirable history of our present difficulties."[38]

Lincoln was obviously delighted to have the Brownings in Washington, old friends whom he could absolutely trust. He knew that the Illinois senator would never betray a confidence, never leak information to his colleagues or to the press, never even hint that he had inside information. He was also aware that Eliza Browning was equally loyal to him. She thought him "one of the wisest men of the age." When a pro-Confederate aunt in Kentucky lamented that "a Sectional President [was] in the chair; Surrounded by an unscrupulous Set," she replied tartly that she had had "many conversations with the President about the State of things in our Country" and was sure that "we have great reason to thank God that we have Such a man at the head of affairs, at such a time."

Browning was almost the only man in whom the President felt he could confide freely. For instance, at their first meeting after Browning arrived in the capital, Lincoln, after reading the message he was about to send to Congress, went on to reminisce about his role in the events that had led up to the outbreak of hostilities. Upon learning from Major Robert Anderson that it was impossible either to defend or to relieve Fort Sumter in Charleston harbor, he had consulted his general in chief, Winfield Scott, and his cabinet, all of whom, with the exception of Postmaster General Montgomery Blair, had urged him to evacuate the fort. He himself conceived the idea of sending supplies to the fort, with no attempt to reinforce it, giving notice to Governor Francis Pickens of South Carolina. "The plan succeeded," the President told Browning. "They attacked Sumter—it fell, and thus, did more service than it otherwise could."[39]

This account, which has fueled the debates among historians as to whether Lincoln intentionally provoked the Civil War or did everything a reasonable man in his position could do to avoid it, Browning carefully recorded in his diary, where it remained unseen for nearly three-quarters of a century. It affords an opportunity to reflect about the value of Browning's diary as a historical source and about the nature of his relationship with Lincoln. Since Lincoln made no notes of this conversation—or, indeed, of any of his conversations with Browning—the diary remains our only source for what was said. Of Browning's general accuracy, there can be no doubt. Page after page of his voluminous record—there are 1,398 printed pages of the *Diary*—can be confirmed in detail. But here and elsewhere, Browning did not purport to give Lincoln's exact words; writing his record some hours after he left the President, he was summarizing or paraphrasing the conversation. There is no way to tell whether that summary accurately reflected what Lincoln said—or, for that matter, whether it reflected what Lincoln intended to say. Then, too, there is always the possibility that Lincoln knowingly misled Browning. Lincoln never lied, but he often tried out different versions of events with different visitors; by hearing himself, he was able to select the version that was most convincing.

With this segment of Browning's diary, there is a further problem. Months before the firing on Fort Sumter, he had urged Lincoln to make sure that, if conflict occurred, the South should appear to be the aggressor, so that Northerners would rally unanimously to the Union cause. Hearing Lincoln's account of the events that led up to the outbreak of hostilities may have seemed to Browning a vindication of "the plan" he had urged. In other words, Lincoln could have intended to give an account of how he exerted presidential leadership against the wishes of his generals and councils; Browning may have heard it as an account of how his—Browning's—strategy succeeded in making the Confederacy seem the aggressor in starting the war. The point here is not to split hairs over this particular conversation—significant as it was—but to warn against accepting all of Browning's accounts as revelations of Lincoln's thoughts.

The warning is necessary because during the next eighteen months, except when Congress was not in session, Browning had more private conversations with the President than any other senator. In June 1862, for instance, Browning conferred with the President no fewer than sixteen times. Often his purpose was to transact routine business, such as the appointment of a constituent to a pursership in the navy. A member of the Senate Committee on the Territories, Browning consulted Lincoln about such matters as the appointment of Indian agents and the completion of a treaty with the Delaware Indians.

Frequently when Washington was breathlessly awaiting news from the battle front, Browning went to the White House to learn how the Union troops were faring. Often on these visits, the President would detain him to discuss the military situation. After the first battle of Bull Run, Lincoln told how public opinion and the cabinet had pressed him to order General Winfield Scott to advance against Richmond. He yielded, and defeat followed. But, Lincoln admitted sadly, had Scott been allowed to conduct the military operation according to his own judgment "this would not have happened."[40] Later, during the winter of 1861–1862, when General George B. McClellan, who replaced Scott, failed to take the offensive, the President confided to Browning that "he was thinking of taking the field himself" and had devised the strategy of threatening all the Confederate positions "at the same time with superior force, and if they weakened one to strengthen another[,] seize and hold the one weakened etc."[41] In April, when Lincoln became so "impatient and dissatisfied with McClellan's sluggishness" that he wrote him a severe letter about the "indispensable necessity" for him to strike a blow at the Confederacy, he read it first to Browning for approval.[42] When McClellan finally did get under way, Browning received almost daily briefings on his progress from the President, who told him in confidence of appalling losses before Richmond. As the summer progressed, Lincoln revealed to Browning his growing distrust of McClellan. By July, he said he "was satisfied that McClellan would not fight." "If by magic," he told Browning, "he could reinforce McClelland [sic] with 100,000 men to day he would be in an ecstasy over it, thank him for it, and tell him that he would go to Richmond tomorrow, but that when tomorrow came he would telegraph that he had certain information that the enemy had 400,000 men, and that he could not advance without reinforcements."[43]

From time to time during these visits, the President would bring up what he called "the negro question." He and Browning agreed that the Union commanders should not, and would not, return to slavery the runaways who were already beginning to flock to the federal armies, but they could not devise any plan for taking care of the fugitives. Believing that whites and freed African-Americans could not live peacefully side by side, both men favored "colonization"—that is, transporting the freedmen back to Africa or to the Caribbean. "They must take care of themselves," they concluded, "till the war is over, and then, colonize."[44] Both believed that the institution of slavery could not long survive the war, and Lincoln told Browning of his plan to offer gradual, compensated emancipation, over a period of twenty years, to the border states of Delaware, Maryland, Kentucky, and Missouri, to which, he said, should be connected "a scheme of colonizing the blacks some where on the American Continent."[45]

They also discussed foreign affairs, in which Browning, as a member of the Senate Committee on Foreign Relations, had a special interest. In December 1861, when news reached Washington of an impending crisis with Great Britain after American commander Charles Wilkes seized two Confederate envoys, James M. Mason and John Slidell, aboard the British ship *Trent,* Browning immediately set about preparing for the President a memorandum on the international law covering the case. Browning's initial reaction was bellicose: if England was "determined to force a war upon us why so be it."[46] But after he discussed the matter with the President, he calmed down, and they "agreed that the question was easily susceptible of a peaceful solution if England was at all disposed to act justly with us."[47] Both men favored arbitration.

Important as such conferences on weighty issues were, Lincoln may have gained more from Browning's social visits to the White House. Browning became the indispensable guest at most White House dinners and social functions. Many of these Browning enjoyed, though he was much put out when, attending the Lincolns' crowded New Year's Day reception in 1862, a pickpocket stole his purse containing between fifty and one hundred dollars in gold.[48] Very often on Sundays, after meeting Browning at Dr. Phineas Gurley's First Presbyterian Church, one or both of the Lincolns would invite him back to the White House for an informal meal. Concerned for her husband's health, Mary Lincoln encouraged Browning to take a ride with him in the late afternoons, sometimes on horseback but more frequently in the presidential carriage. When there was no time for such recreation Browning began to make a habit of dropping by the White House after dinner, often as late as nine o'clock. After paying his respects to Mrs. Lincoln, he would go to the President's office, where Lincoln was often at work, and the two men would exchange news and political gossip or simply reminisce. To this old friend, Lincoln talked more freely than to any other person about what Browning termed "his domestic troubles." Aware that Mary was spending extravagantly, both on White House furnishings and on her personal wardrobe, the President confided to Browning "that he was constantly under great apprehension lest his wife should do something which would bring him into disgrace."[49]

In February 1862, the ties between the Lincolns and the Brownings became even closer, when Willie, the Lincolns' second, and perhaps most promising, son, fell ill, probably of typhoid fever, and died. The Brownings were out of the city but returned at once on hearing the news. President and Mrs. Lincoln sent their carriage for them immediately. They learned that "Tad" (Thomas), the Lincolns' youngest son, was also seriously ill, and they found Lincoln "in very deep distress at the loss of Willie, and agitated with apprehension of a fatal termination of Tad's illness."[50] While Mrs. Browning attempted to console Mary Lincoln, Browning comforted her husband, sending him off to rest while he watched at Tad's bedside. After Willie's funeral, which Mary, prostrate with grief, could not attend, Browning accompanied the President, Robert, his oldest son, and Lyman Trumbull, the senior Illinois senator, to the cemetery. That evening, both Brownings returned to the White House, where they sat up with Tad until two o'clock in the morning. The Brownings stayed with the Lincolns for about a week.

Three months later, both the Lincolns were still grieving over the loss of their son. After church on one Sunday in June, Lincoln invited Browning back to the White House to show him some papers of little Willie that he had just found: "memoranda of important events, inauguration of Gov [Richard] Yates, inauguration of the President, dates of battles, deaths of distinguished persons etc."⁵¹ Browning was the only person outside the family with whom Lincoln shared these treasures.

Lincoln was also more candid with Browning than to others about the state of his health. Though a robust, vigorous man, he found his presidential duties exhausting, and he was worn out by his long working hours. Repeatedly on these private visits, Browning found him suffering from headaches or simply depressed and despondent. Sometimes Browning could change his mood by encouraging him to talk about books and poetry. On one such occasion, both men quoted lines from Thomas Hood, the English comic writer, and Lincoln asked whether his friend remembered one of his favorites. When Browning said no, Lincoln sent for a volume of Hood's poems and read the whole of "The Haunted House" aloud, pausing from time to time to comment on passages that struck him as particularly felicitous. He then went on to read "The Lost Heir" and the "Spoilt Child." "His reading was admirable and his criticisms evinced a high and just appreciation of the true spirit of poetry," Browning judged, and both men enjoyed Hood's humor. After an hour and a half, Browning took his leave "in high spirits and a very genial mood," and the President too felt better able to face "the annoyances and harrassments of his position."⁵²

Sometimes not even Browning could cheer his friend up. Once in July 1862, he found the President looking "weary, care-worn and troubled." Though Lincoln said he felt "tolerably well," Browning expressed his concern "that troubles crowded so heavily upon him, and feared his health was suffering." Lincoln held him by the hand and pressed it, saying in a very tender and touching tone: "Browning I must die some-time." Troubled by "a cadence of deep sadness in his voice," Browning responded: "Your fortunes Mr President are bound up with those of the Country, and disaster to one would be disaster to the other, and I hope you will do all you can to preserve your health and life." When the two men parted, both had tears in their eyes.[53]

IV

At any point during his presidency, Lincoln could have kept this close friend at his side by offering him one of the many appointments available in his administration, but he did not do so. Ironically he came closest during the early days of his first term, before Browning was named Senator. When Lincoln was inaugurated, there was already one vacancy on the U.S. Supreme Court, and a month later, the death of Justice John McLean of Ohio created another. By general agreement, these would be filled by Westerners, and Browning longed for one of them. He had prided himself on standing outside the political arena, neither seeking nor desiring a federal office, but now, in early April 1861, he overcame his scruples and wrote Lincoln—"not without a great deal of embarrassment and hesitation"—to ask for the appointment. This, he reminded the President, was "an office peculiarly adapted to my tastes," and he pledged, "There is nothing in your power to do for me which would gratify me so much as this."[54]

Two months later, when the President had failed to respond to his entreaty, Eliza Browning entered the lists. Without consulting her husband, she said, she wrote the President a personal letter, seeking the appointment for Browning. Claiming that in the past he had not been fully appreciated "owing in part, to his Great Modesty, and unselfishness in not pushing himself forward," she insisted that he was "one of the Wisest best men in the Nation . . . , an unselfish Patriot, & not a miserable office Seeker." She reminded the President that Browning had labored so diligently for Republican success as to affect his health and his ability to attend to business. "We have no incum [*sic*] except from his profession," she lamented, and Browning's investments in land would become "valuable only when we are under the sod." She pleaded with the President to "gratify a sincere friend and devoted wife."[55]

There is no record that Lincoln answered either of the Brownings' letters. When Ohio Republicans pressed him to appoint their favorite, Noah H. Swayne, the President "frankly said that he must appoint Mr. Browning."[56] Repeatedly, he remarked that if the Western Circuit of the Supreme Court could be divided, so that Ohio and Illinois were in different circuits, he would be pleased to appoint both Swayne and Browning. But congressional support for reorganizing the judiciary was lacking, the Ohio congressional delegation was unanimous for Swayne, and Illinois Republicans were divided in their support for Browning. In the end, the President named Swayne to the Court.

Lincoln made a second Supreme Court nomination in July 1862, when he selected Samuel F. Miller, who was favored by the Iowa delegation. Again Browning was left out.

Twice passed over, Browning was under consideration for Lincoln's third Supreme Court nomination, to replace Justice John Archibald Campbell, who resigned to go with the Confederacy. This time, he had considerable support. During his brief service in the Senate, he had made a reputation as an effective legislator. "My relations with all the members have been of the kindest character," he noted when he left that chamber in 1863, "and I find my attachments to them stronger than I had supposed."[57] He had backers in the cabinet, where his old friend Attorney General Bates concluded that he was "a proper man" for the Court.[58] Justice Swayne gave quiet endorsement of his candidacy, and even aged Chief Justice Roger B. Taney judged that his appointment was "probable" though not certain. The President was reported as saying: "I do not know what I may do when the time comes, but there has never been a day when if I had to act I should not have appointed Browning."

But this time there was organized opposition in Illinois. Browning, with his patrician manners and his elegant dress, had never been popular among Republicans. "I should have liked him better if he had been a little less conscious of his own superiority," one of them reflected.[59] Browning's moderate course on slavery and emancipation and his opposition to con-fiscation acts that would seize the property and slaves of rebels alienated the more radical Republicans. Claiming that Browning represented "only the secesh [secessionists] of Illinois—Republicans detest and despise him"—Joseph Medill, editor of the powerful *Chicago Tribune,* thundered: "His elevation to the Supreme Bench will be the most unpop-ular act of Mr. Lincoln's life."[60]

Illinois Republicans hostile to Browning favored the candi-dacy of David Davis and began a campaign on his behalf. William Butler, with whom Lincoln and Browning had boarded during their early years in Springfield, joined Jesse K. Dubois, the Illinois state auditor, who was a neighbor of the Lincolns, in writing the President of their "Decided Preference" for Davis over all other candidates.[61] Leonard Swett, one of Davis's closest allies in Bloomington, pointedly compared the judge's diligent efforts for Lincoln's nomination in 1860 with Browning's tepid support. He asked the President: "Should not a man in power remember those men, and discriminate in favor of those men, who throughout his life have been as true as steel to him?"[62] Hearing that Lincoln still favored Browning, Swett made a special trip to Washington to promote Davis's claims. He promised to renounce any claims he might have for public office if Lincoln appointed Davis.[63]

Adding to these pressures against Browning's nomination was the surprising opposition of Mary Lincoln, who had long been close to both the Brownings. She told Swett when he visited Washington that she favored Davis because Browning had become "distressingly loving."[64] What she meant is not clear. Still mourning over the death of Willie, she had grown increasingly unstable and unpredictable. Perhaps she misinterpreted Browning's overly elaborate efforts at condolence. He tended, as Edward Bates remarked in an entirely different context, to use "language quite too florid" for a man of his gravity, and she may have misunderstood his effusive flattery. At any rate, as a correspondent wrote David Davis, "Mrs Lincoln is your warm friend and . . . presses your claims upon the President seeking every opportunity to put in a good word and . . . is unceasing in her endeavours for your appointment."[65]

These personal and political pressures may have had less influence on Lincoln than his reluctant conclusion that Browning, though a valued friend, lacked the judicial temperament. So long as Browning was in Washington and visited the White House almost every day, his opinions were sound, conservative, and almost identical to those of the President. For instance, he dropped his fierce plan to make the conquered South over as a black protectorate and sided with the most moderate Republicans in opposing confiscation of rebel property and emancipation of the slaves. But when Congress was in recess and he returned to Quincy, his judgment, no longer subject to Lincoln's direct influence, tended to become erratic.

The most marked indication of what Lincoln viewed as Browning's ideological unreliability was his defense of the proclamation General John C. Frémont issued on August 30, 1861, announcing that the slaves of all Missourians who supported the rebellion were "hereby declared freedmen." Lincoln viewed Frémont's action as unconstitutional, a violation of the Confiscation Act the Congress had just passed establishing specific procedures for the sequestration of enemy property, and an encroachment on his presidential powers, and he asked Frémont to rescind his proclamation.

As we have seen, Frémont's proclamation divided Lincoln's closest friends. Herndon rejoiced when it was issued and berated Lincoln for revoking it. Speed thought it a deplorable action, which would cost Lincoln much support in the border states. Browning's views were like Herndon's. He wrote to the President from Quincy: "Fremont's proclamation was necessary and will do good. It has the full approval of all loyal citizens of the West and North West."[66] When he learned that the President had overruled the proclamation, he lamented his action. Granting that there was "no express, written law authorizing it," he wrote Lincoln, "its revocation disheartens our friends, and represses their ardor."[67] In a thirteen-page foolscap letter, he insisted that Frémont's action was justified by "universally acknowledged principles of international political law . . . [and] the laws of war as acknowledged by all civilized nations."[68]

Lincoln was astonished by Browning's letters. They were the last thing he expected from a man who prided himself on his conservatism and his adhesion to the letter of the Constitution, from a man who only months before had worked closely with the President to make the Confiscation Act as lenient and as strictly legal as possible, from a man who so frequently endorsed the President's positions that he was known as Lincoln's spokesman in Congress. He wrote Browning a carefully reasoned defense of his action, insisting that Frémont's proclamation was "simply 'dictatorship.'" "Can it be pretended that it is any longer the government of the U.S.—any government of Constitution and laws," he asked rhetorically, "wherein a General, or a President, may make permanent rules of property by proclamation?"[69]

Pointedly, he urged Browning to "give up your restlessness for new positions" and to back him "manfully on the grounds upon which you and other kind friends gave me the election, and have approved in my public documents."[70]

Browning responded defensively that he had written Lincoln "frankly and candidly," intending at all times to be "both kind and respectful," but that it was obvious that he had succeeded only in annoying the President. "In all kindness," he protested, "I am not conscious of any 'restlessness for new positions.'" "For us, new positions are not necessary," he continued, reminding Lincoln, a bit loftily, that "a firm adherence to old ones is."[71]

Lincoln evidently recognized that his appeal for Browning's unconditional support had failed. When the time came for an appointment to the Supreme Court, he chose Davis, not Browning.

V

THOUGH Lincoln passed over Browning three times in making appointments to the Supreme Court, he still could have kept his friend near him by offering him some other position in the executive branch, such as a cabinet post.[72] Indeed, during the winter of 1862–1863, there were rumors that he was to replace Caleb B. Smith as Secretary of the Interior.[73] In an unexplained reversal, Mary Lincoln favored his appointment. During a private carriage ride, she said, according to Browning's diary, that the President "was anxious to have Mrs Browning and myself in Washington, and the only thing that would prevent him offering me the place would be the fear of having it said he was giving everything to Illinois, but she thought he would do it—She knew he wished to."[74] In December, Postmaster General Montgomery Blair congratulated him on the presumed appointment. When Browning replied that the President had never mentioned the subject, Blair said the appointment was settled and urged Browning to accept. "He then said it was very important that the President should have a personal friend in the cabinet upon whom he could rely."[75]

It does not appear that Lincoln himself ever gave serious consideration to such an appointment. Indeed, he and Browning had gradually been drifting apart since midsummer 1862. After Congress adjourned, Browning returned to Illinois, where he spoke frequently in support of what he thought were the President's plans. He defended Lincoln, McClellan, and Secretary of War Edwin M. Stanton from what he called "wicked newspapers" and claimed—contrary to what he had learned from Lincoln himself—that "all had each other's confidence." He opposed any attempt by the Congress or the military to emancipate the slaves, favoring instead Lincoln's proposal for gradual emancipation in the border states, accompanied by colonization. As for arming the freedmen, he said "the President would do it when there was a necessity for it" but predicted that if Lincoln acted "one-half the loyalists of the Union would fight against it."[76]

Browning's speeches offended many Republicans. The moderate *New York Times* called him one of "the pro-slavery sticklers for the Constitution," who "would not abolish slavery even to preserve the Union," and charged that Browning was exhibiting a spirit "in thorough sympathy with the secession movement."[77] What was more important for Browning's political future, many Illinois Radicals regarded him as a traitor. Illinois Governor Yates, to whom he owed his Senate appointment, said that Browning "by no means" represented his views and expressed disapproval of his course.[78]

Self-righteous and confident that he was voicing Lincoln's views, Browning paid no attention to these warning signs. He reported to the President that he was everywhere received enthusiastically because his listeners thought he represented the President. "You are very strong among the people, both Republicans and Democrats," he assured Lincoln, "and can do anything which your free and unbiased judgment shall deem necessary to give success to our arms, and crush the rebellion." Many in Browning's audiences expressed the deepest interest in the President's health and well-being. Often they said earnestly: "I hope God will spare him to our unhappy Country—he is our Washington."[79]

Clad in his armor of self-righteousness, Browning paid more attention to his own opinions than he did to those of the

President. Had he been more sensitive, he would have noted, even before he left Washington, that Lincoln's views were slowly shifting. In July, he had vigorously lectured the President on the iniquity of the Second Confiscation Act, which called for the seizure of the property of Confederates and the liberation of their slaves, and had urged—even demanded—that he veto it. Lincoln responded that he would give Browning's views "his profound consideration"—and three days later signed the bill. Again, in his last conversation with the President before leaving Washington, when he urged leniency toward Unionists in the South, he might have learned from Lincoln's exclamation that "there was but little Union sentiment" in the Confederate states and that the self-styled Unionists actually "sympathized with and aided treason and rebellion."[80]

In fact, Lincoln was changing course. It had become clear to him that moderate measures and conciliatory policies were failing. As early as July, he privately told Secretary of State Seward and Secretary of the Navy Gideon Welles that it was going to be necessary to emancipate the slaves if the Union was to win the war. He began drafting a proclamation but held it until a Union victory. On September 22, after McClellan checked the Confederate invasion of the North at Antietam, he issued his preliminary emancipation proclamation. It was followed on September 24 with a vigorous proclamation suspending the privilege of the writ of habeas corpus throughout the North.

Browning was thunderstruck. These were not the actions of the President he had known and with whom he had worked so closely. Abruptly he dropped his speaking tour in Illinois and abandoned his campaign supporting Republican congressmen and legislators. To the dismay of his Republican friends, he welcomed an invitation to address a group of Democrats in Monmouth, Illinois, explaining that from the beginning of the war, he had determined "to divest myself of the character of a political partizan." Though he did not, in fact, speak to the group, he loftily informed his political supporters "that the great masses of the democratic party are as patriotic and as true to the institutions of their fathers, as the republicans."[81] In October he promised to speak at a Union (i.e., Republican) rally at Quincy, but he found the speakers who preceded him such extreme abolitionists that he left the meeting. Just before the election, he did address a rally in Quincy, but in a non-committal tone, advising his hearers to vote for the best ticket, leaving them to infer that he did not know which ticket was the best.[82]

It came as no surprise to Browning that the Democrats swept Illinois in the November election, choosing a solidly Democratic legislature and congressional delegation. Already under attack from the Radical wing of his own party, Browning knew this meant an end to his Senate service, and he would return to Washington a lame duck. During the fall, before the Congress reassembled, he discussed Lincoln's proclamations with his friends and found, almost without exception, that they too considered them unfortunate. Judge Thomas Drummond of Chicago, who had been a contender for a Supreme Court appointment, thought the Emancipation Proclamation was probably unconstitutional and "could do no possible good and certainly would do harm."[83] John Todd Stuart, Lincoln's first law partner, agreed that the "most unfortunate" proclamations had kept many Democrats from supporting the Union ticket.[84] Republican Senator William Pitt Fessenden of Maine, whom

Browning met on the train back to Washington, said the Emancipation Proclamation was "at best, but brutum fulmen [an empty threat]," while the suspension of habeas corpus was "an exercise of despotic power."[85]

On his return to Washington in November, Browning frankly told Lincoln of his disappointment with his conduct. The masses of the Democratic party had been behind the President, he said, until he issued his "disasterous [sic]" proclamations. They "had revived old party issues—given them a rallying cry"—and the result was Republican defeat. "To this," Browning noted tersely in his diary, "he made no reply."[86]

After that, Browning felt so alienated that he could not bring himself to discuss these matters further with the President. Their frank talks on public affairs ended. Eventually, in April 1864, after Lincoln explained privately to him the reasons that had impelled him to order emancipation, Browning grudgingly conceded in his diary: "I have no doubt he was honest & sincere in what he did, and actuated by conscientious views of public duty."[87]

This disagreement did not mean that Lincoln and Browning broke off relations, exchanged angry words, or had a bitter quarrel. Lincoln never held grudges. Browning continued to be regularly invited to White House social functions—though he now grumbled that he did not approve of the Lincolns' having dinner parties on Sundays.[88] In his diary, he began to call Lincoln's scheme to end the war by gradual emancipation and colonization a "hallucination."[89]

After the Union defeat at Fredericksburg on December 13, 1862, Browning found himself involved in a caucus of Republican senators, which deplored the way that Lincoln was conducting the war. Given secret information by Secretary of the Treasury Salmon P. Chase, they claimed that Secretary of State Seward was exercising a backstairs influence on the President, coddling generals who did not truly support the Union cause and undercutting Lincoln's emancipation policy. They proposed to censure the administration and to demand the removal of the Secretary of State. A few of Seward's friends were able to block the motion, but when the Secretary learned what was going on, he immediately submitted his resignation to the President.

Browning's part in the caucus was hardly heroic. According to his diary, he told the senators that Seward ought to be removed if he was guilty of the offenses with which he was charged, but that he did not believe he was guilty. Then, if one can believe his report, he urged sending a deputation of senators "to have a full, free, and kind interview with the President—to learn the true state of the case—give him their views &c.," because, he said, he "knew there was no more honest, upright, conscientious man than the President, and that I knew him to be in favour of the most vigorous prosecution of the war."[90] No doubt Browning believed that he had said what he wrote, but none of the other participants in the caucus—and several left detailed recollections—made any mention of his remarks. Senator Fessenden, who wrote out a full account of the caucus proceedings, recorded only that Browning "said a few words, rather expressing a want of readiness to act upon so important a resolution than any opinion on the subject."[91] Browning's tribute to Lincoln is also suspect, since he forgot to include it in his journal for that day but added it, almost as an afterthought, when he wrote his entry for the next day.

The caucus adjourned without taking action. When it reassembled, more senators expressed a want of confidence in

the administration and some were willing to vote for a resolu-
tion asking Lincoln to resign. In the end, with only Preston
King dissenting, they voted to send a delegation to the White
House to urge "a change in and partial reconstruction of the
Cabinet." Browning voted for the resolution.[92]

The next day, Lincoln cornered Browning on one of his routine visits to the White House and asked about the purpose of
the caucus. He did not complain about Browning's failure to
defend his administration, though it was clear that he had a
pretty good idea of what had gone on. "What do these men
want?" Lincoln demanded, and he was not appeased when
Browning told him "what we did yesterday was the gentlest
thing that could be done. We had to do that or worse." "They
wish to get rid of me," Lincoln replied angrily, "and I am sometimes half disposed to gratify them." Browning could only
counsel: "Be firm and we will yet save the Country."[93]

Not a member of the senatorial delegation that visited the
President, Browning did not witness how skillfully Lincoln
managed to blunt criticisms and deflect attacks on his administration, so that he kept his cabinet intact. But he was certainly aware of Lincoln's unhappiness over a confrontation
that, the President said, left him "more distressed than any
other event of my life." Failing to recognize that the crisis was
over and that Lincoln had emerged stronger than ever,
Browning in the next few days tried to persuade the President
to "save himself and the Country" by appointing to his cabinet
conservative men from both parties.

Lincoln said he "could not afford to make a new cabinet"
and added, significantly, that a cabinet composed of the class
of conservatives Browning proposed "would give him trouble,
and be in his way on the Negro question."[94] At this point in

Browning's diary, a passage has been largely deleted, so that there remain only a few phrases: "his present cabinet," "satisfied he will have no other as long as he can avoid it," and "He is not equal to the. . . . "[95]

During the next few weeks, as rumors of reconstituting the cabinet swirled around Washington and Browning's name was frequently mentioned for the post of Secretary of the Interior, it seems never to have occurred to Browning that his own record of opposing emancipation and of failing fully to support the administration made him exactly the kind of man the President said would "cause him trouble, and be in his way."

VI

AT the end of January 1863, Browning presented the credentials of his successor, a Democrat, and left the Senate. He had some regrets, but he was not altogether unhappy. "I rejoice to get away for I fear that I can do no good here. . . . I am despondent, and have but little hope left for the Republic."[96] His disenchantment with Lincoln was so widely known that Governor Horatio Seymour of New York, a leading Democratic critic of the administration, urged Browning to return home by way of New York City and Albany, desiring "exceedingly" to confer with him on political matters.[97] Doubtless Seymour was hoping to build a coalition of War Democrats—those who supported the Union efforts in the war but were sharply critical of Lincoln's policies, especially on emancipation—and moderate Republicans. Browning was not ready to defect, but, returning to Illinois, he willingly listened to suggestions that Lincoln and his administration were ruining the country. He thought that the arbitrary arrests of civilians under the suspension of the writ of habeas corpus meant "the substitution of military for civil authority" and amounted to "virtually an overthrow of the Government."[98] When General Ambrose Burnside, acting on Lincoln's authority, suppressed the antiwar *Chicago Times*, he called it "a despotic and unwarrantable thing." Believing that radicalism in both parties was subverting the government, he suggested a plan, similar to Seymour's, of creating a new party of the center, composed of moderate Republicans and conservative Democrats, which would stand for "the suppression of the rebellion, the restoration of the union, and the reestablishment of the authority of the constitution and laws."[99] Notably missing from his plan was any mention of support for the administration or any endorsement of emancipation or equal rights for the freedmen.

By the end of 1863, bored with Quincy, Browning returned to Washington as partner in a law firm with three other conservative Republicans and became, in effect, a lobbying agent. Now only a former senator, he found he had much less influence. To a Quincy resident who asked his assistance in getting a federal job, he observed: "It is hard for an outsider, who holds no office himself, to get offices for others. The members of Congress gobble up everything that is going."[100] His affairs necessarily brought him fairly frequently to the White House, but now he rarely had long personal conversations with Lincoln. For the most part, his contacts with the President were businesslike and brief, and he learned he could not rely too heavily on old friendship. Presenting the case of a Mississippi woman, a refugee now in Missouri, who wanted the federal government to assign to her a number of freedmen sufficient to harvest the crop on her cotton plantation, Browning argued that her plea was "reasonable and just." Lincoln exploded in anger, saying that her losses were caused by the rebels, that there were many others who suffered more than she, and remarked "with great vehemence that he had rather take a rope and hang himself than to do it."[101]

As the 1864 presidential election approached, Browning resisted efforts to persuade him to campaign for Lincoln's reelection. Of course, he took no part in the attempt of some Radical Republicans to create a new party that ran General Frémont in opposition to Lincoln, but he watched more sympathetically as the Democrats moved toward nominating General McClellan, in whose patriotism and entire fidelity to the Union he expressed confidence.[102] At a Quincy rally to celebrate Sherman's capture of Atlanta, he coupled insistence that the war must be vigorously prosecuted with a plea that the "erring brethren" of the South should be treated with "great indulgence." Pointing out that Browning was careful not to mention "his former political friend and associate, Abraham Lincoln," the *Quincy Whig & Republican* claimed that his speech was "a studied and systematic effort at trimming and dodging."[103] A Baltimore paper reported that he was about to come out for McClellan, because he considered him the best general the country had produced. The story was sufficiently important that one of Browning's partners felt it necessary to explain to Lincoln that his statement had been misrepresented: "He merely said, that if Genl. Fremont or Genl McClellan were elected he would not commit suicide."[104]

Privately, Browning wrote to an Illinois friend that he could not support McClellan because, in his opinion, the Democratic platform virtually recognized Southern independence.[105] But he ignored a plea from Representative William

Pitt Kellogg to issue a joint statement declaring that "there is real[l]y but one course left to those who value the integrity of the union above all other considerations and that lies in the way of the reelection of Mr Lincoln."[106] Not until a month before the election could Browning bring himself to publish a letter that expressed a high opinion of McClellan but announced that he could not support his election on a platform that looked "only to separation and the recognition of the Confederate Government." The letter did not mention Lincoln.[107]

There is no record of how Browning voted, but two months before the election, he wrote to a conservative colleague: "You know, strange as it may seem to you, that I am personally attached to the President, and have faithfully tried to uphold him, and make him respectable; tho' I never have been able to persuade myself that he was big enough for his position. Still, I thought he might get through, as many a boy through college, without disgrace, and without knowledge and I fear he is a failure."[108]

After the election, Browning's interviews with Lincoln were infrequent. When he did see the President on behalf of one of his clients, he found Lincoln "pleasant" and "very kind," but the old intimacy was gone. On the evening of April 14, 1865, he waited for an hour at the White House to see Lincoln but was unsuccessful. His journal records merely: "He was going to the Theatre."

After Lincoln's assassination, Browning grieved sincerely over "the heaviest calamity that could have befallen the country."[109] During the years that followed, he cherished the memory of his friend—even while he collected scurrilous gossip about poor Mary Lincoln, who was desolated by her husband's death. Looking back over his relations with Lincoln through so many years, he concluded: "Our friendship was close, warm, and I believe sincere. I know mine for him was, and I never had reason to distrust his for me. Our relations to my knowledge were never interrupted for a moment."[110]

Lincoln never wrote an epitaph for his friendship with Browning. He was so nonjudgmental that, had he done so, it probably would have been kind. But perhaps he might have quoted William Blake:

> Friendship oft has made my heart to ache
> Do be my Enemy for Friendship's sake.

"BEYOND THE PALE OF HUMAN ENVY"
Lincoln and William H. Seward

ON November 16, 1862, Virginia Woodbury Fox recorded a delicious piece of gossip in her diary. "Tish," she reported—referring to her friend, Leticia McKean, a Washington socialite—told her: "There is a Bucktail soldier here devoted to the President, drives with him, and when Mrs. L. is not home, sleeps with him." "What stuff!" Mrs. Fox appraised the rumor.[1]

This item was brought to my attention by Professor Ari Hoogenboom, who was preparing a biography of Virginia Fox's husband, Gustavus Vasa Fox, the Assistant Secretary of the Navy. I tucked away his letter in the voluminous files I was collecting for my Lincoln biography but passed along copies to several Lincoln specialists. Matthew Pinsker, who was writing a history of the Soldiers' Home, just outside Washington, identified the soldier in question as David V. Derickson of the

150th Pennsylvania Volunteers, known as the "Bucktails" because of the insignia they attached to their uniforms, and the indefatigable C. A. Tripp looked into the story with a view to adding another chapter to his history of Lincoln's sexual life.[2]

They both discovered that there was a little more to the story than Mrs. Fox's unsubstantiated second-hand report. On arriving in Washington in September 1862, two companies of the Bucktail regiment were detailed as a permanent guard for the President at the Soldiers' Home, where he and Mrs. Lincoln tried to escape the summer heat of the capital. Lincoln himself cared little about having such a guard, but Mary Lincoln constantly worried about protecting him. When Robert E. Lee, fresh from his victory at Second Bull Run, invaded Maryland, Secretary of War Edwin M. Stanton also grew concerned about the President's safety and insisted that he be accompanied on his daily journeys between the Soldiers' Home and the White House. So on the day after the Bucktails took up their duties and encamped outside the Soldiers' Home, the President asked Derickson, the captain of Company K, to ride with him in his carriage as he drove back to the city. Asking him about his residence, his occupation, and his military service, Lincoln was obviously much taken with the captain and designated him as his regular escort.

According to Derickson's recollections, which were not published until 1888, he saw the President almost every day during the next four months. The captain reported to the Soldiers' Home at about 6:30 or 7:00 every morning, where he usually found Lincoln having breakfast, before other members of the household were up. Often the President was reading the Bible or "some work on the art of war." The two men drove into the city and returned about five o'clock.[3] Lincoln, Derickson claimed, brought him into his White House office and talked freely about the progress of the war. He introduced Derickson to military commanders, like General Henry Wager Halleck, and also to the members of his cabinet. It is certain that, after the battle of Antietam, Lincoln asked Derickson to join the small party that accompanied him to view the battlefield. In a familiar Brady photograph showing the tall President in his stove pipe hat facing the much shorter McClellan before a tent on the Antietam battleground, Derickson stands off to the President's right.

When the weather grew cooler, the Lincolns returned to the White House, and, on November 1, Captain Derickson and his company were scheduled to be replaced in their choice assignment as the presidential guards. But Lincoln insisted that they stay, writing that Derickson and his company "are very agreeable to me, and while it is deemed proper for any guard to remain, none would be more satisfactory to me than Capt. D. and his company."[4] In the spring, Derickson, desiring to return to his family in Pennsylvania, asked to be transferred to the newly created Provost Marshal's Bureau, and on April 18 he left the President's guard.

All this sounds pleasant and innocuous enough, but Tripp and Pinsker found additional information on Derickson's relationship to the President in an 1895 volume, *The History of the 150th Regiment, Pennsylvania Volunteers, Second Regiment, Bucktail Brigade,* by Thomas Chamberlin. Chamberlin, who had been Derickson's immediate commanding officer in Washington, wrote of the "marked friendship" that Lincoln developed for the officers of the Bucktail regiment: "Captain Derickson, in particular, advanced so far in the President's confidence and esteem that, in Mrs. Lincoln's absence, he frequently spent the night at his cottage, sleeping in the same bed with him, and—it is said—making use of his Excellency's night-shirts!"[5]

It is hard to know what to make of all this. Mrs. Fox's diary entry reports a rumor; obviously neither she nor her friend had any firsthand evidence. Hers is the only remark in the vast contemporary literature that even hints that Lincoln had unusual sexual interests, and her comment, "What stuff!" indicates that she thought that Tish's gossip was nonsense. Chamberlin's book was published four years after Derickson's death. His story can be neither confirmed nor denied, though Chamberlin was an honorable man, whose rather dry regimental history is not filled with gossip. So far as is known, no member of Derickson's regiment, which included his son, rose in wrath to denounce Chamberlin's story. Yet Chamberlin himself did not quite endorse the tale of the captain and the presidential nightshirt, pulling back to write "it is said" to indicate some doubt and adding an exclamation mark to indicate, if not its absurdity, at least its oddity.

As I try to reconstruct this episode, I start with the certainty that all the Lincolns found comfort in the presence of a company of fresh, young Pennsylvanians almost at the door of their summer residence. Tad Lincoln, who was about nine years old, was especially taken with the soldiers, who played with him, fed him, pampered him, and "commissioned" him their 3rd lieutenant. When the War Department threatened to replace the Bucktails with another regiment, Tad indignantly protested and persuaded his father to write his letter praising Derickson and his company and urging that they remain as his guard.[6] Mary Lincoln, too, was generally pleased to have the Bucktails protect her family. Though she sometimes complained of the noise from their nearby camp and objected to their pampering of Tad, she was always fearful for the safety of her husband and was glad to have him guarded.

Lincoln's role in the story was more complicated. Though he had no fears for his own safety and would have preferred not to have a military guard, he, like Tad, found the Pennsylvania soldiers delightful and enjoyed visiting their camp and talking with them. In the fall of 1862, their presence was especially reassuring. These were taxing months for the President: Lee's invasion of Maryland threatened the security of the national capital until McClellan checked the Confederates at Antietam; the Emancipation Proclamation, which the President issued on September 22, produced a furor throughout the North; McClellan's failure to follow up on his victory caused a reshuffling of the Union high command; General Ambrose P. Burnside's attempt to smash the Confederate army at Fredericksburg proved a disastrous failure; and in December, the Republicans in the U.S. Senate branded Lincoln's conduct of the war a failure and demanded that he reorganize his cabinet.

For Lincoln, this was the loneliest period of the war. In October, Mary Lincoln went to New York City for a month, shopping and helping her friend Elizabeth Keckley raise money for the Contraband Relief Association, and Tad was with her for part of that time. Robert was attending Harvard College. The President had no close friends in Washington. Browning, who came nearest to being a confidant, was off in Illinois; anyway, he was estranged after the Emancipation Proclamation. It is scarcely surprising that Lincoln looked to his military guard for company and conversation. To avoid eating alone in the empty fourteen-room cottage, he often invited officers to dinner or breakfast.

The President developed what Aristotle would call an enjoyable friendship with Derickson, who was an amiable, undemanding companion. Nine years younger than Lincoln, twice married, and the father of nine children, Derickson came from a prominent family in Meadville, Pennsylvania. He, like Lincoln, had been active in the formation of the Republican party. At the outbreak of the war, he enlisted as a private in the Pennsylvania Erie Regiment and served out his ninety-day enlistment. In 1862, when Lincoln issued a call for 100,000 more troops, he helped raise the new Bucktail regiment and was elected captain of Company K. Stout and genial, he had what H. S. Huidekoper, the colonel of the regiment, called "most pleasing manners." With a twinkle in his eye, Lincoln told Huidekoper that he and Derickson were "getting quite thick."[7]

Derickson shared something of Lincoln's sense of humor. For instance, when Jesse Winans, from Derickson's home county, came to Washington to visit his six sons in the army, who averaged six feet in height, he asked the captain to introduce him to the President. Knowing the President's fondness for measuring heights with other tall men, Derickson told Lincoln he had a visitor with *"thirty-six-feet-of-sons* in the army," and Winans was promptly admitted to the President's office. Another time Derickson introduced a fellow Pennsylvanian with the remark that he was often complimented on the fact that he resembled Lincoln, and the President, after inspecting his visitor, said: "I don't see just where that compliment comes in, as either of us would make a good subject for a comic almanac."[8]

Suffering from insomnia, Lincoln sometimes talked with Derickson until late into the night. I think it is hardly surprising that he may on occasion have asked the congenial captain to share his bed; in those days, it was not unusual for men to sleep together. And it is possible—though neither man ever mentioned it—that he offered his guest a nightshirt. That their relationship was friendly, not sexual, is suggested by the ease with which their association was ended when Derickson returned to Pennsylvania. They never saw each other again, though Derickson from time to time wrote the President about Pennsylvania support for a second term, pledging that "every thing promises well in this District for the elections." In 1864 he was chosen as a Pennsylvania delegate to the Republican national convention, which renominated Lincoln, but was unable to attend because of his provost marshal duties. He wrote Lincoln that he attributed his unanimous selection more "to the fact that I was known to be your warm friend than to my own personal popularity."[9]

I

ON the last full day of Derickson's service in the presidential guard, he put on a review of his company on the south lawn of the White House for the benefit of the President and Secretary of State William H. Seward, with whom Lincoln would come to enjoy a closer and more significant friendship.[10] In the early days of the Lincoln administration, no one could have predicted that they would get along. Before 1860, Lincoln and Seward had met only once, when both were making campaign speeches for Zachary Taylor in Boston. Seward's strong emphasis on the need to contain slavery impressed Lincoln, who was still pushing the old Whig issues of tariffs and a national bank.

If we can believe the Seward family tradition, Lincoln told Seward that night: "I have been thinking about what you said in your speech. I reckon you are right. We have got to deal with this slavery question, and got to give much more attention to it hereafter than we have been doing."[11] Of course that was a recollection many years after the event, and it ignored the fact that Lincoln had long been opposed to slavery.

Their paths did not cross again until 1860, when Seward was the front-runner for the Republican presidential nomination and Lincoln was a quiet dark horse. Lincoln's victory at the Chicago convention was a shock and a humiliation for Seward, who had counted on the nomination as a proper culmination of his years of service to the Whig and then the Republican party. In public, he managed to take his defeat philosophically and wrote a correspondent who grieved over his loss that a wise man "might well seek rather to have his countrymen regret that he had not been President than be President."[12] But he was deeply mortified, and occasionally he could not control his true feelings. Months after the convention, when a Wisconsin congressman warned there would be general disappointment if, as Secretary of State, he failed to give a diplomatic post to Carl Schurz, Seward burst out: "Disappointment! You speak to me of disappointment. To me, who was justly entitled to the Republican nomination for the presidency, and who had to stand aside and see it given to a little Illinois lawyer. You speak to me of disappointment!"[13]

After the Republican convention, Seward sulked for several weeks, but finally allowed Thurlow Weed, the New York boss who for years had been his mentor, to persuade him actively to join the canvass for the Republican national ticket. He made an extensive campaign tour of the Northwestern states. On

October 1, his train reached Springfield, Illinois, where he and Lincoln had a stiff, formal meeting that lasted only twenty minutes. A critical journalist wrote that the two men acted "as if each was afraid of his own virtue in the presence of the other."[14] But both were political professionals, and they managed to seem cordial. Seward promised the audience that his home state of New York, where he had been governor and senator, would give a majority of 60,000 or more for "your neighbor Abraham Lincoln," and in Cleveland, three days later, carried away by his own rhetoric, he announced that he had found Lincoln "eminently worthy of the support of every honest voter, and well qualified to discharge the duties of the Chief Magistracy."[15]

Though patently insincere, Seward's endorsement probably helped the Republican ticket, and once Lincoln was elected, he felt obliged to reward the New York senator for his support. Somewhat reluctantly, but feeling "under moral, or at least party, duress," Lincoln offered Seward the premier post in his cabinet, the office of Secretary of State.[16] After some feigned reluctance, Seward accepted, and from that point he and Thurlow Weed attempted to take over the management of the President Elect. Weed made two visits to Springfield in order to push for appointments he favored, and Seward kept up a barrage of letters offering Lincoln advice on his cabinet, on patronage, and, as one Southern state after another withdrew from the Union after Lincoln's election, on handling the secession crisis. Through Edwin M. Stanton, President James Buchanan's attorney general, Seward was kept abreast of the vacillation and trepidation that secession caused in the White House. When the newly formed Confederate States of America sent commissioners to Washington to negotiate the surrender of Fort Sumter in Charleston harbor, the last major fort in the Southern states still in federal hands, it was natural that they turned to Seward as the spokesman of the incoming administration. Nearly everybody assumed that Seward would become the "premier" of the new administration, really running the government while Lincoln simply followed his advice.

If the inexperienced President Elect, who was still in Springfield, chafed at Seward's assumption of authority, he gave no outward sign, but he quietly let it be known that he would not entrust all the patronage in New York State to Weed, whose political machine was thought to be corrupt. He paid little attention to Seward's activities until he arrived in Washington and learned that his Secretary of State designate wanted to control the makeup of his cabinet. Specifically Seward objected to the appointment of Salmon P. Chase, the Ohio Republican who had been one of his strongest opponents for the presidential nomination. When Lincoln persisted, Seward wrote him tersely, just two days before the inauguration: "Circumstances which have occurred since I expressed to you in December last my willingness to accept the office of Secretary of State seem to me to render it my duty to ask leave to withdraw that consent."[17]

Lincoln quietly pocketed Seward's letter. Telling John G. Nicolay, his private secretary, "I can't afford to let Seward take the first trick," he acted as though he had never received it.[18] On the evening before his inauguration, he gave a dinner for members of the administration who would be sworn in the next day, where both Seward and Chase were guests of honor. Then, once the inauguration ceremonies were over, he asked Seward to countermand his resignation, citing both the public interest and his own personal feelings. Weed, along with other friends, thought Seward should stand firm, fuming: "If Mr Lincoln knew how entirely the hopes of the whole country are resting on yourself he would open his eyes."[19] But Seward yielded and withdrew his resignation. Lincoln had weathered the first cabinet crisis of his administration.

II

During his first few days in Washington, Lincoln had arrived at a shrewd understanding of the personality of his Secretary of State. The President was neither a psychoanalyst nor a biographer, but he recognized intuitively that Seward would defer to an authority figure. As his harshest critic, Secretary of the Navy Gideon Welles, once remarked, Seward throughout his life identified with stronger characters and clung to them "as the ivy to the oak."[20]

Seward's father was a domineering, controlling man, who attempted to plan every detail of his son's life. So powerful was his influence that years later, after Seward had graduated from Union College, had become a successful lawyer, and had married and started a family, he dropped everything when his father wanted his company on a trip to Europe. Judge Elijah Miller, Seward's law partner in Auburn, in upstate New York, was another powerful figure to whom Seward deferred. Before permitting his daughter Frances to marry Seward, the judge stipulated that she could not have a house of her own but must live with him in his impressive mansion. A little later, Seward met Thurlow Weed, who became the editor of the *Albany Evening Journal* and the mastermind behind Seward's successful races for governor and senator. So closely did Seward identify himself with Weed that he was once heard to say: "Seward is Weed and Weed is Seward. What I do, Weed approves. What he says, I endorse. We are one."[21]

Unlike these other authority figures, Lincoln was younger than Seward, by nearly nine years, but both his appearance and the position he occupied made people think of him as—and call him, behind his back—"Old Abe." In time, Seward came to defer to him too.

What Lincoln did not yet know was that, along with Seward's general submissiveness to authority, he also had brief eruptions of rebelliousness. After his father scolded him for his large tailor's bills while at Union College, young Henry—as his family always called him—sneaked off to Georgia, where he took a job as a school teacher. When his father found him, he returned docilely to college and graduated with distinction. Similarly, Henry violated his explicit pledge to his father-in-law and built a small, separate house for Frances and his growing family. Miller's displeasure, Frances's discomfort, and Henry's absence so much of the time on business and politics quickly put an end to that experiment, and the Sewards moved back into the Miller mansion. Similarly with Weed, he broke from the traces from time to time to express ideas the party boss did not approve. For instance, he did not consult Weed before giving his celebrated 1858 speech that announced an "irrepressible conflict" between freedom and slavery. The phrase gave Seward an undeserved reputation for radicalism, but, under pressure from Weed, he gradually moderated his position. In the secession crisis, he favored a conciliatory approach toward the South.

Lincoln's first direct experience of Seward's unpredictable rebellious streak came on April 1, 1861, when he received a remarkable memorandum from his Secretary of State, "Some Thoughts for the President's Consideration." Claiming that after nearly a month in office the new administration lacked any clear policy, either domestic or foreign, Seward wrote that the President had been spending too much time on minor patronage matters and urged him to make it clear that the real issue before the country was not slavery but union or disunion. On the domestic front, Seward proposed removing federal troops from Fort Sumter in order to calm Southern opinion. In foreign affairs, he noted that both France and Spain had initiated ventures in the Caribbean and urged that the United States seek explanations from both powers. If they were not forthcoming, Congress should be convened and war declared. Whatever policy was adopted, it required "energetic prosecution," whether by the President or a designated member of his cabinet. "It is not in my especial province," Seward concluded disingenuously. "But I seek neither to evade nor assume responsibility."[22]

Lincoln might have made this memorandum the occasion for dismissing his Secretary of State, but he chose not to do so. Perhaps he recognized that for all its impertinence, it contained a considerable measure of truth.[23] He had indeed been too preoccupied with patronage; since this was the first Republican administration, the demands for office were incessant and overwhelming. He saw the wisdom of making Union, not slavery, the question before the country, though he was not convinced that surrendering Fort Sumter was the best way of strengthening Unionist sentiment in the South. Seward's ideas about foreign policy, if not solicited, were not entirely unauthorized. After all, when Lincoln first arrived in Washington, he had told his designated Secretary of State: "Governor

Seward, there is one part of my work that I shall have to leave largely to you. I shall have to depend upon you for taking care of these matters of foreign affairs, of which I know so little, and with which I reckon you are familiar."[24] Lincoln certainly agreed with Seward that French and Spanish adventurism in the Western Hemisphere had to be challenged, though he was far from ready to think of declaring war. Finally, he must have considered Seward's memorandum a private document, not a public manifesto. It contained no suggestion that the Secretary wanted to break up the cabinet or to go public with his discontents.[25] So Lincoln, as was his way, wrote out a careful, thoughtful response, pointing out that the administration did indeed have a policy on secession—a policy announced in his inaugural address, in which Seward had concurred—and that on foreign policy issues, the members of the administration had been acting "all in perfect harmony." To Seward's suggestion that he, or the President, or some other member of the cabinet must energetically prosecute the government's policy, Lincoln replied flatly: "I remark that if this must be done, I must do it."[26]

It was a perfect rebuke—but after finishing it, Lincoln did not send it. The only known copy is in his papers, not in those of Seward. He may not even have read his reply aloud to Seward, but instead they probably discussed the issues face to face. Neither man ever mentioned this episode again. Indeed, nobody else ever knew of it until decades later, when John G. Nicolay and John Hay, in the course of research for their massive *Abraham Lincoln: A History,* uncovered the documents in Lincoln's private papers.

It was, nevertheless, an instructive encounter for both men. Alerted to the Secretary's unpredictability, Lincoln began to give more scrutiny to the diplomatic despatches Seward drafted. For instance, in May 1861, he closely edited what has become known as Seward's "bold remonstrance" to the British government against holding any official intercourse with the Confederate commissioners who had been sent abroad to secure international recognition. Seward wrote that British recognition of the Confederacy might lead to intervention in the American Civil War, and he threatened: "We from that hour shall cease to be friends and become once more, as we have twice before been forced to be, enemies of Great Britain." Lincoln circled the passage and marked it: "Leave out." Then, to make sure that the despatch could do no harm, he directed that it be sent to the American minister, Charles Francis Adams, for his "guidance only, and not [to] be read or shown to any one."[27]

Reluctantly Seward accepted most of the changes that Lincoln directed and toned down his most belligerent statements. As instructed, he marked the despatch to Adams, "Not to be shown or read to the British Secretary of State." But—indicating that his rebellion had not quite subsided—he directed the American minister: "You will keep back nothing when the time arrives for its being said with dignity propriety and effect."[28]

III

AFTER that episode, which clearly established that the President, not the Secretary of State, directed American policy, Lincoln and Seward worked together as useful friends. Initially, it was not an easy relationship for either man. Lincoln was aware of Seward's long history of leadership, of his standing in the Republican party, of his disappointment over rejection at the Chicago convention, and of his recent erratic behavior. Adding to these concerns was Mary Lincoln's strong dislike of the Secretary, whom she referred to as "that hypocrite Seward," that "dirty abolition sneak."[29] Sure that Seward's every move was calculated to give him the Republican nomination in the 1864 election, she snubbed Mrs. Seward when she called to pay her respects during one of her infrequent visits to Washington.[30]

But Lincoln knew that he needed Seward and began a systematic campaign to win his loyalty and even his affection. When Lincoln tried to be charming, he was irresistible, and he knew how to court Seward. Aware of the Secretary's self-importance and vanity, he encouraged Seward to drop in at the White House nearly every day, and when the two men did not meet, they exchanged frequent brief notes about schedules, appointments, and the like.

Lincoln made a point of consulting Seward even on concerns remote from the work of the State Department. Early in the war, troubled over disloyalty and even sabotage in the North, he asked Seward's advice about suspending the writ of habeas corpus, so that suspected Confederate sympathizers and spies could be arrested and held without trial, and he listened as the Secretary insisted that "perdition was the sure penalty for further hesitation."[31] Before overruling Frémont's proclamation freeing the slaves of rebels in Missouri, Lincoln made a point of consulting Seward and indicated that he felt reinforced by his approval. In 1862, when the White House was flooded with letters and petitions demanding the removal of General McClellan, Lincoln sent them over to the State Department for Seward to read.

Whether, in fact, Seward's advice on such matters affected Lincoln's actions is hard to determine, but it is clear that the more deeply the Secretary felt involved in such decisions, the more strongly he supported his Chief. Initially, he had a dim view of Lincoln. The Secretary thought he had "no system, no relative ideas, no conception of his situation—much absorption in the details of office dispensation, but little application to great ideas."[32] He complained that Lincoln did not know how to delegate authority and tried to do all the work of the executive branch himself. But, taken into Lincoln's confidence, he came to feel that the President was learning his job and concluded that Lincoln's magnanimity was "almost superhuman." Within a few months of taking office, Seward did an about-face. "Executive skill and vigor are rare qualities," he told his wife. "The President is the best of us"—though he could not refrain from adding: "but he needs constant and assiduous coöperation."[33] The next year he was even more positive, writing Weed that Lincoln was "wise and practical,"[34] and by 1863, he eulogized the President to the New York diarist, George Templeton Strong, as "the best and wisest man he has ever known."[35]

IV

WHILE the President was wooing the Secretary, Seward was assiduously cultivating his special relationship to Lincoln. After their initial confrontation, he understood that Lincoln did not like arguments and disagreements with his advisers. Accordingly, as Secretary of State in charge of arranging cabinet meetings, he saw to it that very little major business was brought before the group. Instead, he would meet privately with the President, so that, as critics like Welles complained, he could whisper in Lincoln's ear, "patronizing and instructing him, hearing and telling anecdotes, relating interesting details of occurrences in the Senate, and inculcating his political party notions."[36] Explaining to John Hay, Lincoln's private secretary, his preference to serve as a behind-the-scenes adviser, Seward said he willingly left to others the role of publicly urging the President to act and of "running before and shouting for the coming events." He resolved that he would "stay behind, to do with and for the President what seemed best, to share with him the criticism and the risk and to leave the glory to him and to God."[37]

More clearly than anyone else except perhaps Herndon, Seward glimpsed Lincoln's driving ambition—"a little engine that knew no rest," in Herndon's frequently quoted phrase— and understood that, almost from the day of his inauguration, Lincoln wanted, and was working for, a second term. He recognized that he would not tolerate a Secretary of State who was a potential rival. Accordingly, in the winter of 1861, when a number of his friends in Philadelphia proposed to form a William H. Seward Club for 1864, Seward promptly rebutted this "partisan movement" in a widely circulated public letter. Upon entering Lincoln's cabinet, he explained, he had "renounced all ambition" and "all expectation of future personal advantage, in order that the counsels I might give to the President, in such a crisis, should not only be, but be recognized as being, disinterested, loyal, and patriotic."[38]

Aware of the First Lady's hostility, Seward made a point of befriending the Lincoln boys, Willie and Tad, knowing how dear they were to their father's heart. Once he brought them kittens, which they loved, as did their father, who let the pets climb all over him. Seward liked to close his office at four o'clock to take a carriage ride around Washington, and he often persuaded the busy President to accompany him. Frequently, they drove out to the ring of forts that General McClellan had erected to protect the capital, where they both enjoyed chatting with the soldiers and their officers.

Seward worked hard to make himself indispensable to the President. He advised Lincoln on presidential social protocol: the color of gloves to be worn on special occasions, the time for formal White House dinners, the etiquette of calling cards, the proper way to address titled foreigners. On occasion, he instructed Lincoln to put on his coat to welcome a foreign dignitary and mildly scolded him for not doing so when Dr. Francis Lieber came to award him an honorary degree from Columbia College (later Columbia University) in New York City.[39] He screened candidates for the dozens of diplomatic missions and consular offices. He scheduled appointments for ambassadors of foreign countries to make formal visits to the President. He provided drafts of letters of congratulation or condolence to be sent to foreign rulers and proclamations of days of prayer or thanksgiving.

The Secretary did not confine his activities to work properly belonging to his own department; he meddled in the business of nearly every other cabinet officer. Sometimes his intervention was much needed, as at the War Department, where Secretary Simon Cameron proved hopelessly inept. At other times, it was distracting and even harmful. When Lincoln authorized Secretary of the Navy Gideon Welles to prepare an expedition for the relief of Fort Sumter, Seward, without telling either Welles or the President, diverted the *Powhatan*, the most powerful ship in the fleet, for his own attempt to re-inforce Fort Pickens in Florida.

As a result, Seward was distrusted by his cabinet colleagues. Chase had long been his political enemy and rival. Welles believed he was so eager to direct, to be the premier, the real executive, that "with all his shrewdness and talent," he at times became "the victim of his own vanity and conceit."[40] Montgomery Blair, the Postmaster General, thought him "an unprincipled liar—the truth not in him." Attorney General Edward Bates complained bitterly of his "hasty and blundering manner."[41] But such friction in his cabinet bothered the President hardly at all. For years, he had learned to live with what a later generation would call cognitive dissonance—in his own family, in his law practice, in his political career—and he found the process stimulating, not distracting.

Aware that he was widely disliked not merely by his fellow cabinet members but by members of Congress, Seward in his private correspondence adopted a tone of self-pity coupled with self-importance. Lamenting that the "country so largely relying on my poor efforts to save it . . . refused me the full measure of its confidence, needful to that end," he complained to Mrs. Seward: "I am a chief reduced to a subordinate position, and surrounded with a guard, to see that I do not do too much for my country, lest some advantage may revert indirectly to my own fame."[42] He subscribed one of his letters to Weed: "ever your unfortunate friend, who has faith in everybody, and enjoys the confidence of nobody."[43] At the same time, he was sure he was the indispensable man. As he wrote to his wife in August 1861: "I look back, and see that there has not been a day since last January, that I could, safely for the Government, have been absent." Three months later he wrote her: "The responsibility resting upon me is overwhelming."[44]

Seward was careful, however, not to express these emotions to Lincoln, and he presented to the President, as to the public at large, a persona of calm, invincible optimism. Never allowing himself any expression of discouragement or defeat, he thought it his duty to seem cheerful. In his house on Lafayette Square, diagonally across from the White House, he regularly had guests for dinner, entertaining them with excellent food and wine—his enemies said he drank too much—and even more with his endless fund of supposedly confidential news and gossip. He was at his best in his drawing room after supper, comfortable in his easy chair and surrounded by billowing smoke from his inevitable black cigar. After a drop of brandy, he would regale his guests with irreverent and often profane comments on the day's happenings, punctuated by hearty cursing of his opponents. Seward liked company, but he also thought his social life a duty. "In this confusion of nations and of men," he explained to his daughter, "I must be calm, undisturbed, hopeful of all things, and gracious in every way."[45]

V

In routine diplomatic affairs, Lincoln was usually willing to follow Seward's advice, but on important foreign policy questions, the President made the decisions. In so doing, he handled the Secretary with great finesse, allowing Seward to appear to shape policy—and perhaps to believe that he did so. Nowhere was Lincoln's skill more evident than in the crisis that arose when American naval captain Charles Wilkes, in November 1861, stopped and boarded the British mail packet *Trent* off the coast of Cuba and removed from the ship two Confederate envoys,

James M. Mason and John Slidell, who were going to Europe in the hope of securing recognition for the South. Coming at a low point in the fortunes of the Union war effort, Wilkes's act was at first hailed as a victory, and Seward, like most other Northerners, was "elated and jubilant over the capture."[46]

Lincoln faced a dilemma. Though he was not versed in the intricacies of international law, reflection convinced him—just as it convinced Browning—that Wilkes's rash act had been an affront to the British flag and that only by releasing the Confederate envoys from Fort Warren in Boston harbor, where they were being held, could he avoid European intervention in the American conflict. But he also knew that giving up Mason and Slidell would outrage American public opinion.

Deeply troubled but reluctant to act, Lincoln took the unusual step of putting the whole issue before the cabinet, in a meeting on December 15, to which Sumner was invited, in order to read his latest private correspondence from England warning of the danger of war. All recognized the issue was a grave one, and Lincoln warned of the folly of having "two wars on his hands at a time." But there was no consensus, and the meeting adjourned until the next day.

In his own mind, Lincoln had already determined to release Mason and Slidell, but before doing so, he needed to make sure that he had the unqualified support of his Secretary of State. The British distrusted Seward. According to a widely circulated rumor, he had told the Duke of Newcastle that if he ever became Secretary of State, it would be his duty to insult Great Britain. Once in office, he had lived up to that threat. He had continued to assail European powers so vehemently that the British minister, Lord Lyons, felt obliged to warn his superiors "that it may be impossible to deter this Government from offering provocations to Great Britain, which neither our honour nor our interest will allow us to brook."[47] But in the *Trent* crisis, Seward behaved with discretion, and he seemed to suggest at the cabinet meeting that the two Confederate envoys must be surrendered. After the other members of the conference left, Lincoln said: "Governor Seward, you will go on . . . preparing your answer, which . . . will state the reasons why they ought to be given up. Now I have a mind to try my hand at stating the reasons why they ought not to be given up. We will compare the points on each side."

The next day at another cabinet meeting, Seward was ready with a strong argument for releasing Mason and Slidell. As the President said later, Seward had "studied up all the works ever written on international law, and came . . . loaded to the muzzle with the subject."[48] Some members of the cabinet expressed unhappiness with his conclusions, and Secretary Chase said release of the envoys would be "gall and wormwood" to him. But all agreed that it had to be done.

After the meeting adjourned, Seward asked the President, "You thought you might frame an argument for the other side?" Slyly, Lincoln smiled and shook his head, unwilling to reveal that he had maneuvered the Secretary of State into adopting the position that he had favored all along: "I found I could not make an argument that would satisfy my own mind, . . . and that proved to me your ground was the right one."[49]

VI

VALUABLE as Seward's wisdom was, Lincoln was perhaps even more impressed by the Secretary's loyalty. After his initial aberrations in 1861, Seward yielded unquestioningly to his chief—just as he had done to his father and to Judge Miller. As Gideon Welles unkindly observed: "He was subordinate to Abraham Lincoln and deferred to him as he had deferred to Thurlow Weed—conformed to the views of the former as he had for thirty years to those of the latter."[50]

This did not mean that Seward always agreed with the President. He remained firmly convinced that the central issue of the war was not slavery but the preservation of the Union. This, of course, was a view that Lincoln shared with him at the outset of the war, and one that the President publicly maintained as late as August 1862, when he wrote his celebrated letter to Horace Greeley announcing that his "paramount object" was neither to maintain nor to destroy slavery but to preserve the Union. But, as we have seen, under pressure of repeated military reverses and under unflagging criticism from Radicals who insisted that only an emancipation proclamation could bring about Confederate defeat, he gradually changed positions. In July, on a carriage ride with Seward and Welles, Lincoln told his two most conservative advisers that he "had about come to the conclusion" that an emancipation proclamation was "absolutely essential for the salvation of the Union."[51]

Seward regretted Lincoln's decision, because he believed that the preservation of the Union, rather than the destruction of slavery, should remain the administration's war aim. In the summer of 1862, at about the time that Lincoln confided his intention to issue an emancipation proclamation, his Secretary of State wrote an ill-considered despatch to Charles Francis Adams, the American minister to Great Britain, attacking both the Southern secessionists and the Northern abolitionists, "acting in concert together," as equally responsible for the war.

When that document was published, antislavery men were outraged, and the President was obliged to offer the feeble apology that, though Seward usually read important letters aloud to him before sending them, he had no recollection of this particular despatch.[52]

Like Browning, Seward saw no need for an emancipation proclamation. In his view, slavery was already a dying institution; every advance of the Union armies was a step toward freedom. Referring to Radical Republicans in the Congress such as Sumner, Benjamin F. Wade, and Zachariah Chandler without naming them, he ridiculed those who think "that success is obtained by the indulgence of passionate and revengeful utterances in laws and proclamations, without bayonets to enforce them." "It is mournful," he lamented, "to see that a great nation shrinks from a war it has accepted and insists on adopting proclamations, when it is asked for force."[53]

Loyal to the President, Seward made no public statements—unlike Secretary Chase, who constantly leaked his discontents to congressmen and newspapermen. On July 23, when Lincoln announced to the full cabinet that he intended to issue an emancipation proclamation, Seward raised only the question of timing. To launch the proclamation at this particular moment, after the severe reverses experienced by the Union army, he said, would make it seem "our last *shriek,* on the retreat."[54] Lincoln agreed and withheld the proclamation until after McClellan's victory at Antietam.

Seward doubted the wisdom as well as the efficacy of both Lincoln's preliminary proclamation of September 22 and his final proclamation of January 1, 1863, declaring the slaves in the rebel states free. In a private conversation with Thomas Ewing of Ohio, Seward spoke of "the pernicious influence of the proclamation," and he told Browning that "the proclamations were unfortunate, and that we would have been nearer the end of the war and the end of slavery both without them."[55] Agreeing with Browning that the proclamation divided the North while uniting the South, he said he was reminded of the man who, after the Revolution was over, insisted on raising a Liberty pole in his village. When neighbors asked if he could not feel free without it, he replied, "What is liberty without a pole?" What, Seward asked rhetorically, is a war without a proclamation?[56] When the artist Francis B. Carpenter planned his huge painting of the reading of the Emancipation Proclamation as the crowning event of Lincoln's administration, Seward earnestly protested. Carpenter should have painted the cabinet meeting that decided to relieve Fort Sumter; that was "the significant act of the administration."[57]

To the end of his life, Seward believed that the Emancipation Proclamation had been a useless mistake, and he claimed that—because it applied only to Southern territory that was not under Union military control—it had not freed a single slave. But he never made any public objection to Lincoln's policies. Instead, he discouraged all rumors of dissent among Lincoln's advisers, remarking, "There is but one vote in the Cabinet, and that is cast by the President."[58]

VII

SEWARD needed Lincoln's support in 1862 as pressure mounted to remove him from the cabinet. The movement originated in the long-standing feud among New York Republicans led by Seward and Weed, on the one hand, and by Greeley,

David Dudley Field, the antislavery law reformer, and James A. Hamilton, son of the first Secretary of the Treasury, on the other. It grew when Sumner, who had hoped to be Secretary of State himself, grew furious over what he took to be Seward's mishandling of foreign relations. It reached a climax when word of Seward's opposition to an emancipation proclamation leaked out. But the real force behind the movement to oust the Secretary of State was the public perception that the war was going badly and that Lincoln was incompetent. Some outspoken critics attacked the President directly; more sought to remove Seward and put in his place a more forceful advocate of emancipation—probably Salmon P. Chase—who would, in effect, run the government.

The first blast in the war against Seward took place in September 1862, when a delegation of anti-Seward Republican leaders from New York descended on the White House to demand the reorganization of the administration and, especially, the ouster of Seward, who was thought not to have his heart in the war. Lincoln gave them an angry reception. "You, gentlemen," he said, "to hang Mr. Seward would destroy the government." They went home empty-handed.[59]

But by fall, after the Democrats made large gains in the fall congressional elections and after General Burnside suffered a disastrous defeat at Fredericksburg, the anti-Seward movement gained new strength. "Seward must be got out of the Cabinet," Joseph Medill, publisher of the *Chicago Tribune*, announced. "He is Lincoln's evil genius. He has been President *de facto,* and has kept a sponge saturated with chloroform to Uncle Abe's nose."[60] On December 16, Senate Republicans held the extraordinary caucus that I have described in the previous chapter, in order to review the failures of the Lincoln administration and to deplore Seward's "back-stairs influence which often controlled the apparent conclusions of the Cabinet itself." Seward's friends were able to block unanimous adoption of a resolution of censure, and the caucus adjourned until the next day.[61]

When New York Senator Preston King told Seward about the caucus, he exclaimed: "They can do as they please about me, but they shall not put the President in a false position on my account."[62] Immediately he wrote Lincoln a brief note: "I hereby resign the office of Secretary of State of the United States and have the honor to request that this resignation be immediately accepted."[63] His son, Frederick, the Assistant Secretary of State, sent an identical note, and the two men began packing books and papers in preparation for their return to Auburn.

The next day when the senators reassembled, tempers were high, and, fed by secret reports from Secretary Chase that Lincoln failed to consult his cabinet on important issues, the Republican caucus appointed a committee to meet with the President. That evening he had to listen to their complaints that he had entrusted conduct of the war to "men who had no sympathy with it or the cause"—meaning Seward—and to allegations that he did not regularly consult his cabinet on important issues. The meeting adjourned inconclusively, but Michigan Senator Zachariah Chandler rejoiced that they were going to oust Seward, "the millstone around the Administration."[64]

The following morning Lincoln outlined the situation to members of the cabinet. Senators considered Seward "the real cause of our failures," he explained. "While they believed in the Pres[iden]t's honesty," he said in his quaint language, "they seemed to think that when he had in him any good purposes Mr. S[eward]. contrived to *suck them out of him unperceived.*"[65] He asked the cabinet members to meet him again that evening.

When they arrived at the White House, they were surprised to find the Senate delegation in the anteroom. In a long session, the senators aired their grievances and again complained—largely on the basis of Chase's reports—that the President had failed to consult his cabinet before making significant decisions. Blandly, Lincoln polled the cabinet members, asking whether they had been consulted on important issues. One by one, they agreed that they had indeed been consulted. Chase faced a dilemma: if he agreed with his colleagues, the senators would realize that his complaints against Seward were groundless; if he disagreed, his disloyalty to the President would be evident. Blustering that he had not come to be grilled before the Senate committee, Chase reluctantly—and falsely—said that there was no lack of unity in the cabinet and that he had indeed been consulted on important matters—"though perhaps not so fully as might have been desired." With the case against Seward undermined, the senators left.

The next day, Chase, aware that his position was untenable, came to the White House with his own letter of resignation. Lincoln quickly seized it. "This . . . cuts the Gordian knot," he said triumphantly. "I can dispose of this subject." When a visitor expressed the hope that he would not accept either Seward's resignation or Chase's, the President paused and reddened and said abruptly: "If one goes, the other must; they must hunt in couples."[66] He insisted that both men remain in the cabinet.

VIII

SEWARD'S exemplary behavior during the cabinet crisis cemented his relationship with Lincoln. Both men saw that they needed each other. From this time, there was an easy informality about their association that had hitherto been lacking. With increasing frequency, Lincoln would drop by unannounced at Seward's house in the evening, often accompanied by his secretary, John Hay. Because Frances Seward was ill and usually away in Auburn, Seward was often at loose ends. So was Lincoln, especially now that he no longer had Captain Derickson as a companion. The two men, laying aside formality and titles, would talk for hours, Seward leaning back in his easy chair, smoking his cigar, and Lincoln resting his long legs on the fireplace fender.

Seward told his son, Frederick, that during one of their evening conversations, Lincoln said that he hoped to see the Secretary as his successor in the White House. That would gratify Seward's friends who had been so disappointed in 1860, and they would "find all made right at last." "No," Seward recalled that he had replied; "that is all past and ended. The logic of events requires you to be your own successor."[67] Like other historians, I find this story very doubtful. Of course, it is possible that Lincoln was testing Seward, who was being courted by Thurlow Weed and other conservative New Yorkers, to become the candidate of Moderate Republicans and Union-loving Democrats in 1864. At about the same time, Lincoln did dangle before Democratic Governor Horatio Seymour of New York the prospect that if he cooperated with the administration and used his powers against the rebellion, "he would be our next President."[68] But the Seward story is out of character for both men, and there is no corroborative evidence for it. I am inclined to believe that Seward misunderstood the President or, in telling the story to his children, indulged in a bit of fancy.

Quite apart from possible political advancement, the relationship between Lincoln and Seward, which had initially been a rather stiff but useful friendship, developed into a truly enjoyable one. It never became what Aristotle called a perfect friendship, with sharing of intimate hopes and problems. It is very difficult for men in midlife to make new, close friendships, and it is especially hard when the relationship is unequal. As Aristotle observed, a king has no friends. At any point, the President could have dismissed his secretary of state. Their friendship therefore was close, warm, and even affectionate— but not intimate. There is, for example, nothing to suggest that Lincoln ever discussed with Seward the problems of his sometimes turbulent marriage, or that Seward ever talked with the President about his own neurasthenic wife, who most of the time felt too unwell to live in Washington. But the two men liked each other and enjoyed each other's company.

One of the things that bound these dissimilar men together was their sense of humor. Seward loved to tell of the time he discovered Lincoln polishing his shoes and remarked that in Washington, "we do not blacken our own boots." "Indeed," the President replied, "then whose boots *do* you blacken, Mr. Secretary?"[69] Both men were storytellers. Lincoln's fund of anecdotes was apparently endless; Seward's was smaller. As the President once said, a little scornfully, "Mr. Seward is limited to a couple of stories which from repeating he believes are true."[70] But the Secretary laughed uproariously at Lincoln's tale of the Presbyterian minister back in Illinois who sought to drive out a Universalist rival. "There is [a] man in this town,"

he said from his pulpit, "who is preaching all kinds of heresies—he even preaches a doctrine that *all men are to be
saved*—but *we,* brethren, *we look for better things."*[71] And the
Secretary was vastly amused when the coachman on one of
their very bumpy carriage rides cursed his horses so profanely
and vehemently that the President called out: "Driver, my
friend, are you an Episcopalian?" Astonished, the driver
replied: "No, Mr. President, I ain't much of anything; but if I
go to church at all, I go to the Methodist Church." "Oh, excuse
me," replied Lincoln, "I thought you must be an Episcopalian
for you swear just like Secretary Seward, and he's a church-
warden."[72]

To all appearances, they formed a strangely ill-matched pair.
Lincoln's crag-like face, even though partly hidden behind his
unfortunate beard, made him distinctive, and wearing his ever-
present stove pipe hat, he towered nearly a foot over his
diminutive Secretary. Seward was very short, and now that his
once-red hair had turned gray, looked "rusty." His clothing, one
observer unkindly remarked, was "made apparently twenty
years ago and by a bad tailor at that."[73] Henry Adams described
him in a famous passage as "a slouching slender figure; a head
like a wise macaw; a beaked nose; shaggy eyebrows; unorderly
hair and clothes; hoarse voice; offhand manner; free talk, and
perpetual cigar."[74]

I like to imagine these two on one of their occasional strolls
down Pennsylvania Avenue, unaccompanied by secret service
or armed guards, even though they were in the capital of a
nation at war. Seward is as usual effervescent and loquacious;
Lincoln, slow spoken and reserved. But then Lincoln raises his
hand to point to a sign overhanging the street: "T. R. Strong."
"Ha!" Lincoln exclaims, "T. R. Strong, but coffee are stronger."

And both break into whoops of laughter at the atrocious pun. The incident may be apocryphal—but it is true in spirit.[75]

IX

AFTER the cabinet crisis of 1862, nothing interrupted the growing friendship between Lincoln and Seward. By the end of Lincoln's life, nearly all of his original advisers had been replaced: Cameron was ousted from the War Department for incompetence and alleged corruption; Caleb B. Smith was such a mediocrity in the Department of the Interior that nobody noticed his departure; Chase had to leave when it became clear that he could not run the Treasury Department and at the same time campaign against Lincoln for the 1864 Republican nomination; Bates resigned, after failing to persuade Lincoln to appoint him Chief Justice after the death of Roger B. Taney. At the end, only Seward and Welles remained—the two cabinet members whom Lincoln considered personal friends.

Lincoln and Seward were almost inseparable during these years. Seward was one of the few cabinet members to accompany Lincoln to Gettysburg in November 1863 for the dedication of the national cemetery. The night before the ceremony, the President read to him the draft of his Gettysburg Address and asked for his criticisms. But Seward was far too clever to claim any credit. The next day, when a man who had just heard Lincoln's address asked Seward whether he had a hand in drafting it, the Secretary replied that no one but Abraham Lincoln could have made that speech.[76]

In 1863 and 1864, the war was far from over; some of the

heaviest fighting occurred in these final years. During these perilous times, Seward steadfastly supported Lincoln in every way he could. Fearing that the off-year elections of 1863 could further strengthen the Democrats, he publicly urged every "patriot citizen," whether he in the past had been "a Democrat or a Whig or Republican, or Conservative or Radical," to stand behind the administration.[77] Returning to Auburn to cast his vote, Seward urged his fellow citizens to support the Republican ticket. Sustaining the administration, he said, would help bring the war to an end. "There can be no peace and quiet, until Abraham Lincoln is President of the whole United States."[78]

Hostility toward Seward did not disappear during these final years of the war. The Ohio Republican, Joshua R. Giddings, reported that most members of Congress regarded him "as *drunk* or *crazy*."[79] The abolitionist orator, Anna E. Dickinson, stigmatized him "as a traitor to his first principles and a traitor to the nation."[80] Powerful Republican Senator Zachariah Chandler also believed Seward "a traitor *out* and *out*" and suspected that he was "plotting for the dismemberment of the government."[81]

But these attacks lacked both the organization and the ferocity of earlier assaults, and Seward's foes were obliged to resort to indirection. At the June 1864 Republican national convention, there was a strong movement, led by Seward's enemies, to nominate Daniel S. Dickinson for Vice President. A former senator and lieutenant governor who loyally supported the administration, Dickinson was able, and he might bring former Democrats to vote the Republican ticket, but his chief asset was that he was a New Yorker. If he received the nomination, it was generally conceded that Seward would have to resign; New York could not claim both the Vice Presidency and the State Department. The attempted coup quietly collapsed when Lincoln, without overtly intervening, allowed the nomination of Andrew Johnson of Tennessee.[82]

Seward was the only cabinet member to accompany Lincoln when he met emissaries from the Confederate government at Hampton Roads, Virginia, in February 1865. Facing Alexander H. Stephens, the Vice President of the Confederacy, R. M. T. Hunter, the president pro tem of the Confederate Senate, and John A. Campbell, a former associate justice of the U.S. Supreme Court who was now Confederate Assistant Secretary of War, aboard the *River Queen,* Lincoln and Seward discussed possible terms for ending the war. Seward's role was carefully supportive and subordinate. When Stephens proposed a joint attack by the United States and the Confederate States on Mexico, where the French had established a puppet regime under the Emperor Maximilian, Lincoln refused, and Seward reinforced his statement by quoting a firm passage from Lincoln's first inaugural address, declaring that the war could end only after the defeat of the Confederacy. Then the Confederates asked whether the Emancipation Proclamation freed all the slaves in the South or only those in the specific locations designated in that document, and Seward surprised them by reporting that only a few days before, the Congress had passed the Thirteenth Amendment, which abolished slavery.

That effectively ended the conference, but Seward had the last word. When the Confederate emissaries were returning to their steamer, which was to take them back to Richmond, Seward sent a freedman in a rowboat with a basket of champagne, and the Southerners waved their handkerchiefs in acknowledgment. Speaking through a boatswain's trumpet, Seward called out: "Keep the champagne, but return the negro."[83]

X

ON April 5, 1865, Seward was injured in a carriage accident while driving in Washington. In addition to having severe bruises and lacerations, he suffered a broken arm and a fractured jaw, which required a metal brace to hold his head still. Lincoln had gone with a small party on the *River Queen,* to visit Grant's army and to enjoy a brief respite from the labors that had exhausted him. When he heard the news, his first inclination was to return at once to Washington, but Mary Lincoln reassured him that Seward's injuries, though severe and painful, were not life threatening.

On his first evening after returning to Washington, Lincoln visited Seward in his sickroom. He found his friend almost unrecognizable, swathed in bandages, experiencing pain at every movement. "You are back from Richmond?" Seward whispered, unable to move his jaw. "Yes," said the President, "and I think we are near the end at last." Then he stretched his long form across the bed and leaned on his elbow, so as to bring his face near Seward's, and told him of his stay with Grant's army, where he had visited a hospital with 7,000 patients and had shaken the hand of every one. He said that he "worked as hard at it as sawing wood."[84] Then he went on to tell of his visit to Richmond, the captured Confederate capital.[85]

After half an hour or so Seward dozed off, and Lincoln silently left. The two men never saw each other again.

Seward wrote little expressing his deepest feelings or commenting on his friendship with the President. He was not a truly reflective man. At the beginning of the Civil War, he had bought a blank diary, so that he could record his thoughts and actions; he made an entry for only one day. He frequently wrote to members of his family, but he did not dare fully to express his feelings or ideas because he feared that his letters might be intercepted, that they might be published, and that they might convey information to the Confederates. "I cannot talk on paper, with safety, of the incidents and interests of the day in which I am engaged," he explained to his wife. "Even the common topics of political conversation must not be touched upon, lest somebody should fall upon the manuscript and make treason out of it."[86] But in the days after Lincoln's reelection in 1864, Seward let down his guard to give his final judgment of his great friend: "The election has placed our President beyond the pale of human envy or human harm, as he is above the pale of ambition. Henceforth all men will come to see him as . . . I have seen him—a true, loyal, patient, patriotic, and benevolent man."[87]

VI

"ABRAHAM REX"

Lincoln and His
Private Secretaries

ONE evening in early 1864, Lincoln, accompanied only by his private secretary, John Hay, strolled across Lafayette Park to visit Seward in his library.[1]

"No bad news, I hope, Mr. President?"

"No," replied Lincoln. "But Hay happened to find a book that amused us; so I told him we would walk over to Seward's and read it to him and have a laugh over it."

Hay produced a Portuguese guide to English conversation, *English as She Is Spoke,* and read aloud some of its queer inverted sentences. The little book was so unbelievably bad that for the next half-century, it was reprinted as a masterpiece of hilarity. It contained sentences, in Portuguese, like this: "Let's go faster. I never saw a worse animal. It doesn't want to go either forward or backward," with the purported translation in English: "Go us more fast never I was seen a so much bad beast; she will not nor to bring forward neither put back." For a few minutes, the President of the United States and his Secretary of State gained respite from the horrors of war in hearty laughter.[2]

I

IT was not unusual, during the final year of the war, for Hay to accompany Lincoln almost everywhere. The President was lonely, and much of the time he had nobody else to talk to. Mary Lincoln, wrapped in unending grief after the death of Willie in February 1862, largely lived in a world of her own. Browning was alienated. Seward, often busy with his own family and with his State Department duties, was only occasionally available. For relaxed, enjoyable conversation, Lincoln increasingly turned to the two young men who served as his assistants and private secretaries.

Of the two, only the elder, John George Nicolay, had the official title of Private Secretary. Lincoln had known Nicolay since the campaign of 1856, when he employed him as owner of the *Pittsfield* (Illinois) *Free Press* to do some quick printing for the Republican campaign. After that, Lincoln kept an eye on the young newspaperman, recommending him to Horace Greeley as a correspondent who was "entirely trust-worthy."[3] When Nicolay came to Springfield as principal clerk for Ozias M. Hatch, the Illinois secretary of state, Lincoln saw a great deal of him, because Hatch's office served as a kind of unofficial Republican campaign headquarters. After Lincoln received the Republican nomination for President in 1860,

Nicolay volunteered to help the candidate in answering letters.

It soon became clear that Lincoln was going to be burdened with heavy expenses during the campaign, in order to provide refreshments for Republican dignitaries visiting Springfield and to handle his enormously increased correspondence. Several of his Illinois associates contributed to a fund, which eventually amounted to five thousand dollars, to help pay campaign expenses and to provide full-time clerical help.[4] Nicolay, who warmly admired Lincoln, had hoped to write a campaign biography of the Republican candidate but was bitterly disappointed when he learned that the assignment had gone to a young Ohio writer, William Dean Howells. He checked his grief when Hatch told him, "Never mind. You are to be private secretary."[5] He received a salary of $75 a month.

For the next few months, Nicolay worked very hard in the governor's office in the statehouse, to which Lincoln had removed after his nomination. He helped receive visitors, tried to keep Lincoln on schedule, ran some minor political errands for the candidate, and—most of all—handled the mail, which began to come in at the rate of about fifty letters a day. With Lincoln he developed some form letters to answer routine inquiries: "Your letter to Mr. Lincoln of [　] and by which you seek his assistance in getting up a biographical sketch of him, is received. Applications of this class are so numerous that it is simply impossible for him to attend to them."

After the election, the volume of Lincoln's mail increased even more, and Nicolay could not handle it all. John Hay, whom Nicolay had known since their boyhood in Pittsfield, Illinois, and who was now rather desultorily studying law in the office of his uncle, Milton Hay, volunteered to help him. They worked well as a team, and Lincoln evidently was satisfied with them. Characteristically, though, he made no commitments as the time for leaving Springfield neared. "I am gratified to be able to tell you that I have renewed evidence that Mr. Lincoln reposes entire confidence in me, which I deem a sufficient guaranty that my present confidential relation to him will be continued," Nicolay wrote his fiancée, Therena Bates, in December 1860, "though not a word has been said by either of us since the election."[6] Eventually, though, the President Elect did offer him the post of private secretary, at the salary of $2,500 a year. The appointment was the first official act of Lincoln's administration.

Adding Hay to the presidential staff was more complicated. When Nicolay first suggested Hay's appointment, Lincoln replied, "We can't take all Illinois with us down to Washington." Milton Hay smoothed the way for his nephew by promising to pay his expenses in Washington for six months, and Lincoln agreed, saying, "Well, let Hay come."[7] Initially, Lincoln thought he would pay Hay's salary himself, but it was finally worked out that Hay would receive an appointment as a clerk in the Department of the Interior, assigned to duties in the White House, at a salary of $1,500 a year (later increased to $1,800). In 1864 he was commissioned as major and assistant adjutant general, assigned to the Executive Mansion.

II

NICOLAY was twenty-nine years old when he assumed his duties in the White House. Born in Bavaria, he had come to America with his parents in 1838. Orphaned at an early age, he had an impoverished childhood in central Illinois. With only about two years of schooling, he was essentially self-educated, but he worked himself up from printer's devil (that is, an apprentice) to owner of the *Pittsfield Free Press*. Unimpressive in appearance, he was so thin that his 125 pounds seemed scarcely to cover his 5-foot 10-inch frame. His face was covered with a thin, rather straggly beard, which concealed what might have been a pleasant smile; he rarely laughed. In bad health most of the time, he cultivated a brusque, dyspeptic manner, and visitors to the White House often thought him "sour and crusty." "If he is sick," a New Yorker complained to Lincoln, "he has a right to be cross and ungentlemanly in his deportment, but not otherwise." Others lamented that the President had appointed a "nobody" as his private secretary, instead of "a man of refinement and culture."[8]

To some extent, the complaints were justified, because Nicolay had a reputation for acerbity. A fellow newspaperman described him as a "grim Cerberus of Teutonic descent" who guarded the entry into the President's office.[9] He bristled at any suggestion that, as the President's secretary, he was either inefficient or partisan. When an old friend like David Davis complained that his letters were not reaching the President, Nicolay drafted a blistering reply: "A moment's reflection will convince you that the President has not the time to read all the letters he receives; and also, that say of a hundred miscellaneous letters, there will be a large proportion, which are obviously of no interest or importance. These the President would not read if he could." Only then did he go on to assure Davis that his letters "always received a special attention not only from the Secretaries, but from the President himself." The letter was so acrid that Lincoln evidently stopped it. It is in Lincoln's own papers, marked "Not sent."[10]

Apart from Nicolay's health, there were good reasons for his frequent brusqueness to visitors. He had the nearly impossible job of trying to manage the schedule of a President who defied management. In his first month in office, Lincoln insisted on working, on average, twelve hours a day—and his private secretaries had to keep the same hours. Finally they persuaded the President to limit his business hours from 10:00 in the morning to 3:00 in the afternoon, but even then he frequently broke the rules he had agreed to. It was equally difficult to control the stream of visitors who flocked to the White House daily, asking the President's help in finding jobs, in securing promotion, in passing legislation, and, later, in locating relatives in the army, and in securing pardons from court-martial sentences.

It is little wonder that, after a month or so in the White House, Nicolay in his letters to his fiancée began complaining of exhaustion and lamenting that he was "constantly worked to death, and yet doing (accomplishing) nothing."[11]

III

JOHN Hay was the almost exact opposite of Nicolay. Perhaps that was the reason they got along so well together. Though Nicolay was six years older than Hay, they had become best friends as boys in Pittsfield and renewed their friendship when they both moved to Springfield. For the four years of the Civil War, they shared a large room on the second floor in the East Wing of the White House, initially taking their meals with the Lincoln family but later dining at Willard's Hotel and the Metropolitan Club. In all that time, there is no record that they ever exchanged sharp words or grew angry with each other.

While Nicolay cultivated an image of distance and maturity, Hay looked—and wanted to look—perpetually boyish. Visitors to the White House described him as "a comely young man with peach-blossom face." The favored son of doting parents in Warsaw, Illinois, carefully educated at Brown University, and fostered by his wealthy uncle, Hay was self-assured and held decided opinions on all subjects. He filled his office as assistant private secretary to the President with a careless grace, feeling this was not his true vocation, since he aspired to be a poet. He moved easily in Washington society, but for all his air of flippancy, there is no record that he ever leaked confidential information he gleaned in the White House. He could be a model of tact. Hay maintained the difficult balance of preserving a close friendship with Robert Todd Lincoln, the President's oldest son, who was not on affectionate terms with his father, even while he was becoming one of the President's closest confidants. Hay could also exhibit great delicacy of feeling. When he spotted Fanny Seward, the shy teen-aged daughter of the Secretary of State, standing forlornly alone at a White House reception, he went to her side and expressed a hope that she did not know everybody "because it was so pleasant to tell who people were." For the rest of the hour, the two young people gossiped about the celebrities Hay pointed out, and Fanny confided to her diary that Hay was "Very witty—boyish in his manner, yet deep enough—bubbling over with some brilliant speech."[12]

These two young men, neither of whom had any experience in politics or in public life, formed the staff of the President of the United States. Their duties included arranging—or at-

tempting to arrange—the President's schedule, greeting important visitors to the White House, screening out cranks and
other undesirables, and delivering the President's messages to
the Congress. Dealing with the voluminous mail was their
heaviest responsibility, and from time to time, they had to bring
in other assistants to help. William O. Stoddard, a former editor of the *Central Illinois Gazette,* had an appointment as "Secretary to the President to Sign Land Petitions," but, since there
was little work for his office, he helped out when Nicolay and
Hay were overwhelmed. When Stoddard became ill, Edward
D. Neill, another clerk who officially worked for the Department of the Interior, came in to take his place. Late in the war,
Charles Henry Philbrick, a reformed alcoholic with good Illinois Republican connections, joined the staff. He was often
tardy, and Hay thought him lazy.

Like many other confidential secretaries, Nicolay and Hay
thought that they managed their employer. Hay's instructions
to Neill, who sometimes helped in the office when the private
secretaries were out of town, suggest how they saw their role:
"There will probably be little to do. Refer as little to the
President as possible. Keep visitors out of the house when you
can. Inhospitable, but prudent."[13] Both men tended to exagger-
ate the importance of their duties. Because the President on
rare occasions asked them to draft routine letters for him, they
convinced themselves in the years after Lincoln's death that
they had conducted most of his correspondence. When
Herndon asked Hay about Lincoln's habits of work in the
White House, he gave an answer that was as self-promoting as
it was untrue: "He wrote very few letters. . . . He gave the
whole thing over to me and signed without reading them the
letters I wrote in his name. He wrote perhaps half a dozen a

week himself not more."[14] Many years later, Hay further exaggerated his role and told a few friends that he had written some of Lincoln's best letters.*

Nicolay was often irritated by the demands correspondents made on the President's time, but Hay was more likely to be amused. In May 1861, when a truculent state senator in Kentucky solemnly protested because federal troops occupied Cairo, Illinois, just across the Ohio River, Hay received Lincoln's permission to draft a response: "The President directs me to say that the views so ably stated by you shall have due consideration: and to assure you that he would certainly never have ordered the movement of troops, complained of, had he known that Cairo was in your Senatorial district." Hay wanted to add a respectful request from the President that in the future the Kentucky senator would spell "solemly" with an "n," but Lincoln disapproved the change as overkill. So Hay

---

*For years, there has been controversy over Hay's alleged authorship of Lincoln's celebrated letter of November 21, 1864, to Mrs. Lydia Bixby, whose five sons, it was claimed, "died gloriously on the field of battle." Michael Burlingame is the most recent, and the ablest, proponent of Hay's authorship, basing his conclusion, in part, on close textual analysis of the letter, which included words and phrases that are not found elsewhere in Lincoln's writing but that do appear in Hay's. Many other Lincoln specialists disagree. I tend to be skeptical of Hay's claim, which has been filtered through unreliable sources, like Nicholas Murray Butler. On the other hand, I agree with Burlingame that the language of the Bixby letter is not characteristically Lincolnian, and—though this is only a speculation—I attribute the difference in tone to the fact that, unlike other Lincoln letters, which were written after long brooding and careful choice of words, this letter to Mrs. Bixby was probably composed in haste. Governor John A. Andrew of Massachusetts had demanded that "a letter might be written her by the President of the United States, taking notice of a noble mother of five dead heroes," and Lincoln was complying with this request from an important Republican ally. But to prove that I am a true heretic on this matter, I have to say that I have never thought the Bixby letter one of Lincoln's greatest or most moving compositions.

sent off the missive with a concluding paragraph: "Allow me sir to subscribe myself with sentiments of high regards, Your humble Servant John M. Hay Assistant Sec to the President."[15]

Hay handled the visitors who thronged to the White House with a light hand. Once when an obviously demented man demanded to see Lincoln because, as the Son of God, he was carrying a plan to end the war, Hay informed him that the President was busy but that he could come back again the next day, adding—if Hay's memory can be trusted—that it would be a good idea to bring a letter of introduction from his Father.

Though Hay, like Nicolay, was ill from time to time with chills and fever and though he, too, complained of overwork, he clearly enjoyed his years in the White House. Philbrick, the fellow clerk who occasionally helped the private secretaries, grumbled that Nicolay performed the real work in the office while Hay did "the ornamental."[16] But John W. Forney, the newspaperman, captured the situation more accurately when he remarked that Hay "laughed through his term."[17]

IV

THE two private secretaries had some difficulties initially in deciding how, in their private correspondence and conversation, they should refer to Lincoln. "The President" seemed stiff and formal for young men who had known him before his election. "The Chief" seemed more suitable, but presently they replaced that with "the Ancient"—apparently referring to the sobriquet "Old Abe," by which Lincoln (though not in his own hearing) had been addressed for years. Gradually, in deference to the vogue caused by a recent visit of Japanese dignitaries to

Washington, they substituted—probably at Hay's initiative— "the Tycoon," a half-serious, half-affectionate reference to the title that Westerners gave Japanese shoguns, or military commanders, who virtually ruled that country.

Nicolay had been a devoted admirer of Lincoln since their first meeting, and he was proud of his role in helping to elect the first Republican President in 1860. He was aware of Lincoln's historical importance, and, as I have mentioned, he had hoped to write Lincoln's campaign biography. Frustrated in that plan, he and Hay decided to prepare a history of Lincoln's administration, secured a promise of "cordial coöperation" from the President, and began to collect materials for it.[18] There is little evidence that they accomplished much along this line during the war years. Lincoln was always too preoccupied with day-to-day events to help compile a historical record, and Nicolay himself was so busy that he could not find time to keep a regular diary. But he did keep a notebook, in which from time to time he recorded important conversations of the President to which he was witness. His support of Lincoln's policies was unquestioning. When the President came under heavy fire for issuing the Emancipation Proclamation, Nicolay sprang to his defense with a strong editorial in the *Washington Chronicle* that ended: "Abraham Lincoln, the President of the United States, is entitled to the everlasting gratitude of a despised race enfranchised, the plaudits of a distracted country saved, and an inscription of undying fame in the impartial records of history."[19]

Initially John Hay's feelings about Lincoln were ambiguous.[20] From his education in literature and the classics at Brown, he had gained a romantic notion of politics. A great leader, he had been taught, was a man without flaws in his character, and he was usually an aristocrat. It was hard for him to think of Lincoln in this role. After all, Hay had studied law in his uncle's office, which was next door to that of Lincoln & Herndon, and he undoubtedly knew Milton Hay's opinion that the President of the United States was "an old *poke easy,*" who "was said to be henpecked."[21] Anyway, could anything good come out of Springfield, which—anticipating a comment of John F. Kennedy on Washington, D.C.—Hay characterized as "a city combining the meanness of the North with the barbarism of the South"?[22]

Hay had willingly enough joined in the Republican campaign of 1860 and was glad to help his friend Nicolay in handling candidate Lincoln's mail, but even after the election, he had doubts about Lincoln, whom he jokingly called "the Cincinnatus of the prairie." One of the rare public appearances of the President Elect impressed him more favorably, and he told a correspondent in his condescending way: "I am beginning to respect him more than formerly. He maintains a very dignified attitude before all strangers."[23] He did not have to be persuaded to join the President's staff in Washington, though he thought of his job more as a lark than a crusade.

The firing on Fort Sumter and the rapid mobilization for war spurred Hay to begin a diary, which initially was devoted to anecdotes and colorful descriptions, like that of the Kentucky abolitionist, Cassius M. Clay who strode into the President's reception room, wearing, "with a sublimely unconscious air, three pistols and an Arkansas toothpick [a bowie knife with a blade that shut up into the handle] and looked like an admirable vignette to 25-cents-worth of yellow-covered romance."[24]

He also took pleasure in recording—often in a somewhat

patronizing tone—glimpses of the President. He was amused when the Tycoon received a delegation of Pottawatomie Indians and made awkward efforts to make himself understood by speaking bad English: "Where live now?" "When go back Iowa?"[25] He thought it funny when, bringing the President some news, he found him looking out of a White House window at some navy ships puffing up the Potomac, "resting the end of the telescope on his toes sublime."[26]

But as the war grew serious, Hay's interest in keeping a diary—and the time he had for composing his carefully constructed literary images—diminished, and his entries for the rest of 1861 and 1862 became infrequent.

V

FROM the outset Lincoln gave his private secretaries his implicit trust, which they never betrayed. He had always had a fondness for associating with young men, and in Springfield he had been an informal mentor for numerous aspiring lawyers, who looked to him for advice and tactful guidance.[27] Sadly, he could not adequately play his role with his son Robert, with whom his relationship was always troubled. Robert was attending Harvard College and saw his father infrequently. But toward Hay, who was close to Robert's age—and appeared and acted much younger—and toward Nicolay, who was only a few years older, Lincoln extended himself to make them feel at home in the White House and an important part of his administration. Always he treated them both with respect—as colleagues, not as employees. Nicolay he called by his last name, but Hay was usually "John."

Realizing that Nicolay was overworked and that his health was frail, Lincoln, at the height of the Sumter crisis, pulled him out of the White House for a long carriage ride, along with Willie and Tad, the two youngest Lincoln boys. During the early weeks of the war, he took Hay with him to "a very fine matinee at the Navy Yard," where the 12th New York Regiment band played and sang, and then went aboard the *Pensacola,* where they were delighted by the firing of the great Dahlgren gun.[28]

More important, he took them into his confidence about his plans, his hopes, and his disappointments. In April 1861, after the defection of John B. Magruder, who had been in command of one of the batteries defending Washington, Lincoln lamented to Hay: "Three days ago . . . Magruder came voluntarily to me in this room and with his own lips . . . repeated over and over again his asseverations and protestations of loyalty and fidelity."[29] A few days later, he confided that he was developing a military plan for blockading the Southern ports and personally heading an expedition that would "go down to Charleston and pay her the little debt we are owing her."[30] Nothing came of this scheme—Union forces did not attack Charleston until 1863, and, of course, Lincoln did not command the expedition—but he felt he could blow off steam by outlining his plan for his secretaries.

From time to time, the President shared with them his brooding, recurrent thoughts about the meaning of the American conflict. After dismissing Browning's astonishing proposal to subjugate the South and establish a black republic there, he went on to explain to Hay: "I consider the central idea pervading this struggle is the necessity that is upon us, of proving that popular government is not an absurdity. We must settle this question now, whether in a free government the minority have the right to break up the government whenever they choose. If we fail it will go far to prove the incapability of the people to govern themselves."[31]

Lincoln made Nicolay and Hay witnesses to, and to some extent participants in, his long struggle to find a victorious general for the Union armies. They were not involved in his decision, after the Union defeat at First Bull Run (July 21–22, 1861), to put General George B. McClellan in command of the federal forces in Virginia, but by fall they were fully aware of the problems that general's procrastination presented to the President. Their records of their early meetings with McClellan were ominous. In October, when Lincoln, along with Seward and Hay, visited McClellan's headquarters, the general spoke of his plans for an advance. "Dont let them hurry me, is all I ask," he concluded, and Lincoln responded: "You shall have your own way in the matter I assure you."[32]

A little later, Hay witnessed an event that he feared was "a portent of evil to come." The President, accompanied by Seward and Hay, was in the habit of dropping in informally at McClellan's house in the evenings to hear the military news and to talk about plans. On the evening of November 13, they found McClellan was out, attending a wedding, and decided to wait. After about an hour, McClellan came in, heard from the porter that the President was visiting, and, passing the door of the room where his guests were sitting, went upstairs. When he did not return in half an hour, they sent the servant with the message that the President was waiting and received the cool message that the general had gone to bed. Hay was furious over "this unparrallelled [sic] insolence of epaulettes," but the President seemed not to have noticed the snub, "saying it was better at this time not to be making points of etiquette and per-

sonal dignity."[33] But after that time, the President made no
more visits to McClellan's house and required the general to
make his reports at the Executive Mansion.

Any plans McClellan had for an advance were canceled
when he fell seriously ill with typhoid. Then, in February 1862,
when he expected to institute operations at Harpers Ferry, it
was discovered that the pontoons he had ordered to form a
bridge across the Potomac were too large to pass through the
locks on that river. Lincoln was furious, and he allowed his secretaries to witness his angry outburst at General Randolph B.
Marcy, McClellan's chief of staff and father-in-law. "Why in
the [tar]nation, Gen Marcy," he exclaimed excitedly, "couldn't
the Gen. have known whether a boat would go through that
lock, before he spent a million of dollars getting them there? I
am no engineer: but it seems to me that if I wished to know
whether a boat would go through a hole, or a lock common
sense would teach me to go and measure it."[34]

Over the next months, Lincoln shared with his secretaries
his growing disillusionment with McClellan, who led a huge
army down the Potomac to attack Richmond from the east and
eventually came within sight of the Confederate capital, only
to be thrown back to his base at Harrison's Landing. When
Lincoln replaced him as commander in chief with General
Henry Wager Halleck, McClellan sulked and failed to push his
army forward to assist General John Pope in the battle of
Second Bull Run (August 29–30, 1862).

Early in the morning after that battle, Lincoln came to his
secretaries' room as Hay was dressing and said: "Well John we
are whipped again, I am afraid." In a defiant mood, he kept
repeating: "We must hurt this enemy before it gets away."
When Hay made a remark about how bad things looked,

Lincoln replied fiercely: "No, Mr Hay, we must whip these people now. Pope must fight them."[35]

In the near panic after Second Bull Run, Lincoln felt compelled to restore McClellan to command, though he told Hay that the cabinet members were unanimous against him and that, unless the general moved quickly, "this public feeling against him will make it expedient to take important command from him."[36] Though McClellan's quasi-victory at Antietam (September 17, 1862) gave Lincoln an occasion to issue his preliminary emancipation proclamation, the general failed to follow up his success and allowed the Confederate army to escape across the Potomac.

For the next few weeks, as Nicolay told Hay, the President kept "poking sharp sticks under little Mac's ribs," but he could not succeed in getting him to attack Lee's army. Once the fall congressional elections were over, "completely exhausted with McClellan's inaction and never-ending excuses," Lincoln relieved him of his command. "The President has been exceedingly reluctant to do this," Nicolay wrote, reflecting his conversations with Lincoln. "In many respects he thinks McClellan a very superior and efficient officer. This with the high personal regard for him, has let him to indulge him in his whims and complaints and shortcomings as a mother would indulge her baby, but all to no purpose." He is "constitutionally *too slow*," Nicolay wrote, and "has fitly been dubbed the great American tortoise."[37]

VI

LIVING in the same house as these two young men, often sharing meals with them, and working with them for long

hours day after day, Lincoln developed an affectionate friendship for them. To Hay he looked for wit and repartee. The
President was willing to tolerate his ideas, even when they
were half-baked. In the fall of 1861, when Hay, after a visit to
St. Louis, wrote an effusive dispatch for the *New York World*
praising General John C. Frémont as "a born leader" who had
"the qualities which the quick instinct of the people long for,"
Lincoln did not rebuke him, but he showed his opinion of
Hay's views when he overruled Frémont's proclamation eman-
cipating Missouri slaves and removed the general from command. Doubtless he attributed Hay's effusion, which Thurlow
Weed brought to his attention, to youthful enthusiasm.[38]

What he really valued in his young assistant was his sense of
humor. Hay was almost as good a raconteur as Lincoln himself.
Once Hay—"all one bubble," as his fellow worker Stoddard
described him—started to tell a funny story but broke down
before he could finish. Overhearing him, Nicolay, pen in hand,
emerged from his room and asked to hear the tale. As they
exploded with laughter, a voice came from the doorway: "Now,
John, just tell that thing again." The President of the United
States had silently appeared from his office, and at his order
Hay retold his story, as fresh and as funny as the first time.
"Down came the President's foot from across his knee with a
heavy stamp on the floor" recorded Stoddard, "and out through
the hall went an uproarious peal of laughter."[39]

If Lincoln looked to Hay for laughter, he turned to Nicolay
for emotional support in crises. In February 1862, just as the
Lincolns were giving the most spectacular and well-publicized
reception of his administration, their two younger sons, Willie
and Tad, fell ill, probably from typhoid fever. Devotedly the
President and his wife nursed their two little boys over the next

two weeks. Tad held his own, but Willie grew weaker, and, as Nicolay recorded in a brief diary entry on February 18, "the President evidently despairs of his recovery." Two days later, as Nicolay was lying half asleep on the sofa in his office in the late afternoon, Lincoln came in, looking worn and exhausted. "Well, Nicolay," he said, his voice choked with emotion, "my boy is gone—he is actually gone!" Bursting into tears, he went into his own office.[40] Nicolay helped Browning arrange the funeral.

To this growing intimacy between the President and his secretaries there was one main barrier: his wife. Everybody recognized that Mary Lincoln was a complex, difficult person. She was a loyal wife and a devoted mother, and she could be gracious, charming, and witty. But she was unpredictable, and, especially when she was suffering from her recurrent headaches, her outbursts of temper were violent. She had difficulty getting along with people she considered her social inferiors: cooks, maids, draymen, sales clerks in stores. She came to think that her husband's personal secretaries fell into this class.

Before the Lincolns left Springfield, there was no evidence of friction between the wife and the assistants of the President Elect. Indeed, she hardly knew Nicolay, but she evidently thought well of John Hay, who was a great friend of Robert's. Besides, Hay belonged to a good Springfield family, whom Mary considered her social equals. Consequently, in the early days of Lincoln's administration, it was Hay who had the duty of dealing with Mrs. Lincoln. When there were threats on the President's life, whether from a Baltimore mob or from Confederate battery across the Potomac, it was Hay who, as he said, "had to do some very dexterous lying to calm the awakened fears of Mrs. Lincoln in regard to the assassination suspicion."[41]

But before long, she clashed with Nicolay, and Hay not merely took his friend's side but egged him on. He began to refer to Mary Lincoln as the "enemy" and "the Hell-Cat," who, he told Nicolay, "is getting more Hellcattical day by day."[42] There were several grounds for conflict. Nicolay, who was in frequent communication with the State Department, was in charge of White House protocol. It was his duty to screen invitations to White House dinners and make proper seating arrangements according to rank and protocol. Mrs. Lincoln resented what she considered his meddling; she intended to be mistress of her own house.

Her most memorable clash with Nicolay came early in 1864, when she struck from his list of guests at a dinner for the cabinet the names of Secretary of the Treasury Salmon P. Chase, his recently married daughter, Kate, and her husband, Senator William Sprague, regarding them as political rivals of her husband and opponents of his reelection. Nicolay referred the matter to Lincoln, who directed that the three be invited. "Whereat," Nicolay wrote to his fiancée, "there soon arose such a rampage as the [White] House hasn't seen for a year." Stoddard, his assistant, "fairly cowered at the volume of the storm, and I think for the first time begins to appreciate the awful sublimities of nature."[43]

Deciding to exclude Nicolay from the planning, Mrs. Lincoln asked Stoddard to help her, but he did not know how, and she determined to make the arrangements herself. On the afternoon before the dinner, affairs were in a mess, and she had to back down and send for Nicolay, "apologizing and explaining that the affair had worried her so she hadn't slept for a night or two." Smugly the private secretary recorded: "I think she has felt happier since she cast out that devil of stubbornness."[44]

More serious were the disputes over White House financial arrangements. The Executive Mansion was in sad repair when the Lincolns arrived, and Mary Lincoln promptly put herself in charge of spending the $20,000 Congress had appropriated for renovations. On shopping trips to Philadelphia and New York, she bought freely and extravagantly in order to make the White House a showplace, and she ordered the best draperies, rugs, wallpaper, furniture, and china. When the bills began to come in, it was clear that she had greatly overspent the congressional appropriation. A Philadelphia decorator named Carryl demanded payment for handsome Parisian wallpaper for the White House costing $7,000. Lincoln, who had been too busy with the prosecution of the war to pay attention to these matters, was furious. How could Mary overrun an appropriation of $20,000 "for *flub dubs* for this damned old house," especially at a time when soldiers did not have blankets? he exploded. "It was all wrong to spend one cent at such a time," he went on, "and I never ought to have had a cent expended; the house was furnished well enough, better than any one we ever lived in."

He asked who had employed Carryl. When Major B. B. French, the commissioner of public buildings, could not tell him, Lincoln angrily rang his bell and summoned Nicolay.

"How did this man Carryl get into this house?" he demanded.

"I do not know, sir," said Nicolay, ever discreet.

"Who employed him?"

"Mrs. Lincoln, I suppose."

"*Yes,*" Lincoln almost hissed. "Mrs. Lincoln—well, I suppose

Mrs. Lincoln *must* bear the blame, let her bear it, I swear I won't!"[45]

She tried to cover her extravagance by padding White House bills, a trick she learned from an unscrupulous gardener, John Watt. She fired Watt's wife, the White House stewardess, and, claiming that she was now performing the duties of that office herself, demanded Mrs. Watt's salary.[46] But for this shift, she needed the approval of the President's private secretary. Nicolay was out of town at the time, and she approached Hay. "Madame has mounted me to pay her the Stewards salary," he wrote Nicolay. "I told her to kiss mine. Was I right?"[47] Then he refused to turn over control of the White House stationery fund—which amounted to only $1,000 a year—and began to suspect that Mrs. Lincoln was trying to get him fired.

There was justification for the suspicion and animosity that the private secretaries exhibited toward the First Lady. Mary Lincoln had a sharp tongue and an imperious temper, neither of which she made much effort to control. Susceptible to the grossest forms of flattery, she had poor judgment in selecting friends and advisers. Penurious in managing the Lincolns' personal finances, she was extravagant in spending public money. Fearing her husband's anger, she scratched around for ways, ethical or not, to pay her bills.

There is nothing to suggest that either Nicolay or Hay had any understanding of the pressures bearing on Mary Lincoln, and they made no allowance for her emotional volatility or for the impact that Willie's death had on her precarious mental balance. Instead, they quarreled with her and they made fun of her—always, of course, behind her back and out of the hearing of her husband. With the heartlessness of the young, they rebuffed her occasional attempt to make peace. Once when

Mary sent them an invitation to a family dinner, the two secretaries sniffed at it as if it were tainted meat. Reluctantly they agreed to attend—because, as Nicolay explained to his fiancée, one cannot turn down an invitation from the First Lady—all the time worrying that their virtue and their morals might be corrupted.

Behind this never-ending warfare between the President's secretaries and his wife was a feeling of jealousy, which neither party to the conflict articulated or, indeed, fully understood. Now middle-aged and growing stout and doughy in appearance, Mary Lincoln realized that she could no longer command her husband's attention as she once had. His mind was on fighting a war, not on her social triumphs in Washington. She blamed the secretaries for standing between her and her husband.

For their part, Nicolay and Hay regarded Mrs. Lincoln as a nuisance, whose nagging and interference kept the President from his more important duties. They felt he belonged to them, not to his wife.

VII

LINCOLN tried to remain aloof from this domestic discord and exhibited more sensitivity to his secretaries' needs than to his wife's. He recognized that their work, even apart from their battles with Mary Lincoln, was exhausting, and he found that Nicolay's health was as fragile as his temper. So the President made it an unannounced policy to send one or the other of his private secretaries out on fact-finding expeditions, which also served as brief vacations.

In October 1861, deeply troubled by the state of affairs in Missouri, he asked Nicolay, who had gone home to attend to business and to visit his fiancée, Therena Bates, to investigate what he called the "hopeless confusion" in General Frémont's command. Nicolay interviewed several of Frémont's subordinates, as well as Illinois politicians who were familiar with affairs in Missouri, and concluded that Frémont was a "d——d fool," who had "completely frittered away the fairest opportunity a man of small experience ever had to make his name immortal." In contrast to Hay's rapturous depiction of that general's martial air and clear vision, Nicolay's report to the President concluded: "The universal opinion is that he has entirely failed, *and that he ought to be removed*—that any change will be for the better."[48]

The next year, in an attempt to escape the pressure and the summer heat of Washington, Nicolay planned a four- or five-week vacation in Indian country on the Red River, and Hay joked that he must hold onto his scalp lest "your long locks adorn the lodge of an aboriginal warrior and the festive tomtom is made of your stretched hide."[49] The warning was more serious than intended, because by the time Nicolay arrived, the northwest frontier was in turmoil over a major Indian uprising in Minnesota. "We are in the midst of a most terrible and exciting Indian war," he wired the President from St. Paul; "thus far the massacre of innocent white settlers has been fearful a wild panic prevails in nearly one half of the state."[50]

Returning to Washington, he found his associate equally eager to get away. Hay felt like "a used up machine," he said, and he longed for "an exile from Washington to save me from absolute insanity."[51] He was tired of the endless bureaucratic squabblings. He hated to deal with bad-mannered officials, like Lincoln's brusque new Secretary of War, Edwin M. Stanton, who replaced Simon Cameron. "Don't," he begged Nicolay, "in a sudden spasm of good-nature, send any more people with letters to me requesting favors from S[tanton]. I would rather make a tour of a small-pox hospital." He also worried that at a time when most able-bodied young men of his age were in the army, he was still conspicuously a civilian.

He was not able to get away until April 1863, when he ostensibly went on a mission to deliver dispatches from the Navy Department to Admiral Samuel F. DuPont, who was preparing an assault on Charleston, South Carolina. In reality he took a vacation and visited his brother Charles, who was serving in General David Hunter's army. Hay himself saw no action, but he was gratified that Hunter made him acting aide-de-camp with the rank of major. The title, he thought, probably with an eye to his future political prospects, would make his "abolition record" clear, and he was very proud of it. He directed Nicolay that when writing he should "be good enough to remember that I have a pretty extensive handle to my name."[52]

VIII

I AM not sure when Hay's attitude toward Lincoln began to change from detached, slightly condescending amusement to enthusiastic admiration. His sporadic diary entries for 1861 and 1862 give few clues as to his feelings toward the President; indeed, they show rather more admiration for Seward than for Lincoln. But on his trip south in 1863, he began keeping a daily journal, which he continued for the rest of the war, and it is full of observations about the President. Nearly all of them are highly favorable.

Perhaps Hay was simply reflecting the changes that the first two years of the Civil War had brought about: Lincoln had raised the largest and finest armies ever seen on the American continent; he had boldly asserted his authority by overruling Frémont's ill-timed proclamation of freedom and had then removed that disaffected general; he had braved the wrath of Radical Republicans in Congress, whom Hay christened "Jacobins," and blunted their demands for a rapid military advance and a remodeling of Southern society; he had issued his own Emancipation Proclamation; and he had ridden out the storm when Senate Republicans demanded that he fire Seward and reconstruct his cabinet. Though still not the ideal hero of Hay's romantic imaginings, Lincoln had exhibited what Hay had to recognize and admire as "his indomitable will."[53]

Then, too, Hay learned a lesson on his Southern trip. Arriving in South Carolina just after the Confederates repelled an attack by Union monitors in Charleston harbor, he had a long conversation with DuPont, who commanded the federal fleet, and heard that admiral explain the defeat in words almost identical to those Lincoln had used before he left Washington. It was, he wrote Nicolay, "another instance . . . added to the many, of the President having clearer perceptions of military possibilities than any man in the Cabinet or the field. He thought it would fail."[54]

Hay returned to Washington ready not merely to work for Lincoln but to admire and extol him. From this time, his diary and his letters are filled with tributes to the President. After discussing with Lincoln ideas about reconstruction, which the President called "the greatest question ever presented to practical statesmanship," Hay recorded in his private diary: "While the rest are grinding their little private organs for their own glorification the old man is working with the strength of a giant and the purity of an angel to do this great work."[55] He wrote Nicolay in August: "The Tycoon is in fine whack. I have rarely seen him more serene and busy. He is managing this war, the draft, foreign relations, and planning a reconstruction of the Union, all at once. I never knew with what tyrannous authority he rules the Cabinet, till now. . . . I am growing more and more firmly convinced that the good of the country absolutely demands that he should be kept where he is till this thing is over. . . . I believe the hand of God placed him where he is."[56] "The old man sits here and wields like a backwoods Jupiter the bolts of war and the machinery of government with a hand equally steady and equally firm," he wrote Nicolay again the next month. "I do not know whether the nation is worthy of him for another term."[57]

Nicolay was equally devoted. When Lincoln in December 1864 nominated Salmon P. Chase, his former secretary of the treasury, who had fought to win the 1864 Republican nomination for himself, for chief justice, Nicolay wrote his fiancée: "Probably no other man than Lincoln would have had . . . the degree of magnanimity to thus forgive and exalt a rival who had so deeply and so unjustifiably intrigued against him. It is . . . only another most marked illustration of the greatness of the President, in this age of little men."[58]

Like Hay, Nicolay sharply corrected those who questioned the President's ability or challenged his plans. When the editors of the rabidly Radical *Chicago Tribune* complained of a report that Lincoln did not read their paper, Nicolay replied (offering "exclusively my own thoughts and not the

President's") that "he would have been attracted to your journal more frequently as to an old and familiar friend, if it had
not . . . contained so much which he had a right to expect it
would *at least have left unsaid.*" "Was it not to be expected that
those of the President's friends, who knew him long and intimately—who understood his integrity and his devotion to the
country and the cause entrusted to his charge—would at least
abstain from judging him in the blindness of haste, and condemning him in the bitterness of ill-temper?" he asked.[59]

Similarly, when Charles G. Halpine, an Irish-born journalist who wrote for the *New York Herald* under the pen name
Miles O'Reilly, complained that Lincoln was interfering with
military affairs, Hay wrote him stiffly: "You must pardon me
for saying that if the Tycoon had kept his fingers from meddling with the war, we should now have had neither war nor
government I think." All the "trash" that newspapers carried
about cabinet disputes and wrangling over policy, he went on
to say, "looks very silly from an inside view, where Abraham
Rex is the central figure continually. I wish you could see as I
do, that he is devilish near an autocrat in this Administration." "I have to a great extent stopped questioning where I
don't agree with him," he concluded, "content with trusting to
his instinct of the necessities of the time and the wants of the
people."[60]

IX

LINCOLN must have been touched by such loyalty, especially
at a time when he seemed to have so few supporters in
Washington. More and more during the final years of the war,

he turned to his secretaries for advice, for encouragement, and simply for company.

With Hay at his side, he and Judge Advocate General Joseph Holt reviewed the verdicts of the military courts. After one exhausting day in July 1863, Hay reported to Nicolay: "I ran the Tycoon through One hundred Court Martials! A steady sitting of six hours!"[61] The next week, the President was back at the business again, spending six hours with Hay and Holt. "I was amused at the eagerness with which the President caught at any fact which would justify him in saving the life of a condemned soldier," Hay recorded in his diary. "He was only merciless in cases where meanness or cruelty were shown. Cases of cowardice he was specially averse to punishing with death. He said it would frighten the poor devils too terribly to shoot them."[62]

Knowing he could trust his secretaries, Lincoln freely expressed his opinion of generals and politicians. He told them that after his defeat at Chickamauga, General William S. Rosecrans behaved "like a duck hit on the head."[63] When Hay remarked that Benjamin F. Butler, the Massachusetts political general, was a dangerous man, Lincoln agreed but added: "He is like Jim Jett's brother. Jim used to say that his brother was the damdest scoundrel that ever lived but in the infinite mercy of Providence he was also the damdest fool."[64]

More frequently now, he discussed political affairs with his secretaries. He talked with them at length about factional fights among Missouri Republicans, explaining that emotionally he felt closer to the conservatives in that state than to the Radicals, who were "bitterly hostile personally . . . [and] the unhandiest devils in the world to deal with," but he recognized that the Radicals were nearer to him in thought and sentiment and, he added, "after all their faces are set Zionwards."[65]

Sometimes he sought the company of his secretaries simply because he was lonely. He brought both with him to Alexander Gardner's photographic studio, where, Hay recorded, "Nico and I immortalized ourselves by having ourselves done in group with the Presdt."[66] Both secretaries accompanied the President and his wife to the theater, where, on November 9, 1863, they saw John Wilkes Booth playing in *The Marble Heart.*

Because Nicolay's duties kept him close to the White House and because he was often not well, Lincoln more frequently looked to Hay as his companion on small expeditions. They went to church together. They tested the new Spencer repeating rifle together. With Seward, they rode to the Capitol to see Hiram Powers's new statuary on the east pediment; drawing on his own expertise, Lincoln objected to the statue of the wood-chopper "as he did not make a sufficiently clean cut."[67] In the summer of 1864, when Mrs. Lincoln was out of town, the President took Hay to what the secretary called "a Sacred Concert of profane music" at Ford's Theatre, where, Hay recorded, "the Tycoon and I occupied a private box and (both of us) carried on a hefty flirtation with the Monk Girls in the flies."[68]

He enjoyed talking with his secretaries. One evening in July 1863, he had Hay drive out with him to the Soldiers' Home, where the Lincolns spent much of the summer, and, Hay recorded, they "had a talk on philology for which the T[ycoon] has a little indulged inclination."[69] Later that summer, they went to the Washington observatory, where Lincoln looked at the moon and Arcturus, and afterward drove out again to the Soldiers' Home, where, Hay reported, "he read Shakespeare to me, the end of Henry VI and the beginning of Richard III till my heavy eye-lids caught his considerate attention and he sent me to bed."[70]

With these young men, Lincoln felt so relaxed and secure that he could even at times allow himself to be silly. In a euphoric mood over the news that after his defeat at Gettysburg Lee had retreated south of the Potomac, he scribbled a bit of doggerel, "Genl. Lee's invasion of the North, written by himself," which he handed to Hay, who was also a versifier:

> In eighteen sixty three, with pomp,
>   and mighty swell
> Me and Jeff's Confederacy, went
>   forth to sack Phil-del,
> The Yankees they got arter us, and
>   giv us particular hell,
> And we skedaddeled back again,
>   and didn't sack Phil-del.[71]

Hay and Nicolay recorded the President's behavior with fond amusement. After midnight one evening in May 1864, just as Grant was about to launch his great offensive against Lee in Virginia, Lincoln came laughing into the office where his secretaries were still working to show them a caricature, "An unfortunate Bee-ing," in a volume of Thomas Hood's poems he had been reading. He seemed, Hay noted, "utterly unconscious that he with his short shirt hanging about his long legs and setting out behind like the tail feathers of an enormous ostrich was infinitely funnier than anything in the book he was laughing at." "What a man it is!" Hay exclaimed in his diary. "Occupied all day with matters of vast moment, deeply

anxious about the fate of the greatest army of the world, with
his own fame and future hanging on the events of the passing
hour, he yet has such a wealth of simple bonhommie and good
fellow ship that he gets out of bed and perambulates the house
in his shirt to find us that we may share with him the fun of
one of poor Hoods queer little conceits."[72]

X

THE friendship that developed between Lincoln and his secretaries does not exactly fit any one of Aristotle's categories.
Certainly it was enjoyable. For the President, it was also most
useful. In the final year of the war, Lincoln made effective use
of his aides' talents. After he announced his reconstruction
program in December 1863, which looked to the restoration of
Southern states when as many as 10 percent of the 1860 voters pledged to support the Union and accept emancipation, he
encouraged Hay to go with the federal army in Florida in the
vain hope that he could enlist the requisite number of loyal sig-
natures. And in July of the following year, when Horace
Greeley conceived the hare-brained scheme of settling the war
through negotiations with Confederate envoys at Niagara Falls,
he deputized Hay to accompany the erratic editor bearing his
terms for negotiation: restoration of the Union and the abolition of slavery. He knew, of course, that the Southerners could
not accept these terms, and he correctly suspected that they
were not authorized by Jefferson Davis's government. Both of
Hay's missions were therefore unsuccessful, and he received
much blame in the newspapers. "But the Tycoon never minded
it in the least," Hay gaily told Halpine, "and as for me, at my

age, the more abuse I get in the newspapers, the better for me. I shall run for Constable some day on the strength of my gory exploits in Florida."[73]

Nicolay's unsuspected political skills proved especially valuable to Lincoln in the election of 1864. Twice the President sent him to New York on what Nicolay described as "a very delicate, disagreeable and arduous duty" of arranging changes in the customs house officials, who had mostly supported Secretary Chase's candidacy.[74] He became the unofficial manager of Lincoln's reelection campaign, and Republican operatives throughout the North reported to him on the President's prospects in their states. In June, he was Lincoln's personal representative at the Republican national convention in Baltimore, and he successfully fielded insistent demands that the President commit himself to a running mate. After the convention, Lincoln sent Nicolay to Missouri, where the rivalry between Republican factions had affairs in "a pretty bad tangle," the origins of which, he correctly reported to the President, lay in "little else than *personal animosity,* and the usual eagerness to appropriate the spoils."[75]

Though enjoyable and useful, Lincoln's relationship to his secretaries never quite reached the level of perfect friendship. That is hardly surprising. There was too great a gap in age and experience to make total intimacy really possible. Lincoln was old enough to be their father. Then, too, though he held his secretaries in high esteem and they came to revere him, there could be no full equality of feeling because he was their employer and could dismiss them at any time. And there were large areas of thought and emotion that he could not share with these young men. For instance, there is no record that he ever mentioned to either secretary his growing concern over Mrs. Lincoln's mental state, and with rare exceptions they did not bring to his attention their never-ending feud with the First Lady.

Even so, Nicolay and Hay became Lincoln's closest, most loyal friends. They offered him advice, help, and encouragement; they provided engaging, lively company, along with a good deal of the laughter he needed to keep his sanity; and they offered affection, bordering at times on adulation.

XI

EVERYONE knows how the war exhausted Lincoln's strength and aged him prematurely. Less recognized is the effect it had on his assistants. His nerves frazzled by overwork and constant stress, Nicolay became increasingly irascible, calling Washington "the national pig-sty,"[76] and cursing congressmen who wanted favors from Lincoln as a "swarm of gad-flies," sent "to bedevil the President, and to generally retard and derange business."[77] Hay too lost his temper from time to time, blasting Stoddard's "asinity"[78] and insisting that Philbrick work regular office hours. He referred to the Executive Mansion as "the White pest-house" and complained that the odors from the fetid Potomac were so foul that "the ghosts of twenty thousand drowned cats come in nights through the South Windows."[79] "The world is almost too many for me," he lamented to Nicolay.[80]

Recognizing their fatigue, Lincoln realized that his secretaries were young men who needed to think of careers after their term in the White House. He looked kindly on the abortive effort to elect Hay as congressman from reconstructed Florida, and he quietly endorsed Nicolay's plan to get a toe-hold in politics by becoming an Illinois delegate to the 1864 Republican national convention. Neither plan was successful. Nor did anything come of talk that Nicolay would buy the influential *Washington National Intelligencer* or join with Simon Cameron in publishing the *Baltimore Sun*. But it was clear to all that the time was near when both the secretaries would leave what Nicolay called "this labor-ridden and care-burdened town, whose very atmosphere seems infected with some subtle poison fatal to all peace of mind or repose of body."[81]

By February 1865 Nicolay wrote his fiancée that he was "pretty well resolved not to remain here in my present relation." Characteristically, his decision emerged not from any discussion with Lincoln about his future, though he "once or twice alluded to the President about the matter," but "from other causes and considerations"—meaning, probably, his never-ending warfare with Mary Lincoln.[82] The next month, he was named American consul to Paris, at a handsome salary of $5,000 a year, and shortly afterward, Hay was made secretary of the American legation in the same city.

On the night of April 14, 1865, Hay was in the White House with Robert Lincoln, studying Spanish, when he heard the President had been assassinated. Immediately they rushed to the President's side. Hay stood at the head of Lincoln's bed when he died. Nicolay was aboard the *Santiago de Cuba* headed for Havana, seeking rest and recovery, when he learned of Lincoln's death. "It would seem that Providence had exacted from him the last and only additional service and sacrifice he could give his country," he wrote his fiancée, "that of dying for her sake. Those of us who knew him will certainly interpret his death as a sign that Heaven deemed him worthy of martyrdom."[83]

AFTERWORD

WHEN Stephen E. Ambrose interviewed Milton S. Eisenhower about the role he played in his brother's administration, he was told: "Dwight and I discussed every major decision he made. . . . Most persons in leadership authority like to think out loud with someone he deems to be intelligent, well informed, conscious of all the nuances from fiscal policy to political possibility, can be trusted absolutely never to divulge a secret, and whom he admires: it is that kind of person who should be the President's principal confidant."[1]

Many of our greatest Presidents have had such confidants. Among our twentieth-century leaders, I think of Theodore Roosevelt and Henry Cabot Lodge, of Woodrow Wilson and Colonel House, of Franklin D. Roosevelt and Harry Hopkins, of John F. Kennedy and his brother Robert. Some of our least successful Presidents have not had such intimate advisers. Richard Nixon trusted nobody, and Jimmy Carter, after the departure of Bert Lance, had no one in Washington of his own age and experience in whom he could confide.

For most of his time in the White House, Abraham Lincoln also lacked intimate, experienced, trusted friends. At the outset of his administration, he was barely acquainted with the leaders of his own party in the House of Representatives, like Thaddeus Stevens. Except for Orville H. Browning, who presently grew disaffected, he had no close friends in the

Senate either. He might reasonably have hoped for advice and guidance from Lyman Trumbull, the other Illinois Senator, whom he had helped elect, but Trumbull took offense at something he said and vowed never again to visit the White House.

He had expected to rely on James W. Grimes, whom he greatly admired, but the Iowa Senator joined his sharpest critics. Improbably enough, his warmest friendship among the senators was with Charles Sumner, the aloof, doctrinaire spokesman of Massachusetts abolitionism, whom Lincoln respected because of his rigid idealism. Lincoln and Sumner had a friendship that was clearly based on mutual convenience, but, strange as it seems, these two very different men also enjoyed each other's company and, according to Mary Lincoln, used to talk and "laugh together like two school boys." But the President and the Senator disagreed on many major issues, like the timing of the Emancipation Proclamation and plans for reconstruction, and Lincoln did not see Sumner as a sound adviser.

Most members of Lincoln's cabinet were unsuited to the role of presidential confidant. Secretary of the Interior Caleb B. Smith was a nonentity. Postmaster General Montgomery Blair, though able and efficient, was concerned primarily with the promotion of the Blair family. Edward Bates, the attorney general, was too old and too self-centered. Lincoln respected the incorruptibility and efficiency of Edwin M. Stanton, who succeeded Simon Cameron as Secretary of War, but Stanton was too independent and prickly to be a close friend, and at times he seemed to exercise a veto power over the President. At the outset, Lincoln tried to cultivate Salmon P. Chase, but he found his Secretary of the Treasury cold, ambitious, and deceitful.

Lincoln developed real affection for Gideon Welles, his efficient Secretary of the Navy, and felt relaxed enough to call him jokingly "Father Neptune." Though Welles's voluminous diary shows that he admired and respected the President, he was too much a self-contained, undemonstrative New Englander to serve as a confidant. Only with William H. Seward, as we have seen, did Lincoln build anything like an intimate friendship— and even in that, he had to be wary of the occasional flightiness and the rebellious streak exhibited by his Secretary of State.

Lincoln found it hard to develop close friendships in Washington in part because he had had so few during his pre-presidential years. A boy who has no chums becomes a man who rarely has close friends. Except for two or three years when he shared everything with Joshua Speed, Lincoln had had no intimates; he had partners, admirers, acolytes, and disciples, but he had outgrown them all by the time he became President. It is very hard for any man in his fifties who has not previously had confidants to reach out trustingly to establish new, close friendships. For a man invested with power, like the President, the task is even more difficult; he necessarily comes to see each friend as a potential petitioner for public office, for promotion, or simply for publicity, whether for himself or his family.

What difference did it make that Lincoln had so few close friends? Surely if he had been surrounded by friends, he would have lived a happier, less anguished, and less isolated life. But, apart from that, would he have better managed the conduct of the Civil War if he had trusted, confidential advisers? Let me suggest three (entirely imaginary) scenarios:

Scenario 1: During the secession crisis, Lincoln seriously misjudged Unionist strength in the South, believing that the secessionists were a small band of conspirators who would be put down by informed voters loyal to the Union. This was a persistent delusion, which affected his policy during at least the first two years of the Civil War. An informed, trusted adviser with a broad Southern acquaintance (which Lincoln lacked) could have urged him to dispatch respected emissaries into the South to determine the state of public opinion. Instead, after largely ignoring the problem, Lincoln chose to send the bluff, swaggering Ward Hill Lamon and the almost unknown Stephen A. Hurlbut to sound out sentiment in Charleston, South Carolina. Neither accomplished anything useful. Just a little later, the same adviser could have warned the President that Virginia might join the Confederacy unless Unionists were strengthened. In fact, Lincoln did have a private interview with a leading Virginia Unionist, John B. Baldwin, in a last-minute attempt to prevent secession in that state, but his effort came too late, after plans for resupplying Fort Sumter were already under way. "Had this contact been fully worked out at an earlier stage," the great Lincoln scholar J. G. Randall judged, "the possibilities seemed highly significant."

Scenario 2: Lincoln disliked controversy and—astonishing in a man who earned his public name as a debater—was unhappy when he had to argue issues, even with his cabinet advisers. Instead—drawing on his long experience in the courtroom— he developed the technique of preparing mental briefs stating each side of a controversial issue as strongly as possible. Then, before stating a judgment, he liked to test his arguments before an audience. He would often present one version of events to one visitor and the opposing version to the next. For instance, in the summer of 1862, after much reflection, he told Seward and Welles that he had about reached the decision to issue an emancipation proclamation. But at almost the same time, he assured Leonard Swett, an old friend who was visiting from Illinois, that he would issue "no proclamation of emancipation" because that would cause 50,000 Union troops in Kentucky and Tennessee to defect to the enemy. Within days of making both these statements, he wrote one of his most famous letters, to Horace Greeley, which seemed to argue both sides of the issue. Explaining that his "paramount object" was to save the Union, he told Greeley: "If I could save the Union without freeing *any* slave I would do it, and if I could save it by freeing *all* the slaves I would do it; and if I could save it by freeing some and leaving others alone I would also do that." It would be easy to read these contradictory statements—and many of Lincoln's critics did so read them—as indicating vacillation or deceit. But for Lincoln, hearing himself make an argument allowed him better to judge its validity. Surely if he had had a wise, discreet counselor—his own Milton Eisenhower, so to speak—before whom he could test his reasoning in private, his policies would have seemed less confusing and easier to understand.

Scenario 3: During the Republican national convention of 1864, Lincoln maintained a discreet silence on the vice-presidential nominee. That silence killed off the chances for the renomination of Hannibal Hamlin, with whom his relations had been rather stiff but entirely proper. By not voicing an opinion on Hamlin or any other candidate, Lincoln opened the way for the nomination of Andrew Johnson of Tennessee. Nobody knows why Lincoln allowed the convention to select Johnson. My guess is that, like most other American Presidents up until our own time, he did not think much about the office of Vice President and really did not care whom the convention selected. Allowing the delegates to pick Johnson was a mistake. No matter what one says about Johnson's honesty and his bravery in standing up for the Union when his state joined the Confederacy, he was a terrible choice, as the turbulent and bitter years of his administration during the Reconstruction era demonstrated. Here, again, trusted, disinterested friends who looked into Johnson's record as a senator and reviewed his conduct as the controversial, embattled Union military governor of conquered Tennessee could have given the President warning signals.

It is fun to play with these counterfactual scenarios, but all of them have doubtful premises. It is not at all clear that any friend could have guided Abraham Lincoln, with his distrust of intimacy and his unwillingness to confide in others. There was about Lincoln a degree of self-assurance, a reliance on his own abilities, that made it almost impossible for him to bend and seek help from others whom he knew to be his intellectual inferiors. "It is absurd to call him a modest man," John Hay, his private secretary, told Herndon. "No great man was ever modest. It was his intellectual arrogance and unconscious assumption of superiority that men like Chase and Sumner never could forgive."

It is certain that, on some basic issues, no advice from any friend, no suggestions from experience, would have altered Lincoln's policies. He was inflexibly opposed to any expansion of slavery into the national territories, believing that if the peculiar institution was contained, it must ultimately die out. He was absolutely devoted to preserving the Union, and no one could have convinced him to agree to the independence of the Confederacy. Eventually, when he felt compelled to issue the

Emancipation Proclamation, no adviser or confidant could have persuaded him to retract it. As Mary Lincoln said, he was "a terribly firm man when he set his foot down—none of us— no man no woman Could rule him after he had made up his mind."

NOTES

PREFACE

1. And has received it in Jean H. Baker's excellent, perceptive *Mary Todd Lincoln: A Biography* (New York: Norton, 1987). Ruth Painter Randall, *Mary Lincoln: Biography of a Marriage* (Boston: Little, Brown, 1953), is fuller but less critical. *Mary Todd Lincoln: Her Life and Letters,* ed. by Justin G. Turner and Linda Levitt Turner (New York: Knopf, 1972), is an indispensable source.

CHAPTER 1

1. All studies of Lincoln's early life rely heavily on the interviews and letters that his law partner, William H. Herndon, collected shortly after his assassination. These documents are in the Herndon-Weik Collection at the Library of Congress. Fortunately for scholars, Douglas L. Wilson and Rodney O. Davis have published an authoritative, carefully annotated edition of these writings in their invaluable *Herndon's Informants: Letters, Interviews, and Statements about Abraham Lincoln* (Urbana: University of Illinois Press, 1998).

2. *Herndon's Informants,* p. 126.

3. Louis A. Warren, *Lincoln's Parentage & Childhood* (New York: Century Co., 1926), pp. 145–46.

4. *Herndon's Informants,* p. 235; Ida M. Tarbell, *The Early Life of Abraham Lincoln* (New York: S. S. McClure, 1896), p. 44.

5. *Herndon's Informants,* p. 241.

6. Ibid., pp. 103–104.

7. Roy P. Basler and others, eds., *The Collected Works of Abraham Lincoln* (New Brunswick, N.J.: Rutgers University Press, 1953–55), 1:386 (hereinafter cited as CW).

8. Ibid., 4:62.

9. Ibid., 1:379.

10. Ibid., 6:16–17.

11. David Herbert Donald, *Lincoln* (New York: Simon & Schuster, 1995), p. 26.

12. Surprisingly Kenneth J. Winkle, in *The Young Eagle: The Rise of Abraham Lincoln* (Dallas: Taylor Trade Publishing, 2001), pp. 14–15, argues that "Lincoln's experience with parental loss appears thoroughly unremarkable."

13. John Bowlby, *Attachment and Loss,* Vol. 3; *Loss: Sadness and Depression* (New York: Basic Books, 1980), p. 320.

14. *Herndon's Informants,* p. 37.

15. Ibid., p. 134.

16. Ibid., p. 176.

17. Louis A. Warren, *Lincoln's Youth: Indiana Years, Seven to Twenty-one, 1816–1830* (New York: Appleton-Century-Crofts, 1959), p. 98.

18. CW, 4:62. As I have shown in "Education Defective: Lincoln's Preparation for Greatness" (*Lincoln Reconsidered* [New York: Vintage Books, 2001], pp. 63–74), Lincoln exaggerated the deficiencies in his education.

19. *Herndon's Informants,* p. 124.

20. Ibid., p. 131.

21. This discussion relies heavily on the work of Harry Stack Sullivan, *The Interpersonal Theory of Psychiatry* (New York: Norton, 1953), especially chap. 16. For a concise explanation of Sullivan's theories, together with empirical data supporting them, see James Youniss, *Parents and Peers in Social Development* (Chicago: University of Chicago Press, 1980).

See also Robert L. Selman and Lynn Hickey Schultz, *Making a Friend in Youth* (New York: Aldine de Gruyter, 1990). I have also been influenced by the writings of Erik H. Erikson, especially his discussion of Gandhi and his "evil friend," Sheik Mehtab, one of "his counterplayers to whom he gave more of himself than he could afford and from whom he wanted he knew not what." From his intimate but troubled relationship with this unsuitable young man of a different religion and a vastly different background Gandhi developed his classic definition of true friendship as "an identity of souls rarely to be found in the world. Only between like natures can friendship be altogether worthy and enduring." Erikson, *Gandhi's Truth: On the Origins of Militant Nonviolence* (New York: Norton, 1969), pp. 133–40.

22. Catherine L. Bagwell, Andrew F. Newcomb, and William M. Bukowski, "Preadolescent Friendship and Peer Rejection as Predictors of Adult Adjustment," *Child Development* (Chicago: University of Chicago Press, 1930–date) 69 (February 1998): 150–51.

23. CW, 1:320.

24. Douglas L. Wilson, *Honor's Voice: The Transformation of Abraham Lincoln* (New York: Knopf, 1998), p. 53.

25. *Herndon's Informants*, pp. 17–18.

26. Ibid., p. 14.

27. Ibid., p. 73.

28. In *Honor's Voice*, chap. 1, Douglas L. Wilson offers a fascinating account of fighting and wrestling on the frontier.

29. Ibid., p. 20.

30. *Herndon's Informants*, p. 7.

31. CW, 3:512.

32. Wilson, *Honor's Voice*, p. 30.

33. *Herndon's Informants*, p. 353.

34. Ibid.

35. Ibid., p. 394.

36. Ibid., p. 18.

37. Ibid., p. 15.

38. But it was not unusual for a young man in his twenties, unmarried and without steady employment, to be thought of as a "boy." "Up to 1840, men in Springfield married at age twenty-seven, on average." Winkle, *The Young Eagle,* p. 62. The average age in the rural districts was probably lower.

39. Walter B. Stevens, *A Reporter's Lincoln,* ed. Michael Burlingame (Lincoln: University of Nebraska Press, 1998), pp. 5–6.

40. Wilson, *Honor's Voice,* p. 110.

41. *Herndon's Informants,* p. 525.

42. Wilson, *Honor's Voice,* p. 111.

43. *Herndon's Informants,* p. 738.

44. Wilson, *Honor's Voice,* p. 112.

45. Ibid., p. 109.

46. Ibid., p. 110.

47. J. G. Randall, *Lincoln the President: Springfield to Gettysburg* (New York: Dodd, Mead, 1945), 2:341.

48. *Herndon's Informants,* p. 440.

49. Randall, *Lincoln the President,* 2:334.

50. C. A. Tripp, "The Strange Case of Isaac Cogdal," *Journal of the Abraham Lincoln Association* 23 (Winter 2002): 69–77.

51. CW, 5:438.

52. Ibid., 1:118–19.

53. *Herndon's Informants,* p. 18.

54. William H. Herndon and Jesse W. Weik, *Herndon's Life of Lincoln,* ed. Paul M. Angle (Cleveland: The World Publishing Company, 1930), pp. 88–89. [Hereinafter cited as *Herndon's Lincoln.*]

55. *Herndon's Informants,* p. 10.

56. Ibid., p. 528.

57. Donald, *Lincoln,* p. 41.

58. *Herndon's Informants,* p. 173.

59. Ibid., p. 501.

60. Ibid., p. 254.

61. Ibid., p. 32.

62. Ibid., p. 528.

63. Ibid., p. 394.

64. CW, 4:310.

65. Herndon, "Ann Rutledge & Lincoln," unpublished monograph, c. 1887, Herndon-Weik Collection.

66. *Herndon's Informants,* p. 63.

67. Ibid., p. 153.

68. Ibid., p. 507.

69. Ibid., p. 168.

CHAPTER 2

1. The basic sources for this chapter are Lincoln's letters to Speed, published in Roy P. Basler, ed., *The Collected Works of Abraham Lincoln* (New Brunswick, N.J.: Rutgers University Press, 1953–1955) (hereinafter cited as CW); the reminiscences that Speed sent William H. Herndon after Lincoln's death, published, with careful annotation, in Douglas L. Wilson and Rodney O. Davis, ed., *Herndon's Informants: Letters, Interviews, and Statements About Abraham Lincoln* (Urbana: University of Illinois Press, 1998) (hereinafter cited as *Herndon's Informants*); and Joshua F. Speed, *Reminiscences of Abraham Lincoln and Notes of a Visit to California* (Louisville: John P. Morton and Company, 1884). Charles B. Strozier's *Lincoln's Quest for Union: A Psychological Portrait* (2nd ed.; Philadelphia: Paul Dry Books, 2001), pp. 53–65, first brought attention to the profound psychological importance of Lincoln's friendship with Speed. Jonathan Ned Katz, *Love*

Stories: Sex Between Men Before Homosexuality (Chicago: University of Chicago Press, 2001), Chap. 1, is an excellent secondary account. I have also profited from reading C. A. Tripp's unpublished manuscript, "Yours Forever," even though I thoroughly disagree with its conclusions.

2. Speed, "Incidents in the Early Life of A. Lincoln," MS, Illinois State Historical Library.

3. Allen Thorndike Rice, ed., *Reminiscences of Abraham Lincoln by Distinguished Men of His Time* (New York: North American Review, 1888), pp. 294–95.

4. Speed, "Incidents in the Early Life of A. Lincoln."

5. The best biography is Gary Lee Williams, "James and Joshua Speed: Lincoln's Kentucky Friends" (Ph.D. dissertation, Duke University, 1971). There is also valuable biographical information in Robert L. Kincaid, *Joshua Fry Speed: Lincoln's Most Intimate Friend* (Harrogate, Tenn.: Lincoln Memorial University, 1943), which includes all the letters from Lincoln to Speed.

6. Joshua F. Speed to Mrs. Lucy Speed, December 25, 1839, MS in possession of Beverley H. Ballantine, Louisville.

7. Speed, *Reminiscences,* p. 23.

8. CW, 1:254–58, 371–77.

9. Ibid., 1:201.

10. *Herndon's Informants,* p. 476.

11. CW, 1:265.

12. William H. Herndon and Jesse W. Weik, *Herndon's Life of Lincoln,* ed. Paul M. Angle (Cleveland: World Publishing Company, 1930), p. 424.

13. *Herndon's Informants,* p. 499.

14. Ibid., p. 430.

15. John G. Nicolay and John Hay, *Abraham Lincoln: A History* (New York: Century Co., 1890), 1:194. Robert Todd Lincoln agreed that Speed was "the most intimate friend his

father had ever had." John Marshall to Gilmer Adams, October 15, 1912, Speed Family MSS, Filson Historical Society, Louisville, Ky.

16. Herndon, "Miss Rutledge and Lincoln," undated monograph [c. 1887], Herndon-Weik Collection, Library of Congress; Herndon to J. E. Remsburg, September 10, 1887, quoted in William E. Barton, *The Soul of Abraham Lincoln* (New York: George H. Doran Company, 1920), pp. 336–37.

17. Notably by Larry Kramer, who alleges Lincoln "was a gay man and a totally gay man." Kramer claims to have access to a Joshua Speed diary, along with letters in which Speed wrote explicitly about his love affair with Lincoln. The authenticity of this story is highly dubious, since Kramer has not produced the documents or allowed anyone else to see them. But perhaps I am prejudiced, because Kramer calls me a "dried old heterosexual prune at Harvard." For an excellent account, see Carol Lloyd, "Was Lincoln Gay?" *Salon*, April 30, 1999. See also "Big Buck & Big Lick: Lincoln & Whitman," Chap. 7 in Charley Shively, *Drum Beats: Walt Whitman's Civil War Boy Lovers* (San Francisco: Gay Sunshine Press, 1989), and the long essay by W. Scott Thompson, "Was Lincoln Gay?" in History News Network. Thompson concludes: "But make no mistake, Abe Lincoln was gay, and the more evidence is accumulated—or exhumed free of denial—the more we believe the conclusion will be confirmed." Thompson's essay appeared on line at http://historynewsnetwork.org/articles/article.html?id=96.

18. Cf. Gabor Boritt's Introduction to *The Lincoln Enigma: The Changing Faces of an American Icon* (New York: Oxford University Press, 2001), xiii–xxiv.

19. Katz, *Love Stories: Sex Between Men Before Homosexuality*, esp. pp. 60–62 and 402–406, where all the cases are listed.

20. The authoritative study is E. Anthony Rotundo,

American Manhood: Transformations in Masculinity from the Revolution to the Modern Era (New York: Basic Books, 1993). I have also profited from several conversations with Dr. Rotundo on this subject.

21. Caleb Crain, *American Sympathy: Men, Friendship, and Literature in the New Nation* (New Haven: Yale University Press, 2001), pp. 153–59. See also David Deitcher, *Dear Friends: American Photographs of Men Together, 1840–1918* (New York: Harry N. Abrams, 2001).

22. Rotundo, *American Manhood,* pp. 78–79.

23. Rotundo astutely observes: "Among males, romantic friendship was largely a product of a distinct phase in the life cycle—youth." Ibid., p. 76.

24. Titian J. Coffey, in Rice, *Reminiscences of Abraham Lincoln,* p. 241.

25. Michel de Montaigne, in Laurie J. Shannon, "Monarchs, Minions, and 'Sovereigne' Friendship," *South Atlantic Quarterly* 97 (Winter 1998): 92. I have deleted Montaigne's "wives, children," because Lincoln and Speed as yet had neither.

26. Joshua Speed to Mary Speed, October 31, 1841, Speed Family Papers, Filson Historical Society.

27. *Herndon's Informants,* p. 664.

28. Herndon to Jesse W. Weik, December 10, 1885, Herndon-Weik Collection, Library of Congress.

29. Douglas L. Wilson, *Lincoln Before Washington* (Urbana: University of Illinois Press, 1997), p. 117.

30. Ibid., p. 111.

31. Herndon to Jesse W. Weik, January 5, 1889, Herndon-Weik Collection. A part of this story—which Herndon claimed he had firsthand from Speed—was the tale that Lincoln visited a prostitute whom Speed recommended and found, after getting in bed, that she charged five dollars and that he had only three. Refusing the girl's offer of credit, he got up and buttoned

his pants. She called him "the most conscientious man I ever saw." In all probability, this is part of a tall tale, designed to tease Lincoln who was so scrupulously honest, but Herndon, who had no sense of humor, missed the point.

32. Douglas L . Wilson, *Honor's Voice,* pp. 246–47.

33. Herndon, interview with Mrs. N. W. Edwards, January 10, 1866, Herndon-Weik Collection (cf. *Herndon's Informants,* p. 443).

34. Strozier, *Lincoln's Quest for Union,* p. 63.

35. CW, 1:280.

36. *Herndon's Life of Lincoln,* p. 173.

37. *Herndon's Informants,* p. 477.

38. Kincaid, *Joshua Fry Speed,* p. 15.

39. *Herndon's Informants,* p. 444.

40. CW, 1:282.

41. Ibid., 1:289.

42. *Herndon's Informants,* p. 475. In his interview with Herndon, Speed placed Lincoln's "crazy" spell in December 1840, during the special session of the Illinois legislature. It seems more probable that it occurred early in 1841, when the break with Mary Todd seemed irrevocable.

43. This conflates two statements by Speed. *Herndon's Informants,* p. 197; Speed, *Reminiscences,* p. 39.

44. CW, 1:229.

45. Ibid., 1:289.

46. Fiske Kimball, "Jefferson's Designs for Two Kentucky Houses," *Journal of the Society of Architectural Historians,* 9 (1949):14–16.

47. Mildred Fry Bullitt, January 2, 1861, Bullitt MSS, Filson Historical Society.

48. James Speed, response to the toast, "Abraham Lincoln," at the Society of the Loyal Legion, May 4, 1887, typescript, Speed Family MSS.

49. CW, 1:261.

50. Ibid., 1:259–61.

51. Albert J. Beveridge, *Abraham Lincoln, 1809–1858* (Boston: Houghton Mifflin, 1928), 1:320.

52. CW, 1:260.

53. Ibid., 1:320.

54. Ibid., 1:261.

55. Gary Lee Williams, "James and Joshua Speed: Lincoln's Kentucky Friends" (Ph.D. dissertation, Duke University, 1971), p. 30.

56. CW, 1:265.

57. Ibid., 1:266.

58. Ibid., 1:267.

59. Ibid., 1:280

60. Ibid., 1:282.

61. Ibid., 1:280.

62. Ibid., 1:282.

63. Ibid., 1:303.

64. *Herndon's Informants,* p. 431.

65. CW, 1:281.

66. Joshua Speed to his Mother, January 25, 1849, MS, Filson Historical Society.

67. Speed, *Reminiscences,* p. 12.

68. CW, 1:282.

69. Kincaid, *Joshua Fry Speed,* p. 57.

70. CW, 1:325.

71. Ibid., 1:306.

72. Ibid., 1:325.

73. Ibid., 1:305.

74. Ibid., 1:391.

75. *The Story of Farmington* (Louisville, 1997), p. 6; inventory of the Estate of John Speed, December 7, 1840, MS, Filson Historical Society.

76. James Speed to Mary L. Booth, January 10, 1863, MS, Filson Historical Society.

77. My information on Speed's slaveholding is drawn from the invaluable "Joshua Speed: Chronology of Slave Ownership," by Pen Bogart, of the Filson Historical Society, who has generously shared his research with me.

78. CW, 1:322.

79. Williams, "James and Joshua Speed," pp. 51–52.

80. Speed to Lincoln, May 19, 1860, Lincoln MSS, Library of Congress. The Lincoln Papers are now accessible on the Web, as part of the American Memory Project of the Library of Congress, at: http://memory.loc.gov/ammem/alhtml/malhome.html.

81. *CW: First Supplement*, pp. 53–54.

82. Speed to Lincoln, November 14, 1860, Lincoln MSS.

83. Ibid.

84. CW, 4:141.

85. *Herndon's Informants*, p. 475.

86. Dorothy Lamon Teillard, ed., *Recollections of Abraham Lincoln, 1847–1865, by Ward Hill Lamon* (Washington D.C., 1911), p. 286.

87. Speed to Lincoln, May 29, 1861, Lincoln MSS.

88. CW, 4:368–69.

89. Biography of Joshua F. Speed by an unidentified author [probably Thomas Speed], tipped into Thomas Speed, *Memorials of the Speed Family* (1889), pp. 66–71, Filson Historical Society.

90. Speed to Lincoln, September 2, 1861, Lincoln MSS.

91. Speed to Lincoln, September 17, 1861, ibid.

92. Earl S. Miers, ed., *Lincoln Day by Day* (Washington, D.C.: Lincoln Sesquicentennial Commission, 1960), 3:67.

93. CW, *First Supplement*, p. 96.

94. Speed to Lincoln, September 17, 1862, Lincoln MSS.

95. Speed to Lincoln, November 6, 1863, ibid.

96. Speed to Lincoln, September 3, 1861, ibid.

97. Speed to Joseph Holt, September 7, 1861, Holt MSS, Library of Congress.

98. Speed to Lincoln, September 3, 1861, Lincoln MSS.

99. Speed to Joseph Holt, December 8, 1861, Holt MSS.

100. Ibid.

101. *Herndon's Informants,* p. 197.

102. Speed to Lincoln, October 26, 1863, Lincoln MSS.

103. Miers, *Lincoln Day by Day,* 3:79.

104. CW, 1:546.

105. Speed, *Reminiscences,* pp. 32–33.

106. It is not possible to give an exact date for this interview. Speed wrote Herndon on January 12, 1866, that it occurred "about ten days previous to his last inauguration" (*Herndon's Informants,* p. 156). But in his *Reminiscences* Speed said it occurred "about two weeks before his assassination."

107. Speed, *Reminiscences,* pp. 26–27; *Herndon's Informants,* pp. 156–58. In his letter to Herndon, Speed said this was the "last interview but one" that he had with Lincoln. *Herndon's Informants,* p. 156.

CHAPTER 3

1. The facts in this chapter closely follow those I presented in my *Lincoln's Herndon* (New York: Knopf, 1948), which remains the only full-length biography. I was very young when I wrote it and was readily persuaded by Herndon's claim of great intimacy with Lincoln. Now—over half a century later—I have grown much more skeptical, as this chapter shows. In preparing it I have reexamined all my notes on Herndon, have restudied the voluminous collection of his papers in the Herndon-Weik Collection of the Library of Congress, and have analyzed the vast assemblage of documents in *The Law Practice of Abraham Lincoln,* ed. by Cullom Davis and others (3 DVD disks; Urbana, Ill.: University of Illinois Press, 2000).

2. See Lavern Marshall Hamand, "Ward Hill Lamon:

Lincoln's 'Particular Friend'" (Ph.D. dissertation, University of Illinois, 1949), and the excellent biographical sketch in Mark E. Neely, Jr., *The Abraham Lincoln Encyclopedia* (New York: McGraw-Hill, 1982), pp. 177–79.

3. Thomas J. McCormack, ed., *Memoirs of Gustave Koerner, 1809–1896* (Cedar Rapids, Iowa: Torch Press, 1909), 2:113.

4. Ebenezer Peck to Lyman Trumbull, March 21, 1861, Trumbull MSS, Library of Congress (hereinafter cited as LC).

5. Douglas L. Wilson and Rodney O. Davis, eds., *Herndon's Informants* (Urbana: University of Illinois Press, 1998), pp. 346 and 348. I have telescoped two statements Davis gave Herndon on successive days in September 1866.

6. Except where otherwise identified, sources for quotations in the following pages are to be found in my *Lincoln's Herndon*.

7. *Herndon's Informants,* p. 470.

8. Herndon, "Big Me," Herndon-Weik Collection.

9. *Herndon's Informants,* p. 211.

10. Herndon, "Lincoln & Mary Todd," undated monograph, Herndon-Weik Collection.

11. *Herndon's Informants,* p. 407.

12. CW, 1:497.

13. *Catalogue of Articles Owned and Used by Abraham Lincoln. Now Owned by the Lincoln Memorial Collection of Chicago* (Chicago, 1887).

14. My account of the Lincoln & Herndon partnership rests heavily on the admirable "Statistical Portrait" included in *The Law Practice of Abraham Lincoln,* issued on DVD disks by the University of Illinois Press, 2000.

15. *A Letter from William H. Herndon to Isaac N. Arnold Relating to Abraham Lincoln, His Wife, and Their Life in Springfield* (1937).

16. Herndon to Weik, November 13, 1885, Herndon-Weik Collection.

17. William H. Herndon and Jesse W. Weik, *Herndon's Life of Lincoln,* ed. Paul M. Angle (Cleveland: World Publishing Company, 1930), p. 247.

18. CW, 1:115.

19. Herndon to Weik, July 25, 1890, Herndon-Weik Collection.

20. Herndon to Weik, February 18, 1887, ibid.

21. Herndon to Weik, February 11, 1887, ibid.

22. Herndon to Weik, February 9, 1886, ibid.

23. Herndon, "Lincoln as Lawyer Politician & Statesman," undated monograph (c. 1887), Herndon-Weik Collection.

24. Herndon to Weik, December 9, 1886, ibid.

25. *Springfield Illinois Daily Journal,* September 24, 1883.

26. Herndon to Truman H. Bartlett, October 1887, Bartlett MSS, Massachusetts Historical Society.

27. *Herndon's Life of Lincoln,* p. 211.

28. CW, 1:420.

29. Ibid., 1:491.

30. Theodore Parker, *The Effect of Slavery on the American People: A Sermon Preached at the Music Hall, Boston, on Sunday, July 4, 1858,* p. 5.

31. Herndon to Theodore Parker, September 20, November 24, 1858, Herndon-Parker MSS, University of Iowa.

32. Herndon to Weik, December 23, 1885, Herndon-Weik Collection.

33. Herndon to Weik, January 4, 1889, ibid.

34. Herndon to Theodore Parker, July 5, 1858, Herndon-Parker MSS.

35. Herndon, "Analysis of the Character of Abraham Lincoln," *Abraham Lincoln Quarterly* 1 (December 1941): 411–12.

36. Herndon to Parker, September 2, 1858, Herndon-Parker MSS.

37. *Herndon's Informants,* p. 622.

38. Herndon to Weik, February 21, 1891, Herndon-Weik Collection.

39. CW, 3:516.

40. Herndon to Weik, November 14, 1885, Herndon-Weik Collection.

41. Herndon to Lamon, March 3, 1870, Lamon MSS, Huntington Library, San Marino, California.

42. Herndon to Lamon, March 1, 1870, ibid.

43. Herndon to Wendell Phillips, December 28, 1860, Phillips MSS, Houghton Library, Harvard University.

44. Herndon to E. L. Pierce, February 18, 1861, Herndon-Weik Collection.

45. Herndon to Pierce, March 4, 1861, ibid.

46. Herndon to Lyman Trumbull, November 21, 1861, Trumbull MSS.

47. Herndon to John G. Nicolay and John Hay, September 25, 1864, Lincoln MSS.

48. Herndon to Caroline W. H. Dall, January 28, 1862, Dall MSS, Massachusetts Historical Society.

49. *Abraham Lincoln Quarterly,* 1:406–407.

50. By the winter of 1862 Herndon's attitude toward a federal appointment changed. In the sharp economic recession that fall, he went, as he said, "like a thousand others, under pecuniarily." Appealing to the President for help, he was offered a job of about a month's duration at St. Louis, paying five dollars a day and mileage. He declined, because he did not want to leave home. Two years later, he still had hopes for a federal job, and he wrote to Illinois Representative Shelby M. Cullom: "If you see Lincoln tell him for me that if he has any large, honorable, and fat office with a big salary to give away and cannot get any

person on Earth to take it that I'll take and run it on his account, but under no other consideration." The tone was jocular, and Lincoln failed to take the hint, telling Cullom: "If all persons did not bother me more than Herndon I should be a happier man." Herndon, monograph on Lincoln's offer of an appointment, c. 1887, Herndon-Weik Collection.

51. Herndon to Weik, January 16, 1886, Herndon-Weik Collection.

52. Douglas L. Wilson, "William H. Herndon and Mary Todd Lincoln," *Journal of the Abraham Lincoln Association* 22 (Summer 2001): esp. pp. 1–6.

53. Herndon to Weik, October 18, 1889, Herndon-Weik Collection.

54. *Herndon's Life of Lincoln,* p. 390; Jesse W. Weik, *The Real Lincoln: A Portrait* (Boston: Houghton Mifflin, 1922), p. 301.

55. Herndon to Josiah G. Holland, May 26, 1865, Holland MSS, New York Public Library.

56. Herndon to Weik, February 1887, Herndon-Weik Collection.

57. Herndon, "Lincoln as Lawyer Politician & Statesman," undated monograph (c. 1887), Herndon-Weik Collection.

58. Don E. Fehrenbacher and Virginia Fehrenbacher, eds., *Recollected Words of Abraham Lincoln* (Stanford: Stanford University Press, 1996), p. 238.

59. Cf. *Herndon's Life of Lincoln,* pp. 57–58, and Herndon to Weik, December 1, 1888, Herndon-Weik Collection.

60. Herndon to Lamon, February 25, 1870, Lamon MSS.

61. Herndon to Lamon, March 6, 1870, ibid.

62. Herndon to Weik, November 14, 1885, Herndon-Weik Collection.

63. Herndon to Weik, January 19, 1886, ibid. The first record of this alleged conversation with Lincoln I have discov-

ered is in Herndon to Ward H. Lamon, February 25, 1869 [i.e., 1870], Lamon MSS, Huntington Library, where it is dated as "about 1852." In Herndon's incomplete and unpublished fifth lecture on Lincoln, he dated the interview as "in 1846." Copy of MS through the kindness of the Lincoln Studies Center, Knox College.

64. Herndon to Weik, January 19, 1886, Herndon-Weik Collection.

65. Paul H. Verduin, "New Evidence Suggests Lincoln's Mother Born in Richmond County, Virginia, Giving Credibility to Planter Grandfather Legend," *Northern Neck of Virginia Historical Magazine* 38 (December 1988): 4357. I also have greatly profited from a letter Paul Verduin wrote me on October 4, 2000, dealing with this question.

66. In a letter of January 1, 2003, Daniel Stowell, editor of the *Papers of Abraham Lincoln,* has provided me a careful summary of this case, together with copies of the pertinent documents.

67. Herndon to Weik, January 1891, Herndon-Weik Collection.

68. *Herndon's Informants,* p. 431.

69. On this subject I have greatly profited from conversations with Dr. Harold Solomon, of Beth Israel Hospital, Boston, and Dr. Franz von Lichtenberg, of Harvard Medical School.

70. Milton H. Shutes, *Lincoln's Emotional Life* (Philadelphia: Dorrance & Company, 1957), pp. 68–73; Charles B. Strozier, *Lincoln's Quest for Union,* pp. 50–51. Cf. Wilson, *Honor's Voice,* pp. 127–29, and Jean H. Baker, *Mary Todd Lincoln: A Biography* (New York: Norton, 1987), p. 88.

71. Herndon to John W. Keys, April 14, 1886, Ida M. Tarbell Collection, Allegheny College (courtesy Lincoln Studies Center, Knox College).

CHAPTER 4

1. The basic source for this chapter is *The Diary of Orville Hickman Browning,* ed. Theodore C. Pease and J. G. Randall (Springfield: Illinois State Historical Library, 2 vols., 1925–1933). The only biography is Maurice G. Baxter's excellent and succinct *Orville H. Browning: Lincoln's Friend and Critic* (Bloomington: Indiana University Press, 1957). There are numerous letters from Browning to Lincoln in the Lincoln MSS, Library of Congress.

2. Michael Burlingame, *The Inner World of Abraham Lincoln* (Urbana: University of Illinois Press, 1995), p. 105.

3. Theodore C. Pease and J. G. Randall, eds., *The Diary of Orville Hickman Browning* (2 vols.; Springfield: Illinois State Historical Library, 1925–1933), 1:476 (hereinafter cited as Browning, *Diary*).

4. Allan Nevins, *The War for the Union,* vol. 1, *The Improvised War, 1861–1862* (New York: Charles Scribner's Sons, 1959), p. 58.

5. Michael Burlingame, ed., *An Oral History of Abraham Lincoln: John G. Nicolay's Interviews and Essays* (Carbondale: Southern Illinois University Press, 1996), pp. 1–2.

6. Ibid., pp. 3–4.

7. Roy P. Basler and others, eds., *The Collected Works of Abraham Lincoln* (New Brunswick, N.J.: Rutgers University Press, 1953–55), 1:156 (hereinafter cited as CW).

8. Ibid., 1:118.

9. Browning, *Diary,* 1:59, 274, 293, 294.

10. CW, 1:386.

11. Browning, *Diary,* 1:317.

12. Ibid., 1:238.

13. Ibid., 1:327.

14. Ibid., 1:380.

15. Ibid., 1:395.

16. Ibid., 1:410.

17. J. G. Randall, *Lincoln the President: Springfield to Gettysburg* (New York: Dodd, Mead, 1945), 1:160.

18. William E. Baringer, *Lincoln's Rise to Power* (Boston: Little, Brown, 1937), p. 293.

19. Browning, *Diary,* 1:409–10.

20. Browning to Lincoln, June 29, 1860, Lincoln MSS.

21. Maurice G. Baxter, *Orville H. Browning: Lincoln's Friend and Critic* (Bloomington: Indiana University Press, 1957), p. 105.

22. Browning, *Diary,* 1:422.

23. Allen Thorndike Rice, ed., *Reminiscences of Abraham Lincoln by Distinguished Men of His Time* (New York: North American Review, 1888), pp. 605–606.

24. Browning, *Diary,* 1:422.

25. Browning to Lincoln, July 4, 1860, Lincoln MSS.

26. Browning to Lincoln, November 9, 1860, ibid.

27. Browning to Lincoln, January 15, 1861, ibid.

28. Ibid.

29. Browning, *Diary,* 1:453.

30. Browning to Lincoln, February 17, 1861, Lincoln MSS.

31. Browning to Lincoln, March 26, 1861, ibid.

32. Browning to Lincoln, April 18, 1861, ibid.

33. Browning to Lincoln, April 30, 1861, ibid.

34. Ibid.

35. Michael Burlingame and John R. Turner Ettlinger, eds., *Inside the White House: The Complete Civil War Diary of John Hay* (Carbondale, Ill.: Southern Illinois University Press, 1997), p. 19.

36. Browning to Lincoln, April 18, 1861, Lincoln MSS.

37. Browning to Lincoln, March 26, 1861, ibid.

38. Browning, *Diary,* 1:475.

39. Ibid., 1:476.

40. Ibid., 1:485.

41. Ibid., 1:523.

42. Ibid., 1:520.

43. Ibid., 1:563.

44. Ibid., 1:478.

45. Ibid., 1:512.

46. Ibid., 1:515.

47. Ibid., 1:516.

48. Ibid., 1:521.

49. Burlingame, *Oral History,* p. 3.

50. Browning to Isaac N. Arnold, November 25, 1872, Carl Sandburg MSS, Illinois Historical Survey, Urbana.

51. Browning, *Diary,* 1:553.

52. Ibid., 1:542–43.

53. Ibid., 1:559–60.

54. Browning to Lincoln, April 9, 1861, Lincoln MSS.

55. Eliza Browning to Lincoln, June 8, 1861, Lincoln MSS.

56. Harry J. Carman and Reinhard H. Luthin, *Lincoln and the Patronage* (New York: Columbia University Press, 1943), p. 175.

57. Browning, *Diary,* 1:621.

58. Howard K. Beale, ed., *The Diary of Edward Bates, 1859–1866* (Washington, D.C.: Government Printing Office, 1933), p. 244.

59. Thomas J. McCormack, ed., *Memoirs of Gustave Koerner, 1809–1896* (Cedar Rapids, Iowa: Torch Press, 1909), 1:479.

60. David M. Silver, *Lincoln's Supreme Court* (Urbana: University of Illinois Press, 1956), p. 72.

61. Dubois and Butler to Lincoln, September 7, 1862, Lincoln MSS.

62. Swett to Lincoln, January 15, 1862, ibid.

63. Swett to W. H. Herndon, August 29, 1887, in *Herndon's Lincoln,* 3:502–504. Swett's story has been questioned by Willard King (*David Davis: Lincoln's Friend* [Cambridge: Harvard University Press, 1960], p. 195), and it is certain that, contrary to Swett's account, Lincoln did not "at once" appoint Davis.

64. Leonard Swett to his wife, August 10, 1862, David Davis MSS, Illinois State Historical Library.

65. Thomas Sweney to David Davis, June 21, 1862, Davis MSS.

66. Browning to Lincoln, September 11, 1861, Lincoln MSS.

67. Browning to Lincoln, September 17, 1861, ibid.

68. Browning to Lincoln, September 30, 1861, ibid.

69. CW, 4:531–32.

70. Ibid., 4:532.

71. Browning to Lincoln, September 30, 1861, Lincoln MSS.

72. Through Secretary of State Seward, Lincoln did offer Browning appointment as commissioner under the treaty between the United States and Great Britain for the final settlement of the claims of the Hudson's Bay and Puget Sound companies in July 1864. Browning declined. Seward to Browning, July 7, 1864, Browning MSS, Illinois State Historical Library.

73. Browning, *Diary,* 1:591–92.

74. Ibid., 1:595–96.

75. Ibid., 1:605.

76. *Quincy Whig & Republican,* August 9, 18, 1862.

77. Ibid., August 28, 1862.

78. Ibid., September 3, 1862.

79. Browning to Lincoln, August 11, 1862, Lincoln MSS.

80. Theodore Calvin Pease, *The Diary of Orville H. Browning: A New Source for Lincoln's Presidency* (Chicago: University of Chicago Press, 1924), pp. 22–23.

81. Browning to James Strain, September 25, 1862, Browning MSS.

82. Baxter, *Orville H. Browning,* p. 148.

83. Browning, *Diary,* 1:578.

84. Ibid., 1:585.

85. Ibid., 1:587–88.

86. Pease, *Diary of Orville H. Browning,* p. 24.

87. Browning, *Diary,* 1:665.

88. Ibid., 1:592.

89. Ibid., 1:591.

90. Ibid., 1:598–99.

91. Francis Fessenden, *The Life and Public Services of William Pitt Fessenden* (Boston: Houghton Mifflin, 1907), 1:235.

92. Browning, *Diary,* 1:237–38.

93. Ibid., 1:600.

94. Ibid., 1:603.

95. Ibid., 1:604n.

96. Ibid., 1:621.

97. R. Baird to Browning, February 3, 1863, Browning MSS.

98. Browning, *Diary,* 1:631.

99. Baxter, *Orville H. Browning,* p. 154.

100. William S. Warford, "Mission Unaccomplished— Lincoln and an Office-Seeker," *Journal of the Illinois State Historical Society* 53 (Spring 1960): 67.

101. Browning, *Diary,* 1:659.

102. *Quincy Whig & Republican,* October 11, 1864.

103. Ibid., September 5, 1864.

104. Britton A. Hill to Lincoln, October 3, 1864, Lincoln MSS.

105. Carl Landrum, "Lincoln Counted Several Quincyans as Friends During Civil War," undated clipping [c. February 1988], *Quincy Herald-Whig,* Historical Society of Quincy and Adams County.

106. William Kellogg to Browning, September 23, 1864, Browning MSS.

107. *Quincy Whig & Republican,* October 11, 1864.

108. Browning to Edgar Cowan, September 6, 1864, quoted in Baxter, *Orville H. Browning,* p. 158.

109. Ibid., p. 177.

110. Ibid., p. 173.

CHAPTER 5

1. Virginia Woodbury Fox, Diary, November 16, 1862, Levi Woodbury Papers, Library of Congress.

2. For Lincoln's friendship with Captain Derickson, I have relied heavily on two unpublished manuscripts kindly given to me by their authors: Matt Pinsker, "Lincoln's Wartime Retreat" (first draft, 2001), and C. A. Tripp, "What Stuff!" (a chapter for his projected history of Lincoln's sexuality). Dr. Tripp, with his usual generosity, also gave me a copy of Derickson's "Recollections of Lincoln," from the Centennial Edition of the *Meadville* (Pa.) *Tribune Republican,* May 12, 1888. Neither Dr. Pinsker nor Dr. Tripp is responsible for my interpretation of this relationship.

3. Derickson, "Recollections of Lincoln."

4. Roy P. Basler and others, eds., *The Collected Works of Abraham Lincoln* (New Brunswick, N.J.: Rutgers University Press, 1953–55), 5:484–85 (hereinafter cited as CW).

5. Thomas Chamberlin, *History of the One Hundred and Fiftieth Regiment, Pennsylvania Volunteers, Second Regiment, Bucktail Brigade* (Philadelphia: F. McManus, Jr., & Co., Printers, 1905), p. 31.

6. C. A. Tripp, "What Stuff!" unpublished MS, p. 22.

7. H. S. Huidekoper, "On Guard at the White House," *National Magazine* 9 (February 1909): 510–12.

8. Derickson, "Recollections of Lincoln."

9. D. V. Derickson to Lincoln, June 3, 1864, and July 3 [?], 1864, Lincoln MSS, Library of Congress.

10. My account of the Lincoln-Seward relationship draws heavily on two excellent biographies: Glyndon G. Van Deusen, *William Henry Seward* (New York: Oxford University Press, 1967), and John M. Taylor, *William Henry Seward: Lincoln's Right Hand* (New York: HarperCollins, 1991). There is much valuable material in Frederick W. Seward, *Seward at Washington as Senator and Secretary of State* (3 vols.; New York: Derby and Miller, 1891), which fortunately includes many letters from Seward to his wife and family. The William H. Seward Papers, at the University of Rochester Library, are not very revealing on personal affairs.

11. Frederick W. Seward, *Seward at Washington* (New York: Derby and Miller, 1891), 2:80 (hereinafter cited as *Seward*).

12. John M. Taylor, *William Henry Seward: Lincoln's Right Hand* (New York: HarperCollins, 1991), p. 118 (hereinafter cited as Taylor).

13. Glyndon G. Van Deusen, *William Henry Seward* (New York: Oxford University Press, 1967), p. 336 (hereinafter cited as Van Deusen).

14. J. G. Randall, *Lincoln the President: Springfield to Gettysburg* (New York: Dodd, Mead, 1945), 1:248.

15. *Lincoln Lore,* no. 1565 (July 1968).

16. Howard K. Beale, ed., *The Diary of Edward Bates, 1859–1866* (Washington, D.C.: Government Printing Office, 1933), p. 164 (hereinafter cited as Bates).

17. Seward to Lincoln, March 2, 1861, Lincoln MSS.

18. John G. Nicolay and John Hay, *Abraham Lincoln: A History* (New York: Century Company, 1890), 3:371.

19. Thurlow Weed to Seward, March 7, 1861, Seward MSS.

20. Gideon Welles, *Lincoln and Seward* (New York: Sheldon and Company, 1874), p. 18.

21. Ibid., p. 24.

22. Seward, "Some Thoughts for the President's Consideration," April 1, 1861, Lincoln MSS.

23. For a defense of Seward, see Norman B. Ferris, "Lincoln and Seward in Civil War Diplomacy: Their Relationship at the Outset Reexamined," *Journal of the Abraham Lincoln Association* 12 (1991): 21–42. More convincing in the same issue is Richard N. Current's "Comment," pp. 43–47.

24. Frederick W. Seward, *Reminiscences of a War-Time Statesman and Diplomat, 1830–1915* (New York: Putnam, 1916), p. 147.

25. In fact, it is possible that Seward did intend to publish his memorandum, together with what he assumed would be Lincoln's acquiescence in his views, in New York newspapers. Patrick Sowle, "A Reappraisal of Seward's Memorandum of April 1, 1861, to Lincoln," *Journal of Southern History* 33 (May 1967): 234–39. But Lincoln was not aware of any such plan.

26. CW, 4:316–18.

27. Randall, *Lincoln the President*, 2:35–36.

28. For a facsimile of Seward's original draft, Lincoln's emendations, and the final version, see Allen Thorndike Rice, ed., *Reminiscences of Abraham Lincoln by Distinguished Men of His Time* (New York: North American Review, 1888), pp. lx–lxix.

29. Van Deusen, pp. 337–38.

30. Patricia Carley Johnson, ed., "Sensitivity and Civil

War: The Selected Diaries and Papers, 1858–1866, of Frances Adeline [Fanny] Seward" (Ph.D. dissertation, University of Rochester, 1963), pp. 360–61.

31. Taylor, p. 169.

32. Van Deusen, p. 281.

33. *Seward,* 2:575, 590.

34. Taylor, p. 210.

35. Allan Nevins and Milton Halsey Thomas, eds., *The Diary of George Templeton Strong: The Civil War, 1860–1865* (New York: Macmillan, 1952), p. 292.

36. Howard K. Beale and Alan Brownsword, eds., *Diary of Gideon Welles, Secretary of the Navy Under Lincoln and Johnson* (New York: Norton, 1960), 1:136 (hereinafter cited as Welles, *Diary*).

37. Michael Burlingame and John R. Turner Ettlinger, eds., *The Complete Civil War Diary of John Hay* (Carbondale: Southern Illinois University Press, 1997), p. 119 (hereinafter cited as Hay, *Diary*).

38. *Seward,* 3:50.

39. Francis Lieber to Matilda Lieber, July [should be June], 27, 1861, Lieber MSS, Huntington Library.

40. Welles, *Diary,* 1:36.

41. Bates, pp. 291, 230.

42. *Seward,* 3:575.

43. Thurlow Weed Barnes, *Memoir of Thurlow Weed* (Boston: Houghton Mifflin, 1884), p. 408.

44. *Seward,* 2:617, 610.

45. Ibid., 3:114.

46. Welles, *Lincoln and Seward,* p. 185.

47. Lyons to Russell, May 20, 1861, Lyons MSS, Arundel Castle, Sussex.

48. Charles M. Segal, ed., *Conversations with Lincoln* (New Brunswick, N.J.: Transaction Publishers, 2002), p. 380.

49. F. W. Seward, *Reminiscences of a War-Time Statesman,* pp. 189–90.

50. Welles, *Lincoln and Seward,* pp. 43–44.

51. Welles, *Diary,* 1:70.

52. David Herbert Donald, *Charles Sumner and the Rights of Man* (New York: Knopf, 1970), pp. 90, 93.

53. *Seward,* 3:121, 118.

54. Donald, *Lincoln,* p. 366.

55. Browning, *Diary,* 1:612–13, 618.

56. Ibid., 1:609.

57. Hay, *Diary,* pp. 211–12.

58. *Seward,* 2:528.

59. Van Deusen, p. 343.

60. O. J. Hollister, *Life of Schuyler Colfax* (New York: Funk & Wagnalls, 1886), p. 199.

61. The fullest account of the 1862 cabinet crisis is in Francis Fessenden, *Life and Public Services of William Pitt Fessenden* (Boston: Houghton Mifflin, 1907), 1:231–38. I have also treated this episode at length in *Lincoln,* pp. 400–405.

62. *Seward,* 2:146.

63. Seward to Lincoln, December 12, 1862, Lincoln MSS.

64. Browning, *Diary,* 1:600–601.

65. Bates, p. 269.

66. Madeleine Vinton Dahlgren, *Memoir of John A. Dahlgren* (Boston: James R. Osgood and Company, 1882), pp. 383–84.

67. *Seward,* 3:196.

68. Barnes, *Memoir of Thurlow Weed,* p. 428; Stewart Mitchell, *Horatio Seymour of New York* (Cambridge: Harvard University Press, 1938), pp. 273–74.

69. Taylor, p. 189.

70. Segal, ed., *Conversations with Lincoln* (New Brunswick, N.J.: Transaction Publishers, 2002), p. 260.

71. Johnson, "Sensitivity and Civil War," p. 622.

72. Rufus Rockwell Wilson, ed., *Intimate Memories of Lincoln* (Elmira, N.Y.: Primavera Press, 1945), p. 422.

73. Charles Francis Adams, *Autobiography* (Boston: Houghton Mifflin, 1916), p. 59.

74. Henry Adams, *The Education of Henry Adams* (Boston: Houghton Mifflin, 1918), p. 104.

75. P. M. Zall, ed., *Abe Lincoln Laughing* (Berkeley: University of California Press, 1982), p. 33.

76. Taylor, p. 224.

77. Seward to J. A. Roosevelt, April 3, 1863, Seward MSS, University of Rochester.

78. *Seward,* 3:195.

79. J. R. Giddings to "My Dear Son," February 29, 1864, Giddings MSS, Ohio Historical Society.

80. *New York Herald,* May 3, 1863.

81. Chandler to "My dear wife," February 7, 1863, Chandler MSS, Library of Congress; Allan Nevins, *The War for the Union,* Vol. 2: *War Becomes Revolution* (New York: Scribner's, 1960), p. 352n.

82. For a review of the evidence concerning Lincoln's role in this decision, see Donald, *Lincoln,* pp. 505–506 and notes.

83. Theodore C. Blegen, ed., *Abraham Lincoln and His Mailbag: Two Documents by Edward D. Neill, One of Lincoln's Secretaries* (St. Paul: Minnesota Historical Society, 1964), p. 27.

84. Johnson, "Sensitivity and Civil War," p. 872.

85. Seward, *Reminiscences of a War-Time Statesman,* p. 253.

86. *Seward,* 3:23.

87. Taylor, p. 234.

CHAPTER 6

1. The standard biographies of John Hay are William R. Thayer, *The Life and Letters of John Hay* (2 vols.; Boston: Houghton Mifflin, 1916), and Tyler Dennett, *John Hay: From Poetry to Politics* (New York: Dodd, Mead, 1934). The only biography of John G. Nicolay is *Lincoln's Secretary*, by Helen Nicolay (New York: Longmans, Green, 1949). *Inside Lincoln's White House: The Complete Civil War Diary of John Hay* (Carbondale: Southern Illinois University Press, 1997), admirably edited by Michael Burlingame and John R. Turner Ettlinger, is a basic source and supersedes earlier, partial versions of this diary. (It is hereinafter cited as Hay, *Diary*.) Michael Burlingame, ed., *At Lincoln's Side: John Hay's Civil War Correspondence and Selected Writings* (Carbondale: Southern Illinois University Press, 2000), is an important supplement to Hay's diary. (It is hereinafter cited as Hay, *Letters*.) Michael Burlingame, ed., *With Lincoln in the White House: Letters, Memoranda, and Other Writings of John G. Nicolay, 1860–1865* (Carbondale: Southern Illinois University Press, 2000), is very revealing. (It is hereinafter cited as Nicolay, *With Lincoln in the White House*.)

2. Frederick W. Seward, *Seward at Washington as Senator and Secretary of State* (3 vols.; New York: Derby and Miller, 1891), 3:208.

3. Nicolay, *With Lincoln in the White House*, p. xvi.

4. John W. Bunn to Jesse W. Weik, July 26, 1916, Herndon-Weik Collection, Library of Congress.

5. Helen Nicolay, *Lincoln's Secretary*, p. 34.

6. Nicolay, *With Lincoln in the White House*, p. 15.

7. Thayer, *Hay*, 1:87.

8. Nicolay, *With Lincoln in the White House*, p. xvii.

9. Michael Burlingame, *Lincoln Observed: Civil War Dispatches of Noah Brooks* (Carbondale: Southern Illinois University Press, 1998), p. 83.

10. Nicolay, *With Lincoln in the White House,* pp. 65–66.

11. Ibid., p. 55.

12. Patricia Carley Johnson, ed., "Sensitivity and Civil War: The Selected Diaries and Papers, 1858–1866, of Frances Adeline [Fanny] Seward" (Ph.D. dissertation, University of Rochester, 1963), pp. 617–18.

13. Hay, *Letters,* p. 87.

14. Hay to W. H. Herndon, September 5, 1866, Lamon MSS, Huntington Library, San Marino, California. For the full text of this important letter, see Douglas L. Wilson and Rodney O. Davis, eds., *Herndon's Informants: Letters, Interviews, and Statements about Abraham Lincoln* (Urbana: University of Illinois Press, 1998), pp. 330–32.

15. Hay, *Diary,* p. 19.

16. Ibid., p. xv.

17. Ibid., p. 112.

18. John G. Nicolay and John Hay, "Authors' Preface," *Abraham Lincoln: A History* (New York: Century Co., 1890), 1:xii–xiii.

19. Nicolay, *With Lincoln in the White House,* p. 102.

20. Anne Hummel Sherrill, "John Hay: Shield of the Union" (Ph.D. dissertation, University of California, Berkeley, 1967), offers the best account of Hay's changing opinions of Lincoln.

21. Milton Hay to his wife, April 6, 1862, Stuart-Hay MSS, Illinois State Historical Library.

22. Hay, *Diary,* p. xii. President Kennedy called Washington "a city of southern efficiency and northern charm."

23. Hay, *Letters,* p. 5.

24. Hay, *Diary,* p. 8.

25. Ibid., p. 14.

26. Ibid., p. 19.

27. Michael Burlingame, *The Inner World of Abraham*

Lincoln (Urbana: University of Illinois Press, 1994), chap. 4.

28. Hay, *Diary,* pp. 20–21.

29. Nicolay and Hay, *Abraham Lincoln,* 4:142.

30. Hay, *Diary,* p. 11.

31. Ibid., p. 20.

32. Ibid., p. 25.

33. Ibid., p. 32.

34. Nicolay, *With Lincoln in the White House,* p. 72.

35. Hay, *Diary,* p. 38.

36. Ibid.

37. Nicolay, *With Lincoln in the White House,* pp. 90–91.

38. Hay, *Diary,* p. 24.

39. William O. Stoddard, Jr., ed., *Lincoln's Third Secretary: The Memoirs of William O. Stoddard* (New York: Exposition Press, 1955), pp. 166–67.

40. Nicolay, *With Lincoln in the White House,* p. 71.

41. Hay, *Diary,* p. 3.

42. Hay, *Letters,* pp. 18, 20.

43. Nicolay, *With Lincoln in the White House,* p. 124.

44. Ibid., p. 125.

45. Benjamin Brown French, *Witness to the Young Republic,* ed. Donald B. Cole and John D. McDonough (Hanover, N.H.: University Press of New England, 1989), p. 382. Margaret Leech, *Reveille in Washington, 1860–1865* (New York: Harper, 1941), pp. 293–94, offers a spirited account.

46. For a detailed account of Mary Lincoln's financial maneuvers, see Michael Burlingame, "Mary Todd Lincoln's Unethical Conduct as First Lady," in Hay, *Letters,* pp. 185–203.

47. Ibid., p. 19.

48. Nicolay, *With Lincoln in the White House,* pp. 60–61.

49. Hay, *Letters,* p. 25.

50. Nicolay, *With Lincoln in the White House,* p. 88.

Jean H. Baker, of Goucher College, read it so carefully and pointed out how all too frequently I misjudged Mary Lincoln. Charles Strozier brought his superb psychoanalytical insight into my often amateurish musings and helped me avoid some major traps. I was immeasurably relieved when Mark E. Neely, Jr., of Pennsylvania State University, who has an unparalleled mastery of Lincoln literature, assured me that he found no gross errors in my book. Once more Aïda D. Donald, my wife, took time from her own important writing to vet mine, and this book—like all my other books—is the better for her help.

Again I am grateful to Kathryn Blatt, who saved me dozens of errors through her meticulous proofreading of the entire book.

Many thanks, too, to my optimistic and enthusiastic literary agent, John Taylor Williams, of Kneerim & Williams, who had faith in me and in this book.

To all the people at Simon & Schuster who have helped me, I am deeply grateful. Once again it was a pleasure to work with Roger Labrie, who gave my manuscript a careful, detailed reading and helped me catch dozens of errors and infelicities. My chief debt is to my superb editor, Alice E. Mayhew. She not merely had patience with me during the long gestation of this project, but closely read the final manuscript and improved every page by her constructive criticism.

Index